Appalachian Mountain Club
River Guide

MAINE

Third Edition

APPALACHIAN MOUNTAIN CLUB

BOSTON

Cover photograph: Jerry and Marcy Monkman
Cover design: Belinda Desher and Beth Ann Colalella
Book design: Elisabeth Leydon Brady

Distributed by The Globe Pequot Press, Inc., Guilford, CT

Library of Congress Cataloging-in-Publication Data is available.

The paper used in this publication meets the minimum requirements of the
American National Standard for Information Sciences—Permanence of Paper
for Printed Library Materials, ANSI Z39.48–1984.

Due to changes in conditions,
use of the information in this book
is at the sole risk of the user.

Printed in the United States of America.

10 9 8 7 6 5 4 3 2 1   02 03 04 05 06 07

Contents

Preface

Since passage of the Clean Water Act in 1972, Maine's rivers have gradually, then dramatically become cleaner and more pleasant places to be. The federal law, state and local regulations, and perhaps most importantly, the interest and commitment of local individuals have made the difference. The rivers are generally, though not completely, free of industrial pollutants and sewage. Wildlife and fish are returning; foul odors are almost gone.

The rivers in northern and eastern Maine remain as unspoiled as always. You can have day-to-weeks long canoe trips in these areas with minimal intrusions. The Allagash Wilderness Waterway, a federally designated Wild River, is at the center of continuing controversy over access. See Chapter 5 for more information.

This revised *AMC River Guide: Maine* brings up-to-date descriptions of improved water quality in many of Maine's rivers. It also describes improved (or restricted) access and other changes. One of the most exciting changes described here is the removal of the Edwards Dam on the Kennebec River in Augusta. See page 65 for more information.

These are good times for our rivers, but as paddlers rivers are ours to protect. By using the river for recreation, you are an important part of the ongoing protection and care of our rivers. Support legislation to keep water clean and rivers accessible, and remember to Leave No Trace on rivers and all natural areas (see page 354).

Enjoy!

John Fiske

Acknowledgments

Special thanks to Gardner Defoe and Linda Koski for their excellent revisions of the Saint John and Allagash. Thanks also to Zip Kellogg for his on-the-phone help. Everyone was incredibly helpful: Rod Dore, Dwayne Shaw, Betsy Ham, Burnham Martin, Julie Isbill, Becca Roolf, Marcel Polak, Fred Pearson, Shelby Rousseau (Rangeley Lakes Heritage Trust), Zip Kellogg, Judy Hayes (DeLorme), Sue Lincoln, Joe Crowley, Sue Lincoln, Martin Brown, Sherwood Libby, Fred Westerburg, Matt Bernier, Chuck Heffernon, Sunrise County Expeditions, Professional Maine Guides Association.

Introduction

During the last ice age, which ended approximately 15,000 years ago, Maine was covered by glaciers up to one mile thick. These glaciers removed much of the existing topsoil and gouged out the bedrock. When the glaciers retreated, the state we now call Maine was dotted with numerous valleys, rivers, and lakes.

Canoeing and kayaking are excellent ways to enjoy the scenery created by the glaciers. The purpose of this book is to describe Maine's rivers and a few of its lakes. This book should enable the reader to locate put-ins and take-outs for specific river trips, and offer a very good idea of what to expect on the river between the two points. The rivers described range in difficulty from flatwater to Class IV whitewater.

Safety

Although this book was prepared carefully, no guidebook should be used on blind faith. It is a helpful companion, along with a map, to have when you run a river, but it will not prevent every problem.

If you are a new boater, or would like to improve your skills, take advantage of the many outfitters, private schools, and national and local organizations (including the AMC and the Maine Chapter of the AMC), that offer canoe and kayak instruction. Join a local group that run rivers together; boating with a responsible, safety-conscious group will help improve your skills. There are also many books to read on the subject. Ultimately, though, it is your responsibility to know the limits of your skills and to paddle within them. The Safety Code of American Whitewater is included in Appendix A; it contains many good suggestions for safe boating.

Be aware, too, that canoeing and kayaking have changed considerably in the past five years. Today, high-tech boats are being built to deal with the more difficult rapids. More and more, former portages have turned into standard runs for experts. The problem of rating rivers, already made difficult by variations in water levels, is further compounded by the type of boat used. A rapid that is an "easy Class III" to an expert in a specially designed boat with a full set of airbags may still be a portage to many people. In this book, rivers marked "runnable" in high water that have Class III and above rapids are rated for whitewater boats. If you are paddling a flatwater canoe, you should increase the rating at least one class.

If you are attempting rapids that are rated Class III or above, you should consider yourself a whitewater boater and outfit your boat and yourself accordingly.

- Always wear an approved life jacket.
- Use a full set of airbags in your boat.
- Use thigh straps to help keep you stable in the canoe while going through large drops or turbulent water.
- Wear a helmet.
- Learn to self-rescue; then learn an Eskimo roll.
- Check your equipment carefully before leaving home.
- Carry an extra paddle, a throwbag, and a first-aid kit when you paddle.

As a sport, boating involves certain risks that can be minimized with the proper training, forethought, caution, and equipment.

Be Considerate of Landowners

Many put-ins, take-outs, and portages are open for public use. Others require that you cross private property. You will note that many landowners whose property borders popular paddling rivers have posted their property against trespass. Paddlers can prevent additional closings by being thoughtful. Always ask for and obtain permission from landowners; don't damage vegetation; don't park cars where they block roads; pick up litter. Make your portage expeditiously and leave; don't picnic or make a disturbance. Don't expect local residents to be responsible for rescuing you and your canoe or kayak. Dumping boats and getting them pinned on whitewater rivers happen to the best of us. Paddlers should prepare before launching by having suitable equipment, clothing, and a large enough group. Access to put-ins and take-outs is the right of a private landowner and the privilege of the user. Access is becoming limited on some rivers, so it is increasingly important to maintain good relations with property owners.

River Stewardship

Paddlers can get active in efforts to ensure that boat access will be available in the future. Part of doing so involves accepting the responsibilty of thinking of rivers as complex ecosystems serving the needs of many. Nothing guarantees that put-ins and take-outs that exist today will be around tomorrow. Paddlers should be aware of the issues that surround rivers. Water quality, wildlife habitat, drinking water, dams, recreation, and land ownership all affect rivers and the paddling experience.

Fortunately many resources are available to paddlers who are interested in having a role in river stewardship. Local watershed councils and river groups, local conservation commissions, nonprofit recreation groups such as the Appalachian Mountain Club (www.outdoors.org), the American Canoe Association (www.acanet.org), and American Whitewater (www.americanwhitewater.org), and national river conservation groups such as American Rivers (www. amrivers.org) are excellent resources for information on rivers and how to become a steward. By knowing all the facts about river issues, paddlers can be better advocates in protecting the rivers they love.

Using the River Guide

Organization
Each chapter begins with a map that identifies the rivers described in the text. The principal river is described first and then the tributaries in descending (downstream) order. In the coastal watersheds, the rivers are arranged from west to east.

Format for River Descriptions
Each description starts with general information about the river as a whole. Longer rivers are then broken into sections that

are of reasonable length for a canoe or kayak trip and omit unrunnable sections of rivers. These sections are introduced by a boldfaced heading and, in most cases, a table that summarizes significant information about that segment.

Two new additions to the description are the date on which the information was verified by a volunteer river checker and map numbers from *The DeLorme Maine Atlas and Gazetteer*. We recommend that you investigate drops and other obstacles on all rivers.

The tables present significant information about that section of river. In the descriptive text that follows the tables, cumulative distances from the section's starting point are placed within parentheses.

Table Format

Starting Point ➤ Ending Point	Total miles
Description:	(Difficulty of the river in this segment)
Date checked:	(Last date that information was verified as being correct)
Navigable:	(Recommended water levels and seasons)
Scenery:	(What you will see from the boat)
Maps:	(U.S. Geological Survey quadrangles, *The DeLorme Maine Atlas and Gazetteer* map numbers, and other maps)
Portages:	(Where to, when to, and how far to carry)

Terminology: Difficulty of River

The following terms appear opposite the "Description" heading in the summary table and are used to describe the difficulty of the water to be paddled:

Lake The segment being described flows through a lake, or it is necessary to paddle across a lake to reach the beginning of a river.

Flatwater There is little or no current, and the river's surface is smooth and unbroken. Paddling upstream is easy.

Quickwater The river moves fast. Its surface is nearly smooth at high water levels but is likely to be choppy at medium water levels and shallow at low water levels.

Marsh/Swamp Vegetation often obstructs the river. Paddling may be slower than the distance alone would indicate.

Class Difficulty of rapids in a segment is rated according to American Whitewater classifications: I, II, III, or IV. *See Appendix A for a description of these classifications.*

When two or more terms appear together opposite the "Description" heading in the summary table, expect to encounter all of the conditions in that segment of the river. When one of these terms describes water conditions throughout most of the segment, it appears in boldface type.

Judging the difficulty of rapids is subjective. It depends on the type of boat, on how well paddlers read the river, and on how skillfully they maneuver their boats. The difficulty of rapids changes with the water level. A given stretch of rapids may become easier or harder when there is more water in the river. Water level affects different parts of the same river differently. As a general rule, more water washes out a river with low gradient and small rocks, but it generates larger waves and more turbulence in a river that drops steeply through large rocks.

As water level rises, current picks up. Be aware of this. If the river is high and the air and water are cold, increase the rating by at least one, and possibly two classes.

On small rivers, fallen trees present a greater hazard to paddlers than do rapids, especially since their location cannot be documented in advance. Barbed-wire fences frequently cross rivers in rural areas and are hard to spot. Be alert and have your boat under control.

Terminology: Water Levels

The following terms appear opposite the "Navigable" heading in the summary tables. They describe the water level recommended for paddling a particular segment. The dates and conditions most likely to produce the recommended water level follow in parentheses.

Low water There is a clearly defined shoreline below the bank. Small rocky rivers will not be passable, but flatter stretches and rapids in large rivers will be navigable.

Medium water The river extends to the bank, and soft vegetation along the shore may be underwater. Marshy areas may be wet. Larger whitewater rivers, depending on the type of rapids, will be navigable at this water level, and dodging rocks will be the major entertainment.

High water The river is near the top of its defined bank, and alder along the shore may be underwater. This is an acceptable water level for small whitewater rivers.

Very high water Large trees or clumps of smaller ones have their roots in the water. Reaching shore may be difficult or impossible. This water level is recommended only for experts who are familiar with the particular river and its features.

Flood The river overflows its banks and makes pillows on large trees. This stage is dangerous for everyone.

Levels lower than those recommended do not necessarily mean that the river is not runnable; a river for which high water is recommended may be traveled in medium water, but it is likely to be scratchy, and paddlers may have to wade down some sections.

Terminology: Scenery

The following terms are used in the tables to describe the territory that borders the river.

Wild Long sections of semiwilderness, with no more than a few isolated camps and occasional road access. Dirt roads may parallel the river within sight or sound but only for short distances; they do not noticeably alter the semiwilderness atmosphere of the trip. These roads may be closed to the public or altogether impassable.

Forested Banks on both sides of the river look densely wooded, but there are good dirt and asphalt roads that follow along the river or are not far from it. These roads may approach or cross the river frequently. There may be farms and houses nearby, but not many of them are visible from the water.

Rural Farms are visible from the river, and some fields may extend down to the water.

Towns Small and isolated towns border the river. Aside from their effects on water quality, these towns have little impact on the trip.

Settled There are many houses or small buildings within sight or sound of the river.

Urban Multistoried buildings are visible. The shorelines are frequently unattractive.

Maps

Each table includes pertinent topographical maps in 7.5-minute series unless followed by "15" to indicate that they are in the 15-minute series. Topographical maps may be ordered from:

U.S. Geological Survey Information Services
Box 25286, Denver Federal Center
Denver, CO 80225
888-ASK-USGS (888-275-8747)
http://mapping.usgs.gov

The DL indication in the tables stands for *The Maine Atlas and Gazetteer,* which is published by DeLorme and is widely available at bookstores and outfitters. The same company also publishes Maine's official highway map. The publisher's address is:

DeLorme
Two DeLorme Drive
Box 298
Yarmouth, ME 04096
800-511-2459
www.delorme.com

For information on Canadian maps, write to:

Canada Map Office
Policy and Product Promotions Office
Centre for Topographic Information
Natural Resources Canada
615 Booth Street, Room 711
Ottawa, Ontario Canada
KIA 0E9
http://maps.nrcan.gc.ca/

For information on tidal sections of the big coastal rivers, National Ocean Survey charts provide excellent information. Write to:

FAA Distribution Division, AVN-530
National Aeronautical Charting Office
Riverdale, MD 20737-1199
800-638-8972
http://chartmaker.ncd.noaa.gov

Portages

The portages listed include all unavoidable carries (such as dams and waterfalls) and difficult sections where there is usually insufficient water to make them runnable. In addition, some rapids are listed if their difficulty significantly exceeds the rating of that portion of the river. For example,

Portages: 2.5 mi R dam 50 yd
5.0 mi e ledge
(11.75 mi L dam 500 yd)

The first dam is 2.5 miles from the start and should be portaged on the right for 50 yards. The ledge at 5.0 miles from the start can be portaged on either side. The distance will vary with the height of the water and the skill of the paddler. In some cases, it might possibly be run, but it is well above the level of difficulty given in the chart above. The parentheses around the dam at 11.75 miles indicate it need not be portaged by those ending their trip there.

Unlisted portages may occur where there are fallen trees, low snowmobile bridges, or carries around rapids you do not wish to run.

Campsites

Information on campsites is listed as follows:

(6) mi L 5th St. John Pond (near canal) permit
1.5 mi R Red Pine Grove (poor) NMW $ car

a) Parentheses around the distance indicate that the campsite is located off the route normally followed, and opposite or in line with a point 6.0 miles along that route.

b) "L" indicates the left-hand side of Fifth Saint John Pond.

c) The name or location of the campsite is followed by special directions (near canal) or a comment (poor).

d) A fire permit is needed for those sites that are followed by the word "permit." They may be obtained at a Maine Forest Service Ranger Station, including those indicated on the chapter maps.

e) Administering organizations are also noted: Allagash Wilderness Waterway (AWW), Maine Forest Service (MFS), and North Maine Woods (NMW).

f) Fees are charged where the symbol "$" appears, and when a campsite is also accessible by road, the word "car" is written.

Abbreviations

The following abbreviations are used in the summary tables:

ft	foot, feet
mi	mile, miles
yd	yard, yards
L	left
R	right
e	either
cfs	flow of water in cubic feet per second
DL	*The Maine Atlas and Gazetteer*
CNTS	Canadian National Topographical Survey

AWW	Allagash Wilderness Waterway
MFS	Maine Forest Service
NMW	North Maine Woods

Example: How to Read a Summary Table

Smithville ➤ Brownville	3.75 mi
Description:	Class I, II
Date checked:	2001
Navigable:	High water (April to early May)
Scenery:	Forested
Map(s):	Greenwood; DL 15
Portages:	1.5 mi L dam 15 yd
	2.0 mi L two ledges 100 yd

Smithville ➤ Brownville The starting point for this imaginary segment is Smithville. The end point is Brownville.

3.75 mi The total distance to be covered is 3.75 miles.

Description: Class I, II Paddlers will encounter Class I and II whitewater on this segment. Most of the segment is Class II.

Date Checked: 2001 A volunteer river checker verified the description in 2001.

Navigable: High water (April to early May) The river is runnable at high water levels, which are most likely to occur during April and the first part of May.

Scenery: Forested Paddlers will pass between wooded banks, but access roads may exist in the woods, close to the river.

Maps: Greenwood; DL 15 The topographical map for this segment is the USGS Greenwood 7.5-minute quadrangle; *The Maine Atlas and Gazetteer* map number is 15.

Portages:	**1.5 mi L dam 15 yd**
	2.0 mi L two ledges 100 yd

Paddlers will have to carry their boats for about 15 yards around a dam about 1.5 miles from Smithville. The best route for the portage is on the left as you face downstream. There is another portage in 0.5 mile, 2.0 miles from the starting point at Smithville. The best route is also on the left, and paddlers will have to carry their boats about 100 yards to avoid two ledges. The last portage is not the take-out point for the end of this section, however. If it were, it would appear in parentheses to indicate that only those paddlers wanting to continue downriver need to complete that portage.

Security

Crime is common. At put-ins for some popular rivers, close to 100 percent of the parked cars are burglarized. To discourage this, do not leave money, cameras, or other valuables in cars. The first place thieves look is in your bag of dry clothes; leave your wallet at home. Take only the cash and cards you will need, and carry them in a waterproof folder in your pocket. If this is not possible (for example, on an extended trip), pay to park your car at a gas station or at a house.

Time

It's impossible to estimate time realistically for a river trip. Too many factors influence the length of time. For example, the water height affects the speed of the current. The boater may pursue paddling as an athletic endeavor or may prefer to float silently with the current, observing. A small, well-qualified party may scout nothing, while an instruction trip may scout everything. Paddlers may spend time bailing out canoes, taking pictures, or negotiating blowdowns.

On a large river with the current and wind favorably behind, the miles whiz by. A paddler, on the other hand, may take hours to travel a single mile on a small stream blocked with alder thickets and fallen trees. The same mile will require far less time when it is free of obstructions. It is good practice to select alternate end points for a trip, especially on an unfamiliar river.

River Levels in Maine

The water-level information given in the summary tables for individual rivers includes approximate dates, which are subject to wide variation from year to year. Some of the factors that influence water levels are discussed here.

Snow depth, temperature, rainfall, and transpiration are four seasonal factors that affect river levels. Runoff is generally greater and swifter when the ground is frozen. As the snow cover disappears, temperature becomes less important. Once the leaves are out, surface runoff decreases substantially because plants use a great deal of water during transpiration. Conversely, the fall foliage season invariably signals a rise in water levels following rain.

Terrain also must be considered. A river flowing from steep-sided hills and mountains will quickly collect the runoff from rainfall and melting snow. On the other hand, lakes, swamps, and gently rolling hills buffer the spring runoff; the result is an extended paddling season despite the weather. Knowledge of Maine's topography and familiarity with its weather will be helpful to you.

You must also take into account the nature of the river itself. If a river is flat, weather affects navigability only slightly. If the river is steep and full of rapids, then heavy snow, warm temperatures, and moderate rainfall all may be necessary to keep it runnable. Farther north, access to the water in early spring is hindered, first by snow and later by mud. Also, ice shelves along the banks are hazardous in rapids and an inconvenience elsewhere.

If you wish to run rapids in mid-March, coastal Maine is the place to go. By the end of March, the season moves to central Maine. By May, the rivers of northern Maine, which are fed by melting snow, are usually at optimal levels. Sometimes they are passable through Memorial Day, but there have been years when the season is over in late April.

River levels can vary tremendously from season to season, and unusually heavy rainfall can make any river passable at any time. If you do enough canoeing and kayaking, you will probably eventually meet someone who will defend winter boating and will claim that the canoeing season includes any sunny day when the temperature is above freezing.

Over several years, a person who runs a lot of rivers develops a sense of river levels. Those who fish the ocean acquire an instinct for the tides, those who live off the land can almost smell the weather, and so it is with river people. After a while they get to know when a river runs and when it does not.

Water Releases

With many of Maine's rivers passable for only a few weeks in the spring or after an unusually heavy rainfall, releases of water from dams can extend the paddling season in some localities. There are three types of releases. The first type of release comes from dams used to generate power. The West Branch of the Penobscot, the Kennebec, the Androscoggin, and the Magalloway are all runnable throughout the summer because they are used as a source of power.

The second type of release is one scheduled solely for the benefit of paddlers. These are arranged by whitewater clubs. They take place on scheduled weekends during the spring, summer, and fall. The Dead River in the Kennebec watershed is a good example of this type of release.

The third type of release is the annual drawdown of lakes that are used primarily for summer recreation. These releases generally take place in the fall. A drawdown often takes several weeks to complete. Rivers that are drawn down in the fall include the Dead River and the Kennebec River.

Administering Organizations

Allagash Wilderness Waterway
Bureau of Parks and Recreation
286 Water Street
Key Bank Plaza
Augusta, ME 04333
207-287-3821
www.state.me.us

If you are planning a trip on the Allagash Wilderness Waterway, write to the above address. You will receive an excellent map of the waterway and a copy of all rules and regulations pertaining to the Allagash.

Maine Forest Service
Department of Conservation
State House Station 22
Augusta, ME 04333
207-289-2791

In many sections of Maine, the Maine Forest Service has established authorized campsites where fire permits are not needed. However, at many campsites located along the rivers, you will need a permit in order to build a fire. Information regarding many such sites is given in the individual river descriptions. Fire permits may be obtained at the locations shown on the chapter maps. If you have further questions, contact the Maine Forest Service at the address given above.

North Maine Woods, Inc.
P.O. Box 421
Ashland, ME 04732
207-435-6213

North Maine Woods is an organization that was set up to regulate the access to most of the timberlands north of Baxter State Park and west of Route 11. On behalf of the many landowners of that region, North Maine Woods coordinates the uses of the area by companies engaged in logging operations and by the general public seeking recreation. It maintains checkpoints on the roads that give access to the region and at campsites within.

A camping fee is collected at the checkpoints on arrival. Several flying services are authorized to issue permits, and anyone arriving by plane should inquire about this ahead of time. Season registrations are also available.

Because rules and fees are subject to change, write for current information.

Paper Industry Information Office
P.O. Box 5670
15 Western Avenue
Augusta, ME 04332-5670
207-622-3166

This organization will send maps and information on the use of private forest lands and roads owned by the paper companies. Recreation opportunities use company-owned property includes camping, hiking, fishing, and paddling.

Rentals

There are many places to rent boats in Maine. This information is in the Yellow Pages under "Canoes." Canoe and kayak dealers may be able to help you locate distant outfitters.

Suggested Canoe Camping Trips

Miles	Portages	Lake	Quickwater	Class I	Class II	Class III	Passable in summer
33.75	1	X					X
53.0	1–2	●	X	X	●		X
47+/-	0–1		X	●			●
53+			X	X	●	●	
34.0	1–2	●	X	●	●		
44.5+/-	1–2	X			●		X
76.5-	2–8	X	●	●	●	X	
45-	1						
24.5+	0–1	X	X	X	●		●
47.5-	4–6		X	●	●	●	X
43.5+		X	X	X			X
43.25+/-	1		X	●	●		X
33+/-	1	●	X	●	X		X
56-		●	X	X	●	●	X
19.75+	1		X	●			
14.25	0–2	●	●	●	●	●	●
24.0-	2–6	X	X		●	X	X

Symbols: + trip can be easily lengthened   X predominate features
         - trip can be easily shortened   ● occational features

Suggested Whitewater Runs of Class II Difficulty

Chapter	River	Miles	Class III Rapids	Passible in summer
6	**B Stream** (Hammond ➤ Houlton)	4.25		X
2	**Bear River** (North Newry ➤ Newry)	6.75		
3	**Carrabassett** (Kingfield ➤ New Portland)	6.5		
3	**Dead, North Branch** (Chain of Lakes Dam ➤ Eustis)	19.0	2	
8	**Dennys** (Meddybmps ➤ Dennysville)	20.75	1	
8	**Grand Lake Stream** (West Grand Lake ➤ Big Lake)	3.0		X
3	**Kennebec River** (The Forks ➤ Caratunk)	9.0		X
4	**Kenduskeag** (Kenduskeag ➤ Bangor)	16.0	1	
1	**Little Ossipee River** (Davis Brook ➤ ME 5)	11.25		
4	**Nesowadnehunk Stream** (Nesowadnehunk Lake ➤ Campgound 5)	5.0	1	X
4	**Piscataquis River** (Dover Foxcroft ➤ Derby)	18.5		X
3	**Sandy River** (Phillips ➤ Fairbanks Bridge)	17.25	2	X
7	**Sheepscot River** (Whitefield ➤ Head Tide)	6.0		

Suggested Whitewater Runs of Class III Difficulty

Chapter.	River	Miles	Class IV Rapids	Passible in summer
8	**Blue Hills Falls**			X
3	**Carrabassett River** (Kingfield ➤ New Portland)	10.0		
3	**Dead River (under 2,500 cfs)** (Spencer Stream➤ The Forks)	16.0		X
6	**Machias Stream** (Big Machias Lake ➤ Aroostook River)	32.0		
4	**Pleasant River, West Branch** (K. I. Words ➤ Brownville Jct.)	9.75		
3	**Roach River** (Kokad-jo ➤ Moosehead Lake)	6.5		
1	**Saco River** (Limington Rips)	0.5		
4	**Souadabscook Stream** (Vatiades Landing ➤ Hampden)	9.0	1	
2	**Swift River** (Byron ➤ Mexico)	13.0	1	
8	**Union River, West Branch** (Great Pond ➤ Amherst)	11.0	2	
2	**Webb River** (Lake Webb ➤ Carthage)	4.5	1	
2	**Wild River** (Campground ➤ Gilead)	8.0	1	

Suggested Whitewater Runs of Class IV Difficulty

Chapter	River	Miles	Big Water Rapids	Ledge Drops	Passible in summer
6	**Aroostook River** (Fort Fairefield ➤ St. John River)	11.0	X	X	X
3	**Dead River (2,500+ cfs)** (Spencer Stream ➤ The Forks)	16.0	X	X	X
3	**Kennebec River** (East Outlet ➤ Indian Pond)	3.5	X		X
4	**Mattawamkeag River** (Kingman ➤ Mattawamkeag)	12.5	X	X	
2	**Rapid River** (Middle Dam ➤ Lake Umbagog)	6.0			X
3	**Sandy River** (Smalls Falls ➤ South Branch)	5.5		X	

Chapter 1
Lower Saco Watershed

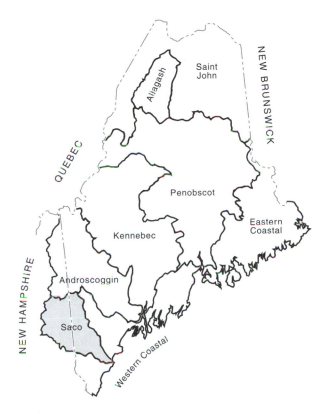

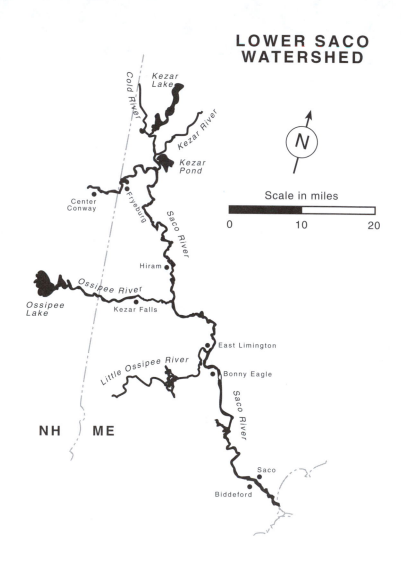

LOWER SACO WATERSHED

N

Scale in miles

0   10   20

Cold River

Kezar Lake

Kezar River

Kezar Pond

Center Conway

Fryeburg

Saco River

Hiram

Ossipee River

Ossipee Lake

Kezar Falls

East Limington

Little Ossipee River

Bonny Eagle

NH   ME

Saco River

Saco

Biddeford

Saco River

The Saco is one of New England's most popular paddling rivers. Melting snow and spring rains provide whitewater boating for the novice to the expert near the headwaters in spring and early summer, while below the Maine–New Hampshire border the river is mostly flat and passable at all water levels. The river begins at Saco Lake just north of Crawford Notch. It drains the southern slopes of the Presidential Range and, in New Hampshire, flows though the Mount Washington Valley. From Conway, New Hampshire, it winds generally southeast to the Atlantic Ocean south of Portland, Maine.

Although settlement along the Saco began early in the seventeenth century, few towns were located next to the river. To this day, it remains a pastoral stream passing through only a few small settlements until it gets almost to the sea. The Saco River Corridor Commission, which cooperates with local communities in matters relating to zoning and land-use planning, offers state-supported protection of the Maine portion of the Saco.

This book does not include the Saco River or its tributaries in New Hampshire, which are primarily whitewater trips. It also does not include the New Hampshire tributaries of the Ossipee River, which flow into Ossipee Lake and are primarily quickwater. Descriptions of these rivers are available in *AMC River Guide: New Hampshire/Vermont.*

The Little Ossipee is a good choice for an overnight trip in the spring. The Saco between Conway and Cornish is very popular for camping trips throughout the paddling season.

Spring whitewater is available on the Ossipee and Little Ossipee, while the Saco at Limington Rips can be used all summer. The Saco has a good current and can be run at all water levels. Flatwater is available on lakes and in pools behind dams.

The Saco River: A History and Canoeing Guide by Viola Sheehan discusses the Saco River in Maine. Available from the Saco River Corridor Association, 207-625-8123, www.srcc-maine.org. for $6.50. It provides an excellent history of the Saco River, and several drawings of the Little Ossipee, Ossipee, and Saco Rivers as a paddling guide.

Center Conway, NH ➤ Hiram, ME	44.25 mi

Description:	Flatwater, quickwater, Class II
Date checked:	2000
Navigable:	Spring, summer, fall
Scenery:	Forested, rural
Maps:	North Conway 15, Ossipee Lake 15, Fryeburg, Brownfield, Hiram; DL 4
Portage:	10.0 mi R Swan's Falls 300 yd
Campsites:	10.0 mi R Swan's Falls AMC $ car
	14.0 mi R Canal Bridge (ME 5) commercial $ car
	23.5 mi L Walker's Falls AMC $
	29.5 mi R Woodland Acres commercial $ car
	29.5 mi L River Run commercial $ car
	35.5 mi R Burnt Meadows commercial $ by reservation only

From Center Conway, NH, to Hiram is the "sandy" Saco, where low water during the summer months exposes many miles of beaches. A quickwater river in a wide valley of farms and forests, it flows alternately along the edges of fields and through stands of pine and swamp maple. There are a few small towns, but none infringe upon the river.

The setting is so peaceful and the water so clean that the Saco attracts people (thousands of them on a nice summer weekend). Because of the large crowds and the impact that high-density use can have on a river, there are river-usage regulations. In additon to the river-use regulations, AMC encourages all paddlers to adopt the Leave No Trace principles outlined on page 354. All trash must be carried out (not buried). Nothing is to be washed in the river; all washing should be done in buckets and the waste water poured on the soil away from the river. Human waste should be buried at least 6 inches deep in topsoil and at least 200 feet from the river's high water mark. Fire permits are required. Only cooking fires on sand bars are allowed; no bonfires are permitted. All fires should be extinguished with water (not covered with sand). The land along the Saco is privately owned. Paddlers need to get permission before wandering. Other than at campgrounds, camping is permitted on unposted sand bars from the Maine state line to Hiram. Never dive head first into the river! The river generally is shallow, even where it looks deep—deaths and serious injuries have occurred far too often on the river.

For further information and maps on the river, contact the AMC campgrounds at Swan's Falls, 207-935-3395, and Walker's Falls, the Saco River Recreational Council, P.O. Box 363, Fryeburg, ME 04037, 603-447-3801, or any of the canoe liveries. Fire permits are available in Fryeburg from the town fire warden. Check on this with the liveries.

There are at least nine other parking sites along the river; some charge fees and others are free; many offer only unsupervised parking. There is parking at Canal Bridge on ME 5, at Walker's Bridge on US 302, at the Brownfield Bridge on ME 160, at Weston's Bridge off ME 113 west of Fryeburg, and at the Lovewell Pond access that is reached by a road that leaves ME 5/113 southeast of Fryeburg and north of a railroad crossing. The *AMC Saco River Trip Leaders' Guide*, $2.00, lists all available parking (as well as complete information and helpful hints for a successful Saco River trip) and is available at the AMC Saco River Campgrounds as well as from the AMC campground registrars. Please be considerate of landowners and park only at designated areas.

Now you are ready for your Saco River trip. The river is clearest in the 17.5 miles from center Conway, NH, to the confluence with the Old Saco. In this section of the river, the current is stronger, the river generally shallower, the banks more open, and the sand bars more numerous. As you approach and pass the Old Saco entering from the north, you will notice that the banks are more heavily forested and the water darker.

Just below the US 302 bridge near Center Conway, NH, soon after the river flows between the abutments of the old covered bridge, there are some Class II rips that are bony in low water. The remaining 9.0 miles to Swan's Falls are mostly quickwater. The main highway approaches the river across from McSherry's Nursery (3.25 mi). The next landmark is Weston's Bridge (6.75 mi). Weston's Bridge and Beach is the Fryeburg town beach. There are organized swimming lessons and activities in the river every day, so paddlers are advised to stay far river right on the outside of the curve. In another 3.25 miles is Swan's Falls (10 mi), where there is a dam that should be approached cautiously in high water. Portage on the right.

About 1 mile past Canal Bridge (14.0 mi), the river swings to the north and a channel enters on the right. The stream can be followed upstream 200 yards or so to Bog Pond, a small and secluded body of water. The next landmark is the Old Saco (17.50 mi), which enters on the left.

The Old Course of the Saco, as the name implies, was once the channel of the river. The Saco today follows a canal dug in 1817 for flood control. The western end of the Old Saco is silted in, but the eastern portion of it still drains Kezar Lake.

From the Old Saco (17.5 mi) quickwater continues for 6.0 miles past Walker's Bridge, US 302 (21.0 mi), and the outlet to Pleasant Pond (23.25 mi) to Walker's Falls (23.5 mi) where the short, easy rapids become flooded out at high water. Pleasant Pond is very close to the river and provides good views of the mountains.

Two miles below Walker's Falls the outlet from Lovewell Pond enters on the right. Then the Saco meanders, passing to the west of Brownfield Bog Wildlife Management area, which is a nesting area for ducks, great blue herons, bald eagles, and other colorful and rare birds. The Inland Fisheries and Wildlife Department has set up rookeries here in an attempt to encourage nesting. Below the ME 160 bridge (29.5 mi) the river continues to meander for the next 13.75 miles to Hiram (43.25 mi).

Hiram ➤ Bonny Eagle Dam (ME 35)   25.25 mi

Description:	Flatwater, quickwater, Class I, II
Date checked:	2000
Navigable:	Spring, summer, fall
Scenery:	Forested, rural, towns
Maps:	Hiram, Cornish, Sebago Lake 15, Buxton; DL 4
Portages:	2.75 mi R Great Falls Dam 0.25 mi
	14.75 mi L Steep Falls 50 yd
	25.25 mi R Bonny Eagle Dam 70 yd
Campsites:	14.75 mi L Steep Falls (at portage)
	15.0 mi R Steep Falls (R turn below old dam)
	19.25 mi Limington Rips (island at top)

The Saco is a fairly large river rising in Crawford Notch. The rapids are much more difficult in high water, especially Limington Rips, which generate big waves. This portion of the river is used much less than the section preceding it. The water is not as clear as it is near Fryeburg, but the scenery is comparable. The occasional rapids are a feature not found on the section from Center Conway, NH, to Hiram.

In the late spring when water levels are generally medium, paddlers can make a nice 20.75-mile run by starting at Kezar Falls, running the Ossipee River to the Saco near Cornish, then continuing down the Saco to the ME 25 bridge in East Limington.

From Hiram there is flatwater for 2.75 miles to Great Falls Dam. **Caution!** In high water, go left of an island after a sweeping left turn. You should land on the right above the dam and portage along the trail there. Two-thirds of a mile below Great Falls Dam there is a Class I rapid at a short left turn. Quickwater continues past the mouth of the Ossipee River (5.75 mi) to the ME 5/117 bridge in Cornish (6.25 mi).

There are riffles just past the Cornish bridge. After 2.75 miles, you reach Old Bald Rapid, a short Class II pitch with large waves in high water. There are more riffles in the remaining 5.5 miles to Steep Falls.

Steep Falls (14.75 mi) is a dangerous 7-foot drop, which must be portaged. You are apt to come upon it suddenly, especially in the fast-moving current of high water. Be alert for the sound of falling water, a glimpse of a house on the left bank, or the sighting of a green girder bridge below the falls. When you notice any of these, get quickly to the left bank where there is a short portage. After the falls, there is 0.25 mile of rapids, Class II in low water, but rougher in high water. The rapids continue under the bridge and past the remains of a dam.

Below Steep Falls, riffles continue intermittently for 1.0 mile, followed by almost 3.0 miles of quickwater to Parkers Rips, a short Class II rapid near a house on the right where the river swings left. In 0.75 mile, you reach Limington Rips, a 0.5-mile set of Class II rapids in low water, but Class III with heavy waves in medium water.

The left-hand side of the island requires more maneuvering and is usually used in low water. The drop is steeper on the right, but scouting is easier, and the shore closer in case of mishap. The take-out above the rapid is also on the right, to a road immediately adjacent. Although the hardest section of this rapid is near the end, below the ME 25 bridge (19.75 mi), most mishaps occur before the bridge.

Just past Limington Rips, the Little Ossipee River enters on the right (20.0 mi). Deadwater continues for the remaining 5.25 miles to Bonny Eagle Dam (25.25 mi) just below the ME 35 bridge. Take out on the right bank near the power house. If you are continuing down the river, portage beyond the building about 50 yards to a gravel path to the river.

Bonny Eagle Dam (ME 35) ➤ Biddeford	19.0 mi
Description:	Lake, flatwater
Date checked:	2000
Navigable:	Spring, summer, fall
Scenery:	Forested, rural, towns
Maps:	Buxton 15, Kennebunk 15, Biddeford 15, Portland 15; DL 2, 3

Portages:	1.5 mi L dam at West Buxton
	6.75 mi R dam at Bar Mills
	10.0 mi R Skelton Dam
	(20.0 mi dams)

More than half of this section consists of deadwaters behind a succession of dams. Near the ME 4A/117 bridge (8.0 mi) at Salmon Falls (flooded out), you enter the third deadwater. As the river opens into the wide lake behind Skelton Dam at Union Falls (10.0 mi), head southeast after a short portage around the dam.

A couple of miles after the ME 5 bridge (14.5 mi), the flatwater is broken by a short rapid. Below the Maine Turnpike (18.75 mi) there is a convenient take-out on the right at Rotary Park (19.0 mi). There are dams in Biddeford and Saco, below which the river is tidal.

Old Course

Kezar Outlet drains Kezar Lake south to Old Course of the Saco, a bit west of the latter's northernmost point. The upper (western) portion of the Old Course is now only a series of sloughs, its entrance from the Saco unidentifiable. The lower portion is kept active by the outlets from Kezar Lake, Charles Pond, and Kezar Pond. Wildlife is abundant; almost every stump and rock is covered with turtles in season.

Kezar Outlet ➤ Saco River		8.0 mi
Description:	Quickwater	
Date checked:	2000	
Navigable:	Spring, summer, fall	
Scenery:	Forested	
Maps:	Fryeburg 15; DL 4	

The current flows briskly, and vegetation covers the bottom, waving sinuously. Red School Bridge on US 5 (4.0 mi) and Hemlock Covered Bridge (6.5 mi) also allow access.

The outlet from Kezar Pond enters left just above the covered bridge. The Saco River is another 1.5 miles.

Kezar Lake Outlet

This route is popular as an access to the Saco River, making an interesting variation. Swimming is not as desirable here as on the main Saco.

Kezar Lake Narrows ➤ Old Course		4.5 mi
Description:	Lake, flatwater	
Date checked:	2000	
Navigable:	Spring, summer, fall	
Scenery:	Forested	
Maps:	Fryeburg 15; DL 4	
Portage:	4.25 mi dam 10 yd	

From the landing at Kezar Narrows, paddle southwest into the lower bay and across it to the outlet (1.75 mi). The lake level is raised by a small dam on the outlet just above the confluence with the Charles River (4.5 mi). The wire grating above it must also be lifted over.

Below the dam, the river flows quickly, passing under a bridge near the confluence. It may be rocky in low water.

Charles River

The Charles River is the outlet to Charles Pond. The river flows from Charles Pond to the outlet from Kezar Lake; they meet and flow together into the Old Course of the Saco.

Charles Pond ➤ Kezar Outlet		1.5 mi
Description:	Flatwater, quickwater	
Date checked:	2000	
Navigable:	Spring, summer, fall	
Scenery:	Forested	
Maps:	Fryeburg; DL 10	

The Charles River leaves from the east side of Charles Pond. It is rockier and wider than the Cold River and may require occasional wading to pass when the Cold River is runnable. It passes under a bridge just above the confluence with Kezar Outlet.

Cold River

The Cold River is a small stream that rises on Baldface Mountain in New Hampshire, flows to Charles Pond, and ultimately to the Saco River. Because it is a narrow stream with a good watershed, it may be run after summer thunderstorms as well as in spring.

Pine Hill Road ➤ Chares Pond	10.0 mi
Description:	Quickwater
Date checked:	2000
Navigable:	Medium water (late spring or after heavy rain)
Scenery:	Forested
Maps:	North Conway 15, Fryeburg, 15; DL 10

Put in from the road to Pine Hill. The river is very small but flows mostly over a smooth, sandy bottom with deep pools here and there. The river flows into the north side of Charles Pond, which is about 0.5 mile in diameter. The outlet, marked by a large rock, is only a few hundred feet to the left. Follow the outlet approximately 1 mile to the road that runs along the Old Course of the Saco.

(For an exciting, if frigid swim, find Emerald Pool, near the AMC Cold River Camp, off ME/NH 113, north of Fryeburg.)

Kezar River

This small stream drains the Five Kezar Ponds in Stoneham and flows southwest to the Old Course of the Saco just north of Kezar Pond.

Number Four ➤ Lovell	2.25 mi
Description:	Quickwater, flatwater
Date checked:	2000
Navigable:	Summer (after a heavy rain)
Scenery:	Forested
Maps:	North Conway 15, Fryeburg 15; DL 10

This stream can be run from here after a heavy summer rain. It is a canoe-width wide at the start, with overhanging bushes.

After 1.5 miles, it opens up into the flowage above the dam at Lovell, with pond lilies and attractive wooded banks.

Paddlers continuing can portage right through a culvert under the highway.

Lovell ➤ Old Channel	3.50 mi
Description:	Quickwater, flatwater
Date checked:	2000
Navigable:	Summer (after a heavy rain)
Scenery:	Forested
Maps:	North Conway 15, Fryeburg 15; DL 10

The bottom is sandy where it circles around Smarts Hill. The river enters Swimming Bog about 2 miles from Lovell and somewhat disappears into it. By keeping to the right-hand channel, you may be able to work through it down to the Old Saco. When the river is up, much of the water overflows into Kezar Pond.

Ossipee River

The Ossipee River flows east for 17.5 miles from Lake Ossipee, across the Maine border, and into the Saco River near Cornish. It has dependable flow in the spring, but by summer the water level is too low to run the lower section.

Ossipee Lake ➤ Kezar Falls	10.75 mi
Description:	Quickwater, Class I, II
Date checked:	2001
Navigable:	High and medium water (spring)
	Low water (passable, some lining at rapids)
Scenery:	Forested, rural, towns
Maps:	Ossipee Lake 15, Kezar Falls; DL 4
Portages:	10.5 mi first dam at Kezar Falls (across island) 30 yd
	10.75 mi R second dam at Kezar Falls 30 yd

Quickwater characterizes this section, although there is one nice rapid just above the NH 153 bridge in Effingham Falls.

There are several more short rapids before Kezar Falls, but for most of the distance the river is smooth. Vacation cottages line the banks near the beginnings and below East Freedom there are more cottages and houses, with a main highway close by on the left bank for much of the distance. Anyone seeking a paddle in remote surroundings will not find it here.

The dam at the outlet of Ossipee Lake is at the end of a side road 0.5 mile west of the junction of NH 25 and 153 in Effingham Falls. Put in below the gatehouse and run down the sluiceway to a pool of slackwater. Soon, there begins 0.25 mile of rapids that are Class II or III, depending on the water level. They are the most difficult on the river, and they lead up to the NH 153 bridge (1.5 mi).

There are 1.5 miles of quickwater past the NH 25 bridge (2.0 mi) to East Freedom, where 0.25 mile of Class II rapids leads under a bridge (4.5 mi) to the Maine border. The remaining distance to Kezar Falls is mostly quickwater with two short Class II rapids, one before and one after the ME 160 bridge in Porter (7.75 mi).

In Kezar Falls, go to the right of the island and take out at a small bridge (10.5 mi). If you are continuing downstream, carry across the island to the foot of the main dam and continue 0.25 mile through the town to the second dam (10.75 mi). Take out on the right, carry across the canal, and put in below the dam.

Kezar Falls ➤ Saco River	6.75 mi
Description:	Quickwater, Class I, II
Date checked:	2000
Navigable:	High and medium water (early to late spring)
Scenery:	Forested, rural
Maps:	Kezar Falls, Cornish; DL 4
Portage:	4.25 mi dam 10 yd

Below the second dam in Kezar Falls, the Ossipee River takes on a different character. It is a scenic run past forests and farms almost all the way to the Saco River, with quickwater or rapids for the entire distance.

When the water level is up, the run from Kezar Falls to the ME 5/117 bridge over the Saco can be made in a little over an hour. But if you continue down the Saco for another 14.0 miles to the ME 25 bridge, you can make a long, scenic trip of mixed flatwater and rapids. Note, however, that Limington Rips, which begin just above the bridge, are severe rapids in high water.

A half-mile east of the ME 25 bridge in Kezar Falls, turn north onto Garner Avenue and take the first right to reach the dam and power station.

Below the dam there are nice Class I and II rapids for 1.0 mile to Which Way Rips, where the river abruptly divides around an island. Quickwater and Class I rapids continue to the first bridge (3.5 mi), with more quickwater to the second (5.5 mi). Below the second bridge and past a few cottages, there are some easy Class II rapids that lead almost to the Saco River (6.75 mi) only 0.5 mile above the ME 5/117 bridge east of Cornish (7.25 mi).

Little Ossipee River

The Little Ossipee is a fairly popular trip in southwestern Maine. It flows east from Balch Pond, a small lake on the Maine–New Hampshire border, to the Saco River just downstream from the ME 25 bridge at East Limington.

In high water, it is an easy two-day trip of 28.25 miles from Davis Brook near North Shapleigh to East Limington just above the confluence with the Saco River. The hardest rapids that are normally run are at Newfield, and they are Class II. Those at Hardscrabble Falls below ME 117 are so difficult that all but the last 100 yards are usually portaged. The section below Ledgemere Dam is usually passable through the summer.

Davis Brook ➤ ME 5	11.25 mi
Description:	Flatwater, quickwater, Class I, II
Date checked:	2000
Navigable:	High and medium water (early spring to late April)

Scenery:	Wild, forested, towns
Maps:	Newfield 15; DL 2

The most remote part of the Little Osipee River is the section above Newfield. Much of the area was burned in 1947, and today it is covered with scrub growth, predominately gray birch. In medium water, all the rapids are shallow, so high water is recommended.

ME 11 crosses the Little Ossipee at the Newfield-Shapleigh town line. Just south of this point, follow Mann Road east for 0.9 mile to the double culvert over Davis Brook.

Alternatively, you can start at the culvert on ME 11. There are rocks inside that are difficult to dodge in the darkness. The first mile to Davis Brook contains shallow rapids, which may be choked with debris and may require short carries.

Davis Brook is a small stream that flows into the Little Ossipee 0.25 mile from Mann Road. Then, in the next 4.25 miles, the main river is a mixture of quickwater and short, easy Class I–II rapids. The river flows through some small meadows, and there is at least one beaver dam.

Approaching Newfield, there is a Class II drop over some ledges. Just east of Newfield, ME 11 crosses Chellis Brook. If the depth of the water over the cement brook bed under the bridge is between 1.25 and 1.5 feet, the Little Ossipee is probably at medium level. In that case, the recommended start is at Chellis Brook, which joins the main river in 100 yards. If the water under the bridge is less than 8 inches, this section will be scratchy in many places.

Most of the remaining 6.25 miles to ME 5 at Ossipee Mills is quickwater with no significant rapids. About halfway down, you pass between the two old abutments of Clark's Bridge.

ME 5 ➤ Ledgemere Dam		5.75 mi
Description:	Lake	
Date checked:	2000	
Navigable:	When lake is full	
Scenery:	Forested	
Maps:	Newfield 15, Buxton 15; DL 2 and 4	

The flashboards on Ledgemere Dam may not be in place, with the result that the level of the lake may be down a few feet. Ledgemere Flowage (renamed Lake Arrowhead by real estate developers peddling house lots) will then have some sections of shoals and extensive mud flats with exposed stumps. In some places, sandy beaches will be exposed. Portions of the lake are attractive, others are not. There are many houses; most of the shoreline is developed.

The lake poses navigation problems. The topographical map shows the normal pool elevation, but the lake usually is kept at full pool.

Ledgemere Dam ➤ East Limington	11.75 mi
Description:	Flatwater, quickwater, Class II
Date checked:	2000
Navigable:	Spring, summer, fall
Scenery:	Forested
Maps:	Buxton 15; DL 2 and 4
Portages:	4.25 mi R Hardscrabble Falls 0.5 mi
	11.25 mi L falls at East Limington 300 yd
Campsite:	4.75 mi R Hardscrabble Falls (end of portage)

The Little Ossipee is much larger below Ledgemere Flowage than it is above it. The banks are heavily wooded all the way to East Limington, and near the end it flows through a small, narrow valley with steep slopes close to the riverbank. The river is mostly flatwater in this section and there are almost no easily runnable rapids. The first of the two ledge drops, Hardscrabble Falls, should be portaged, whereas the second one is just after a logical take-out point near the end of the river.

The current is fast for a mile or so to a short Class I drop. Then it is slow past the ME 117 bridge (1.75 mi) to the second bridge (4.25 mi), which is at the top of Hardscrabble Falls. **Caution!** Stop on the right above the bridge. The falls, which are 0.5 mile long, begin and end with Class II rapids, but the middle section consists of a steep drop over a series of ledges that should not tempt any paddler. The portage follows a rutted dirt road close to the right bank, and makes a sharp right turn after passing a field on the right.

From the end of Hardscrabble Falls (4.75 mi), the river is flat and winding for 6.0 miles to a short Class II drop within sight of, and 0.25 mile above the last bridge on the Little Ossipee. **Caution!** This bridge at East Limington is located just *above* a dangerous pitch. Stop above this bridge (11.25 mi). You should look at the approach, particularly in high water. Take-out and/or portage is on the right *above* the bridge. If you are continuing the last 0.5 mile to the Saco, go across the road and take an old trail that follows the southern bank of the river. Another 0.25 mile of flatwater brings you to the end of the Little Ossipee. Limington Rips is 0.25 mile to the left, and Bonny Eagle Dam is 5.25 miles down the deadwater to the right.

Access at East Limington: The bridge above the last portage on the Little Ossippee is about 1 mile by road from the ME 25 bridge over the Saco River. Heading west from the latter, take the first left.

Chapter 2
Androscoggin Watershed

ANDROSCOGGIN
WATERSHED

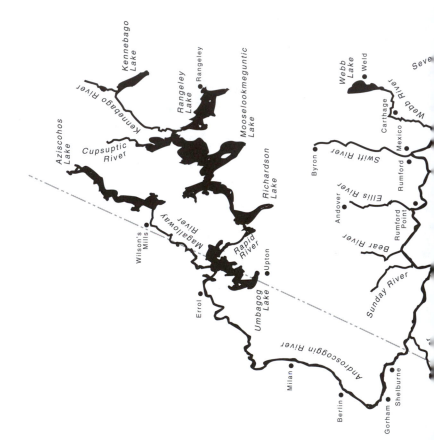

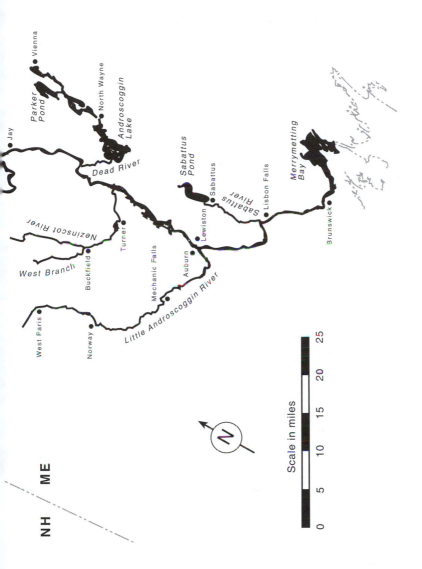

Scale in miles

0 5 10 15 20 25

NH

ME

Vienna

Parker Pond

North Wayne

Androscoggin Lake

Jay

Dead River

Sabattus Pond

Sabattus

Lewiston

Lisbon Falls

Sabattus River

Merrymetting Bay

Brunswick

Nezinscot River

West Branch

Buckfield

Turner

Mechanic Falls

Auburn

Little Androscoggin River

West Paris

Norway

Androscoggin River

After the glaciers in the last ice age retreated some 15,000 years ago, the present-day Androscoggin valley was made up of a chain of lakes linked by short rivers. In time the Androscoggin as we know it emerged. The beautiful valleys, or intervales, along the Androscoggin mark where the lakes once were.

The Abenaki tribe of Native Americans used the river as a means of transportation and as a source of fish. When the Europeans arrived, they used the waterway as a power source and an industrial-waste-and-sewer system. During the first half of the last century, the Androscoggin was one of the most polluted rivers in the United States. The Federal Water Pollution Control Act of 1972, better known as the Clean Water Act, has led the way to a much cleaner river. The main force behind the legislation was Senator Edmund Muskie, who grew up along the Androscoggin in Rumford. In addition, recognizing the need for continuing improvement, the state of Maine enacted the Color, Odor, and Foam Reduction Act in the spring of 1990 to reduce the level of those three pollutants in the rivers of Maine. As the river's water quality has continued to improve, recreational use of the river has grown dramatically. A few sections have rapids that need to be respected, and, as always, water levels affect difficulty. The river's novice-friendly nature, ease of access, and beautiful scenery make the waterway a great paddling river.

The Androscoggin River begins north of Errol at the confluence of the Magalloway River and the outlet of Umbagog Lake. This is no longer a clearly defined spot because the dam at Errol floods many miles up both branches. The lakes in the headwaters form a vast storage area of impounded water to run the mills and power stations on the Androscoggin. This makes summer paddling possible.

Lake Umbagog ➤ Berlin, NH	34.25 mi
Description:	Flatwater, quickwater, Class I, II
Date checked:	2000
Navigable:	Spring, summer, fall; controlled release
Scenery:	Forested, rural
Maps:	Errol 15, Milan 15, Berlin

Portages:	3.75 mi L Errol Dam
	21.75 mi R Pontook Dam
	(34.5 mi Berlin Dam)
Campsites:	4.5 mi R Errol Bridge private $ car
	8.0 mi R Mollidgewock private $ car

This is the clean water section of the Androscoggin. Below the Errol and Pontook Dams two whitewater runs exist all through the summer. Although the runs are neither long nor difficult, they are popular in July and August, with few other whitewater alternatives in new England. The valley is attractive, though not wild because NH 16 follows the river closely almost the entire distance. For this reason, it is rarely used for overnight trips.

Below Lake Umbagog, the river is wide with extensive marshes on both sides. In 3.0 miles, it reaches NH 16 where there is a launching ramp; 0.75 mile beyond this ramp is the Errol Dam (3.75 mi), which is portaged on the left.

The section from Errol Dam to just below the NH 26 bridge, 0.75 mile long, consists of a short rapid, a pool, and another 0.5 mile of easier Class II rapids. Due to the slackwater below where Clear Stream enters on the right (which is immediately after the rapids) and the proximity of the road, these rapids are not as dangerous as the size and difficulty of the river normally would indicate. If you plan to run this section by itself, the best way to reach it is to park your car beside the pool above Errol, run the rapids, and take out on river right either near the bridge or at the end of the rapids.

Below Clear Stream (4.75 mi), there are 3.25 miles of flatwater to Mollidgewock Brook (8.0 mi). Downstream there are 3.0 miles of Class II rapids separated by pools, with mixed smoothwater and riffles for the remaining distance to Pontook Reservoir. There is an access point at the Dummer-Cambridge town line along NH 16. It is a section of old NH 16, and is right along the river. There is a bridge (12.75 mi) just above Seven Islands, with a nice wave. Bog Brook (18.25 mi), which enters on the left, is the next landmark. Portage at Pontook Dam (21.3 mi) on the right.

Caution! At the dam there is a strong, consistent, and dangerous reversal. This hydraulic is more dangerous than it looks; two people have drowned here. Heed the warning signs: Put in at the boat landing 50 yards below the dam, and do not go upstream to play in the reversal! Since the new dam has been in operation, the water level below the dam has been too low to create rapids. The river needs to flow at 1,200 cfs to create Class II rapids. There are pre-arranged water releases on summer weekends, which provide enough water for boating. Call 603-449-2903 for release information. There is a public boat launch at the Paul O. Boffinger Conservation Area, on the right side of the river, 1.0 mile below the Pontook rapids. This area has parking, restrooms, and interpretive signs.

The remaining 10.5 miles have a good current but no rapids. The bridge in Milan can be used as an access point, although the bank is very steep. Park on the left side of the river. The Nansen Wayside Park is also a good access point, with an easy paddle down to Berlin from here. There is a bridge in Milan (27.75 mi). In Berlin, you should take out at the playground (34.5 mi) located on the left below the first bridge, or continue down to the new boat launch and float installed in the summer of 2000 by the Northern Forest Heritage Park. It is on river right, but close to the Berlin Dam, so paddle cautiously.

Berlin, NH ➤ Shelburne Dam		11.50 mi
Description:	Flatwater, quickwater, Class I	
Date checked:	2000	
Navigable:	Spring, summer, fall; controlled release (not recommended, dams)	
Scenery:	Urban, forested	
Maps:	Berlin, Shelburne	
Portages:	7 dams	

The river valley is attractive, with views of the Presidential Range to the southwest and lower mountains to the east. A recommended paddle would be to put-in in Gorham and paddle down to the Shelburne Dam. No portages are necessary, and the views of the Presidential Range in this section are wonderful. The river has been cleaned up substantially. You will hardly be able to discern the difference in water quality in this section from the first section. The seven dams above Gorham may each be portaged individually, or in series.

Shelburne Dam ➤ Bethel   17.75 mi

Description:	Flatwater, quickwater, Class I
Date checked:	2000
Navigable:	Spring, summer, fall: controlled release
Scenery:	Forested, rural
Maps:	Shelburne, Gilead, Bethel; DL 10

The water in this section is less polluted than in the past and the river valley is scenic, with views of the Presidential Range to the southwest and lower mountains to the east. The river can sometimes have an odor, but not everyone can detect it.

Put in below the dam at the bridge on which the Appalachian Trail crosses the river. Two log cribs dominate the view upstream over the dam. There is good current with pleasant riffles for many miles, as the river continually separates around numerous islands.

At 2.75 miles, there is a bridge. Above the next bridge near Gilead (8.75 mi) is the most difficult rapid in this section, dropping past rocky outcroppings. There is a boat launch on river right above this bridge. At 14.0 miles is the Newt's Landing Access site, owned and maintained by the Mahoosuc Land Trust. It is on the south bank and easily recognized by the log steps leading up from the river. Parking and river information are available here. The current continues slower to Bethel and the US 2 bridge.

Bethel ➤ Rumford   23.50 mi

Description:	Flatwater, quickwater, Class I
Date checked:	2000
Navigable:	Spring, summer, fall: controlled release
Scenery:	Forested
Maps:	Bethel, Bryant Pond, East Andover, Rumford; DL 10 and 18
Portage:	(24.25 mi L Rumford car recommended)

This is a beauiful stretch of river, still in the mountains, with fine views in every direction. The river flows through meadows in an open valley, offering many opportunities to enjoy the views. There are many riffles but no major rapids, and the current is good. The views toward Grafton Notch are particularly interesting, and birds are abundant. The river is large, however, so wind can cause considerable trouble.

The best access at Bethel is at the private campground next to the US 2 bridge. Ask for and obtain permission from the property owners before accessing the river. Here the river turns north; it passes a highway rest area just before the Sunday River enters on the left (4.0 mi) in North Bethel. Just beyond the riffle at the mouth of the Bear River entering left at Newry (6.5 mi), the river resumes its eastward course. A newly built boat launch (11.0 mi) in Hanover offers access to this section of the river, which is sometimes used for floatplane launches and landings. The Ellis River enters on the left (13.75 mi) shortly before the bridge at Rumford Point (14.25 mi).

The remaining 10.0 miles to Rumford have a good current and are good going all the way. Another public boat launch is at about mile 23, next to the McDonalds on US 2.

Take out at the bridge above the first dam at the pull-off on the left. Three dams and a major waterfall make it advisable to carry the whole city in one long portage, cutting across the northward loop of the river where the Swift River enters.

Rumford ➤ Livermore Falls	24.0 mi
Description:	Quickwater, flatwater
Date checked:	2000
Navigable:	Spring, summer, fall; controlled release
Scenery:	Forested, rural, towns
Maps:	Rumford, Dixfield, Worthley Pond, Canton, East Dixfield, Wilton, Livermore Falls, DL 19 and 11
Portage:	(24.0 mi 1 dam)

In this stretch, the river is still in mountainous country, although the higher hills have been left behind. The Androscoggin can be accessed easily at the Mexico boat launch on the Swift River, with the Mead Paper Company on the opposite bank for the first mile or so. From Rumford it is 4.0 miles with a good current to the West Pen bridge, then to

Dixfield, where the Webb River enters on the left. A public boat launch on river left is in Dixfield and is the last easy access point. A bridge in Canton is passed at 15.0 miles, then a portage on river left at the Riley Dam (21.2 mi). There is a series of dams owned by International Paper in this region—be attentive! The remaining 5.0 miles to Livermore Falls present no problems. At first, the river remains in a narrow valley, but then gradually the valley becomes more open and the bottom lands wider and more rural. Some 16 miles below Dixfield, Sevenmile Stream enters on the left. There is a big dam at Livermore Falls that is best carried on the left.

Livermore Falls ➤ Auburn-Lewiston	30.0 mi
Description:	Quickwater, flatwater, Class II, III
Date checked:	2000
Navigable:	Spring, summer, fall; controlled release
Scenery:	Rural, towns
Maps:	Livermore Falls, Turner Center, Lewiston 15; DL 11
Portages:	25.5 mi Gulf Island Dam
	26.5 mi Deer Rips Dam
	(29.0 mi dam and cascades)

A boat access site below the dams in Livermore Falls is on river right, about 0.5 mile south of ME 4 bridge. There are two sets of rapids in this section before you come to the twin bridges of ME 219. Just below the bridge is a ledge-type rapid, which should be scouted before running. Portaging is possible through the island that the twin bridges cross. The 6.6 miles from the twin bridges to Center Bridge is wonderful calmwater paddling, with white pine lining the banks. The current is almost nonexistent due to the Gulf Island Pond dam another 9.0 miles downstream. The Turner bridge has a boat launch with parking, but no restroom facilities.

From here, it is all slackwater for 7.0 miles down Gulf Island Pond to the Gulf Island Dam. Many paddlers take out here, but you can continue 1.3 miles more to the Deer Rips Dam, another high dam. Below that is another 2.6 miles to the first dam in Auburn-Lewiston, where there is a long carry on river right around the dam and cascades below.

Gulf Island Pond has an interesting feature a few miles down. In a state-mandated effort to increase oxygen levels in the impounded water, pure oxygen is bubbled into the water through an underwater diffuser. A line of effervescent water crosses the river from bank to bank. An unusual sight.

Auburn-Lewiston ➤ Durham		10.0 mi
Description:	Flatwater, quickwater, Class II, III	
Date checked:	2000	
Navigable:	Spring, summer, fall; controlled release	
Scenery:	Rural	
Maps:	Lewiston 15, Freeport 15, Bath 15; DL 5 and 6	

In this section, the river flows through the rolling country of southern Maine, with less-spectacular but still pleasant rural scenery. The Little Androscoggin River joins with the Androscoggin in Auburn. There is a set of rips, Dresser's Rips, below the confluence of the two rivers that are Class II–III, depending on the water level.

Durham ➤ Brunswick		12.50 mi
Description:	Flatwater, quickwater, Class II	
Date checked:	2000	
Navigable:	Spring, summer, fall; controlled release	
Scenery:	Urban, rural	
Portages:	4.0 mi L Worumbo Falls Dam 0.5 mi	
	7.5 mi R dam at Pejepscot 0.25 mi	
	(12.5 mi R dam at Brunswick)	

A fine public boat launch is found in Durham, on river right. This section of the river is beautiful, and lots of wildlife can be seen. From Durham it is 3.0 miles to the boat launch at the confluence with the Sabattus River, which enters on the left upstream of Lisbon. There are some Class I–II riffles in this section. Another mile brings you to the Worumbo Falls Dam; portage on the left. Another 0.5 mile downstream on river left is the Lisbon Falls boat ramp. Three miles of flat water bring you to the Pejepscot Dam; portage on river right along the trail. A cleverly designed boat slide helps with the steep bank back down to the river downstream of the dam. Most of the remaining 4.0 miles are quickwater. The large red I-95 bridge hums with traffic, and then the Brunswick take-out is at the Mill Street boat landing, on river right. The river is cordoned off with log booms from this point on because of fast current, rapids, and the dam below. For those willing to brave traffic, portage on river right to below the rapids at the 250th Anniversary park. Brunswick's new bike path is also an access point, reachable by Water Street on the right side of the river. You can put in here to explore Merrymeeting Bay, which is tidal. Keep an eye on the weather, as this expanse is wide and unprotected.

Magalloway River

The Magalloway River is a beautiful, wildlife-abundant, little-used river in western Maine. Beginning in Moose Bog near the Canadian Border, the river runs through Aziscohos Lake, then meanders its way into New Hampshire before joining the outlet of Umbagog Lake to form the Androscoggin River. Above Aziscohos Lake, there is no public access.

Aziscohos Lake offers many miles of paddling as well as a number of campsites. Below Aziscohos Dam, the Magalloway River offers both whitewater and flatwater trips, which may be run in combination with trips across Umbagog Lake and/or the Androscoggin River.

Camping in the area is uncrowded but limited to designated areas along the rivers and lakes. Culvert Camps on the Magalloway are administered from Mollidgewock Campground (603-482-3373), 3.0 miles south of Errol.

Aziscohos Dam ➤ Wilsons Mills		3.25 mi
Description:	Class II, III, IV	
Date checked:	2000	
Navigable:	Spring, summer, fall; controlled release	
Scenery:	Wild, forested	
Maps:	Oquossoc 15, Errol 15; DL 28 and 27	

For more information on this stretch, see the *AMC Classic Northeastern Whitewater Guide* by Bruce Lessels.

Although it may look tempting, do not put in just below the dam! Many iron rods are still embedded in the bedrock from logging days and will quickly tear any boat into pieces.

The first few hundred yards are extremely technical and can be bony at low levels. Although it is usually Class III, this stretch can be Class IV at high levels; beyond here, the rapids are less difficult but still technical. After a mile or so, on a left bend, a large ledge drop may form a large hole at high levels. A hunting camp may be seen on the right side. From this point, the river decreases in intensity as it nears the NH 16 bridge at Wilsons Mills.

Wilsons Mills ➤ Androscoggin River	16.25 mi
Description:	Flatwater, quickwater
Date checked:	2000
Navigable:	Spring, summer, fall; controlled release
Scenery:	Forested, rural
Maps:	Errol 15; DL 27

The lower part of the Magalloway offers a leisurely paddle and a chance to observe wildlife and picturesque views. The river is narrow at the start, with a 3-MPH current; it meanders along with views of Aziscohos Mountain on the east, and Halfmoon Mountain and the spectacular granite cliffs on the sides of the Diamond Peaks and Mount Dustin off to the west, looping into New Hampshire for a mile.

Below the confluence with the Diamond River (6.0 mi), the Magalloway River begins to widen; in 0.75 mile it passes under the ME 16 bridge near the Magalloway schoolhouse and back into New Hampshire in another mile. From there, the river wanders, with many side channels to explore and pond lilies galore. The Sturtevant Pond outlet enters in a wide culvert from the left. Farther down, Culvert Camp is on the right. In 3.0 miles, it reaches Umbagog Lake and the Androscoggin River, when the river swings west, away from the highway.

Umbagog Lake

All of the big lakes of western Maine, Rangeley, Mooselook-meguntic, and the Richardson Lakes, drain through the Rapid River into Umbagog Lake and from there to the Androscoggin River. All of these lake levels are artificially raised, creating a dependable reservoir for power generation. They offer public launching ramps, campsites, and many miles of paddling.

Lake Umbagog is an irregularly shaped, shallow lake that is mostly wild, but accessible. Much of the New Hampshire land surrounding the lake lies within the Lake Umbagog National Wildlife Refuge. Bald eagles (one pair) have nested in a tall, nearly dead pine tree on an island near the point where the Magalloway River enters the lake.

Lake Umbagog is a popular, though expensive, place to camp. Settlement is only at the southern end, along NH 26, where reservations for campsites should be arranged.

There are campsites at the Umbagog Lake Campground (Errol, NH; 603-482-7795). Reserve sites and pay a fee at the base camp located where NH 16 skirts the southern tip of the lake.

Camping at Cedar Stump Campground, at the mouth of the Rapid River, is run by Saco Bound/Northern Waters (603-447-2177) in Errol, which can also arrange shuttle service for the Rapid River.

Rapid River

The Rapid River flows from Lower Richardson Lake to Lake Umbagog and offers difficult rapids and clean water in a remote setting. The river flow is regulated at Middle Dam on Lower Richardson Lake by the Union Water Power Company for power generation and paper production on the Androscoggin. Water-release levels for the next 24 hours can be obtained from Central Maine Power's river information line (800-557-3569).

Forest Lodge, the former home of Louise Dickinson Rich, whose book, *We Took to the Woods*, relates her experiences in this region, is on the tote road below Pond in the River. On the northwestern shore of Pond in the River are the remains of the steam tug *Alligator*, which was used to winch rafts of logs across the lake. Some of the rocks in the river have been blasted to facilitate log drives, and their sharp edges can be hazardous to boaters.

The Rapid River would be even more popular if the access were less difficult. Middle Dam can be reached by a 3- to 4-mile paddle across Lower Richardson Lake, whereas the mouth of the Rapid River can be reached by a 6- to 7-mile paddle from Errol. A motorboat shuttle is often arranged by whitewater paddlers. A tote road runs from Middle Dam to Sunday Cove on Lake Umbagog, and shuttle service is available through Lakewood Camps at Middle Dam (Andover, ME; 207-243-2959) for whitewater paddlers wishing to run the rapids or for flatwater paddlers wishing to avoid them. It is also possible to hand-carry boats up to run the last section of the rapids.

Middle Dam ➤ Long Pool		3.0 mi
Description:	Lake, Class II, III, IV	
Date checked:	2000	
Navigable:	Spring, summer, fall; controlled release, 600-2,000 cfs runnable	
Scenery:	Wild	
Maps:	Oquossoc 15; DL 18	

Put in at the whirlpool below the dam or 50 yards downstream at Harbec Pool. The next 0.5 mile is Cemetery Rapids, which contains Class III waves with the right side recommended for the upper half and the left side for the lower half. The next 1.5 miles are Pond in the River. Lower Dam, at the outlet, is mostly gone, and the 2-foot-plus drop can be run if desired. There is a branch road from the tote road for those wishing to start here. Then there is 1.0 mile of Class II–III rapids, scratchy at 600 cfs, to Long Pool, where there is a branch road. Paddlers carrying up from downstream should take the turn just after a few houses on the right.

Long Pool ➤ Lake Umbagog		3.0 mi
Description:	Class III, IV	
Date checked:	2000	

Navigable:	Spring, summer, fall; controlled release, 600-2,000 cfs runnable
Scenery:	Wild
Maps:	Oquossoc 15, Errol 15; DL 18
Campsite:	1.5 mi Cedar Stump private $

The first 1.5 miles have difficult rapids that should be run only by expert boaters with suitable heavy-water craft. Just below Long Pool, the river curves slightly to the right and enters the First Big Pitch, which contains 4- to 6-foot waves (even at lower levels); this should be run to the right of center to avoid a large hole on the left. This is followed by several hundred yards of easier rapids to another difficult but shorter pitch, sometimes known as Elephant Rock because of the large black rock in the middle. After a short, calmer section at Cold Spring, the Third Big Pitch starts (sometimes called the Staircase because of its appearance when viewed from below), with three steps and a pool below each at the lower water levels. This rapid is longer than the first two and leads to Smooth Ledge. Here, a rock dike extends from the right bank, with a hydraulic and a pool below, which is a favored spot for lunch.

Next is an S-turn rapid called Island Rip, which is intricate at 600 cfs and contains larger waves at higher levels. Then come two hydraulics to the right of center called the Jaws of Death. The upper hydraulic is full of air and hard to get out of at 600 cfs (not quite as difficult at 1,200 cfs) and becomes a standing wave at 1,800 cfs. The lower one also should be avoided.

The Devil's Hopyard consists of heavy waves studded with boulders for the next mile. The rapids end abruptly, and just below is Cedar Stump, a primitive campsite that can be reached by motorboat from Lake Umbagog. A carry trail up the river connects to the tote road for those wishing to hand carry. It is about 1.5 miles to Long Pool or 2.5 miles to Lower Dam.

The last 1.5 miles to Lake Umbagog are wide, and the current gradually decreases.

Cupsuptic River

The Cupsuptic River rises in a rugged mountain wilderness on the Maine-Quebec border and flows southward into Cupsuptic Lake, one of the Rangeley lakes. The last 8.0 miles below Big Falls are relatively flat and offer good paddling. Access to the start is by a private road controlled by the Seven Islands Company. Ask for and obtain permission before crossing property lines.

Big Falls ➤ Cupsuptic Lake		8.0 mi
Description:	Flatwater, quickwater, Class I	
Date checked:	2000	
Navigable:	High water	
Scenery:	Forested	
Maps:	Cupsuptic 15; DL 28	
Portage:	6.0 mi R Little Falls 0.25 mi	

A start can be made at Lost Brook field, just below Big Falls. The first mile to Portage Brook has fast current, shallow rapids, and pools. From there to Little Falls, the current moves more slowly and can be paddled either way, as the course becomes more meandering and the balsam banks give way to alder thickets. The river can be reached at the bridge on Lincoln Pond Road. There may be many blowdowns.

Two more miles of slower current bring you to Little Falls. You can put in here to paddle upstream for about 3 miles until blowdowns make further progress impractical. There is a good 0.25-mile portage trail on the right around the falls. The falls has approximately a 5-foot drop, and is not recommended to run. There is a huge boulder in the middle of this 30-foot-wide stretch. Also, this is a historical flyfishing spot. It is common to see 6 to 8 flyfishermen on any given day. A mass of downed trees for 200 yards below the falls makes a carry imperative. There is a portage trail on the right. Below are 2.0 more miles of slackwater to ME 16 and Cupsuptic Lake.

Kennebago River

The Kennebago River rises just east of the high peaks on the Maine-Quebec border and flows south to drain the rugged mountain area north of the Rangeley lakes. In enters Mooselookmeguntic Lake close to the outlet of Rangeley River from Rangeley Lake. The dirt road that follows up the river is not open to the public, but the river can be reached indirectly from the Morton Cut-off Road, right onto Lincoln Pond Road.

The upper and lower sections are relatively quiet, but the middle section is an expert whitewater run in the early spring.

Bear Brook ➤ Kennebago		8.0 mi
Description:	Quickwater, Class I	
Date checked:	2000	
Navigable:	High and medium water	
Scenery:	Wild	
Maps:	Cupsuptic 15; DL 28	
Portage:	(8.0 mi power dams)	

At high water, it is possible to put in at the Bear Brook bridge, which can be reached by the Canada Road. Shallow rapids lead for a distance to Little Kennebago Lake, which is a mile across to the outlet at the south end. There, you can reach a launching ramp via Lincoln Pond Road from ME 16, and Morton Cut-off Road, or from Tim Pond Road from ME 27, north of Eustis. You can paddle upstream aways from this point. The river meanders 3.0 miles to the outlet of Kennebago Lake. It is another mile to the first of two power dams.

Kennebago ➤ Bridge		6.0 mi
Description:	Class III	
Date checked:	2000	
Navigable:	Medium and high water	
Scenery:	Wild	
Maps:	Cupsuptic 15, Oquossoc 15; DL 28	

You need to ask for and obtain permission to drive on a private road opposite the Cupsuptic MFS. Put in below the lower dam at the old settlement of Kennebago. The first 2.0 miles are Class I and II rapids and the last 4.0 are Class III. The rapids are continuous, and you must be able to read them as they are run.

The gauge for this run is on the ME 16 bridge that crosses the Kennebago 1.0 mile north of Oquossoc. A reading of 1.0 on the gauge is medium water and 1.6 and over is high water. At medium water, the river is rocky and technical. At 1.6, many of the rocks are covered and there are large, turbulent, boat-filling waves. There are also some sticky reversals.

Bridge ➤ Mooselookmeguntic Lake	7.0 mi
Description:	Flatwater, quickwater, Class I, II
Date checked:	2000
Navigable:	Medium water
Scenery:	Wild, forested
Maps:	Oquossoc 15; DL 28

The first mile below here is easy rapids, which are probably scratchy in midsummer. This is followed by a good current for the next 2.0 miles to Kamankeag Brook, which can be reached by driving in 5.0 miles on Boy Scout Camp Road, off ME 16. The current slows and the river winds for the final 4.0 miles to the ME 16 bridge and Mooselookmeguntic Lake, passing the Boy Scout camp (no buildings) on the left bank partway down. This is probably the only spot on the Kennebago providing loading areas (and lots of blueberries). Moose are often seen along the river.

From the Boy Scout camp down, it is a predominantly sandy/gravel bottom, and quick moving in the spring, up to Class II. In the summer there would be some dragging. Great fun for families.

A recommended put-in is at Steepbank Pool, with a take-out at ME 16. The Boy Scout camp is halfway down. Steepbank Pool is a historic flyfishing spot, chock full of anglers. Be courteous.

Rangeley River

The Rangeley River is the connecting link between Rangeley Lake and Mooselookmeguntic Lake. It starts at the ME 16 bridge at the northwestern edge of Rangeley Lake, and it looks like a continuation of the lake.

Rangeley Lake ➤ Mooselookmeguntic Lake		1.5 mi
Description:	Class II	
Date checked:	2000	
Navigable:	Medium water	
Scenery:	Forested, town	
Maps:	Oquossoc 15; DL 28	

Lift over the screens and paddle 200 yards to the dam, which should be carried left. The fish ladder has been removed, although the framework remains. Below the dam are fairly continuous Class II rapids to Mooselookmeguntic Lake. These are recommended for spring and early summer.

Wild River

The Wild River drains the Carter and the Baldface-Royce ranges in the White Mountains, flowing northeast to Hastings. There, it is joined by Evans Brook from Evans Notch and then flows north into the Androscoggin River at Gilead.

Wild River Campground ➤ Gilead		8.0 mi
Description:	Class II, III, IV	
Date checked:	2000	
Navigable:	High water (mid-March to mid-April)	
Scenery:	Forested	
Maps:	Bethel; DL 10	

Take US 2 to Gilead, and then follow ME 113 for 2.75 miles to Hastings. If the snow has melted, take the gravel road that turns off to the right at Hastings; the road follows the river to Wild River Campground, which is about 5 miles from the start of the gravel road. To avoid a longer carry (100 yd) from the campground to the Wild, you can put in at Blue Brook, just below the campground. It flows into the Wild after a short distance. If the road is not open to the campground, you can use many alternative put-ins; in most places, the river is just a short carry through the woods. Always remember to ask for and obtain permission before crossing property lines. For information on road conditions, call the Ranger Station at Evans Notch (207-824-2134).

The run is continuous with many rocks, waves, and holes. Two miles from the take-out, where the river turns away from the road (just below a large gravel turnout), is the heaviest water on the trip—Class IV. It is best to scout this section on the way to the put-in. The last mile above the US 2 bridge is an easier, Class II stretch. A few inches more or less water changes the run to dangerously heavy or bony.

Sunday River

The Sunday River rises in the northern Mahoosuc Range and flows southeast into the Androscoggin River at North Bethel. It enjoys a beautiful setting in a small, peaceful valley where the Mahoosucs rise impressively in the background. The waters are perfectly clear.

Above the Pool ➤ Androscoggin River	9.25 mi
Description:	Quickwater, flatwater, Class I, II, III
Date checked:	2000
Navigable:	High water (late April to early May)
Scenery:	Forested, rural
Maps:	Gilead, Bethel; DL 10

Take Sunday River Road toward Ketchum from North Bethel. Shortly before you come to the bridge over Sunday River, there is a woods road that leads to the river and a good put-in spot. The put-in here avoids the unrunnable double-ledge drop that is about 100 yards below the bridge. High water is needed, so the best time is usually around the end of April. This period often coincides with mud season, which can make the access road a Class IV experience.

The rapids are Class II for the first 1.25 miles; then Class III rapids start. There, the river splits into three branches; stop and scout. Most of the water is in the center and left; the run in the center is more difficult than the left. A small, river-wide hydraulic is formed where the branches come together.

Below the pool there is an easy Class III rapid; then the rapids are mostly Class II for the rest of the way to the covered bridge, with a few slightly harder. Watch carefully for downed trees.

There is a new gauge on the downstream, river-right side of the concrete bridge next to the covered bridge.

Below the covered bridge is another mile of easy rapids, and then the current gradually slows to the Androscoggin. The easiest take-out is from a side road on the right, upstream of the US 2 bridge (9.25 mi).

Bear River

The Bear River drains the south side of Grafton Notch. Most of this section is easy rapids, but there are three widely separated Class III ledges.

North Newry ➤ Newry	6.75 mi
Description:	Quickwater, Class I, II, III
Date checked:	2000
Navigable:	High water (April)
Scenery:	Forested, rural
Maps:	Old Speck Mountain 15, Bethel; DL 18 and 10

Put in at the Devil's Horseshoe, which is 0.25 mile north of the tiny settlement of North Newry on ME 26. The Horseshoe is a geologic feature that so much resembles a breached dam that you will question whether its origin was natural. Kayakers may be tempted to run the heavy 4-foot drop through the break.

Busy Class II water starts immediately and lasts for about 0.75 mile, to the point where Branch Brook comes in from under ME 26 on the left. Here there is a 3-foot sloping ledge with a tiny bit of a slot in it. The setup for the slot is a fast S-turn, which is Class III when the water is high.

Fast current and scattered rocks continue for 0.25 mile to a sudden, but straightforward, drop over a 2-foot ledge. The river then runs fast and fairly unobstructed for another mile to a 2- to 3-foot ledge, which produces a strong roller and some haystacks.

The remaining 4.0 miles to US 2 are mostly fast current with occasional rocks or tight corners, none of which rates more than Class II at average mid-April flows. The Androscoggin River is 100 yards downstream of the US 2 bridge.

Ellis River

The Ellis River rises in Ellis Pond and flows westward through the hills into the Andover interval, where it meets the West Branch of the Ellis River. Above South Andover, it is too shallow to run in low water. Unlike the other rivers in this region, it is a stillwater stream which offers an easy trip in enjoyable surroundings.

Andover ➤ Rumford Point	17.0 mi
Description:	Flatwater, quickwater
Date checked:	2000
Navigable:	Medium water
Scenery:	Rural
Maps:	Old Speck Mountain 15, Ellis Pond, East Andover; DL 18

You can put in at the crossing of ME 5 over the West Branch of the Ellis River just below the turn to South Arm. It is a small meadow brook here, winding through the intervale for 2.0 miles to the junction with the main river. It then becomes larger but continues its winding course another 2.5 miles to the bridge at South Andover. For the next 8.5 miles, the river twists through the flat valley bottoms to the bridge at the North Rumford School. The river continues, but with a somewhat less tortuous course for 4.0 miles to the US 2 bridge, only 200 yards above the junction with the Androscoggin River.

Swift River

The Swift River rises in one of the unincorporated townships south of Rangeley and flows south through Byron, Roxbury, and Mexico to the Androscoggin River at Rumford. For the most part, it is too steep to paddle. The river is perhaps best known as a popular place to pan for gold, although more aluminum than gold is now to be found on some rocks. The river rises and falls quickly, making it difficult to determine the best time for paddling. When low, it is impassable, and when high, it is dangerous in spots. At medium water, it is navigable from below the gorge at Byron.

Byron ➤ Mexico	13.0 mi
Description:	Quickwater, Class I, II, III
Date checked:	2000
Navigable:	Medium water (April)
Scenery:	Forested, towns
Maps:	Ellis Pond 15, Roxbury 15, Rumford 15; DL 18 and 19
Portages:	(6.5 mi L Swift River Falls 100 yd) 10.0 mi R dam and ledge 0.5 mi

Put in just below the gorge at Coos Canyon. You can reach the best put-in by turning right off ME 17 onto Tumbledown Mountain Road. After crossing the bridge over the gorge, take the next right, which is just after the bridge, and follow that for 100 yards to the Swift.

There are some sharp turns and drops in the first mile or so below the gorge. Many of these turns and ledge drops offer good playing and surfing spots. The next 3.0 miles to Roxbury are Class I and II and quickwater. One mile below Roxbury (where Walker Brook enters on the left) is a Class III rapid. Here, the point at which the river begins to steepen and become more difficult, is the most interesting and challenging part of the trip. After Walker Brook rapid, the river turns to the right and then back to the left as it passes through a steep-walled gorge. The rapids preceding the gorge can be difficult at any water level, with large waves and rocks protecting the mouth of the gorge. The gorge itself is a Class III ride with a wave train running through the center.

Below the gorge, several Class III drops occur as the river turns sharply and passes over a series of ledges. One mile below the gorge is Swift River Falls. There is a take-out or a portage on the left. These falls cannot be run.

After Swift River Falls, there are quickwater and Class I rapids to Hale, where there is an easy Class II ledge just above the bridge and a heavy Class II–III chute underneath it. Next, an impassable pitch and a dam require a long portage on the right. About 1 mile of Class II water brings you to "Tubbs," and an S-turn drop that is harder than it looks (Class III at high water). The rapids diminish and disappear in the 2.0 miles to Mexico and the US 2 bridge 100 yards above the junction with the Androscoggin.

Webb River

The Webb River rises in Lake Webb in Weld and flows south through Carthage to form the boundary between Mexico and Dixfield, finally emptying into the Androscoggin River at Dixfield. The upper part between Lake Webb and Carthage offers a good spring run for Class III paddlers. The section below Carthage is mostly smoothwater and is usable in all but a dry season.

Lake Webb ➤ Carthage	4.5 mi
Description:	Class II, III
Date checked:	2000
Navigable:	High water (late March to early April)
Scenery:	Forested, rural, towns
Maps:	Weld, Dixfield; DL 19

If you are approaching Lake Webb from the south on ME 142, leave a shuttle vehicle at the take-out (a widening of the road's shoulder just over 0.5 mile past the point where the Webb is first crossed by a small bridge on ME 142). From the takeout, drive north on ME 142 for approximately 4.5 miles to the second ME 142 bridge that crosses the Webb. Check the gauge on the downstream, center abutment of the bridge. A reading of 2 is considered minimal level; anything above 2 will offer a good Class II–III run. The put-in, located 0.75 mile above this bridge, is not much more than a widening of the shoulder on the left side of the road if you are going north.

The put-in is down a steep bank, and the river is narrow.

The rapids begin immediately and continue for most of the 4.75-mile run. The rapids are generally short and rocky and are often followed by pools. There are also a few ledge drops.

Approximately 1.25 miles from the put-in the river narrows and is lined with alder; watch for downed trees and branches that reach into the river.

Next is a small bridge that marks the beginning of a short Class III drop, usually run on the right. The next short section of the run is Class II–III rapids, which offer good surfing opportunities. Below this section are several good Class III rapids full of rocks and waves, with the last rapid being just above a bridge over the Webb at Berry Mills. This rapid is marked by a high bank on the left where the river drops sharply, turns to the right, and then straightens for a short distance before turning back hard to the left.

Below Berry Mills, the river passes through a heavily wooded section where there are multiple channels. The best route is usually on the right. Watch for downed trees in the river. Below the wooded section is one more solid Class III rapid, which leads to the take-out on the right.

Carthage ➤ Dixfield	9.0 mi
Description:	Flatwater
Date checked:	2000
Navigable:	Spring, summer, fall
Scenery:	Forested, rural
Maps:	Weld, Dixfield; DL 19
Portages:	4.0 mi falls short
	8.5 mi falls

Put in at the ME 142 bridge at Carthage. There are 2.0 miles of meadow paddling followed by 2.0 miles more through woodlands to the falls, where a short carry should be made. Below are 4.0 more miles of marshy woodlands leading to a bridge at the beginning of a 100-yard-long rapid near the northern edge of Dixfield. In the next mile, toward the Androscoggin River, is an impassable waterfall just before the point where the US 2 bridge is visible.

Sevenmile Stream

Sevenmile Stream rises in Carthage and flows east and then south to the Androscoggin River in Jay. Its upper stretches are too steep to run, but below East Dixfield it has a few miles of good, navigable sections. It is a relatively small stream and should be paddled early in the season when the snows are still melting on Saddleback Mountain. This is lovely, mountainous country.

East Dixfield ➤ Androscoggin River	8.0 mi
Description:	Quickwater, flatwater
Date checked:	2000
Navigable:	Spring (early April)
Scenery:	Rural
Maps:	East Dixfield, Wilton; DL 19

Put in at East Dixfield from a side road off ME 17. The first 2.5 miles are all rapids but not difficult. The going is almost all through open meadowland. By the time Birchland Cemetery is reached, though, the river has become much quieter, and from there to the Androscoggin River the going is all smooth-water with a fair current. Take out at the ME 140 bridge less than 100 yards above the Androscoggin River.

Dead River

The Dead River is the outlet from Androscoggin Lake to the Androscoggin River. It should not be confused with the whitewater run on the Dead River that flows into the Kennebec River at the Forks. This Dead River is a flatwater paddle and can be done at any season.

Androscoggin Lake ➤ Androscoggin River	7.0 mi
Description:	Flatwater (motorboats)
Date checked:	2000
Navigable:	Spring, summer, fall
Scenery:	Forested
Maps:	Wayne, Turner Center; DL 12
Portage:	5.5 mi dam

The Dead River starts on the northern side of Androscroggin Lake, near the tip of the peninsula that extends almost 2 miles into the lake. It is nearly 2.0 miles down the river to the village of Dead River and the highway bridge. The river then winds and twists for another 3.0 miles to the next bridge, below which are 2.0 more river miles to the Androscoggin River, with an easy lift around a low dam. You may take out at a farm on the left bank just below the mouth or go on down the Androscoggin 3.0 miles to the ME 219 bridge. Remember to ask for and obtain permission before crossing property lines.

Flying Pond   2.5 mi

From the head of Flying Pond in Vienna you can paddle 18.0 miles of lakes and connecting rivers to the Dead River and another 7.0 miles of easy going down the Dead River to the Androscoggin (25.0 miles in all). All the lakes and rivers are flatwater paddling which can be done at any season.

You can put in at Vienna; from there, it is 1.0 mile to the cove on the east short where the outlet is located. There is a long arm of the lake to the south of this, however. The outlet runs through a series of ponds, the last of which is 1.0 mile long and behind the dam at Mount Vernon. The dam must be carried into Minnehonk Lake.

Minnehonk Lake   1.25 mi

From Mount Vernon at the northern end of the lake it is only a short paddle to Hopkins Stream at the southern end.

Hopkins Stream   3.0 mi

There are 200 yards of brook to Horseshoe Pond, the outlet of which takes off just to the right of the inlet. Then it is 3.0 miles down an easy stream of smoothwater to the dam at West Mount Vernon, where a short carry brings you into Crotched Pond.

Alternative Start at Parker Pond   3.75 mi

You can put in at the northern end of Parker Pond where the stream from Whittier Pond crosses under the road at the shore in Vienna. Only the northern end of the pond is in Vienna; the rest is in Fayette, although most of the shores are in Chesterfield and Mount Vernon. The outlet is at the southeastern corner where a short river takes off. After 0.5 mile, there is a dam. Traveling 100 yards more brings you to the millpond behind the dam at West Mount Vernon, 0.5 mile farther on. You can also reach this point from Flying Pond in Vienna and Minnehonk Lake in Mount Vernon by coming down Hopkins stream from the latter. Below this is Crotched Pond.

Crotched Pond	3.75 mi

Crotched pond is sometimes called Echo Lake. Although the outlet is at Fayette on the western bay (where there is a small dam), there is an equally long eastern bay, which also provides a pleasant outing.

Lovejoy Pond	2.5 mi

It is only 2.0 miles from Fayette to the outlet at North Wayne, but there is also a northeastern arm that invites exploration. About 0.25 mile down the outlet river, at North Wayne, you will come to a dam that must be carried.

Pickerel Pond and Pocasset Lake	3.0 mi

Just below the dam at North Wayne, Pickerel Pond begins. It is only 1.0 mile from the inlet at the northeastern end to the outlet at the northwestern end, but a large bay to the south offers access to marshes. Pocasset Lake is 2.0 miles long and wider than some of the upper lakes. The outlet river takes off at Wayne, west of the peninsula that juts into the lake from the south. Here, there are two dams a short distance apart.

Androscoggin Lake	2.5 mi

This is the largest lake in this chain. Although it is only 2.0 miles from the inlet to the outlet, there are many miles of fine flatwater paddling in the large southern and western bays.

Nezinscot River

The Nezinscot River rises in the high hills of Sumner, its East Branch forming the boundary between Sumner and Hartford. The two branches meet just below Buckfield and the main river flows east to the Androscoggin River at Turner. The East Branch below East Sumner is small and quite rocky even in high water. The main river is more placid and can be paddled in any but dry seasons. The river runs through pleasant valleys with open meadows and woodlands.

Buckfield ➤ Androscoggin River	15.0 mi
Description:	Flatwater, quickwater, Class I, II
Date checked:	2000
Navigable:	Spring
Scenery:	Forested, rural
Maps:	Worthley Pond, West Sumner-Buckfield, Poland 15, Turner Center; DL 11
Portages:	8.0 mi dam at Turner (14.5 mi dam at Keens Mills)

Put in at the ME 117 bridge south and east of Buckfield. The next 8.0 miles to the dam at Turner are flat river through open meadows and woodlands, with the river making several big loops a few miles above Turner. Below the dam at Turner is 0.25 mile of Class II rapids over and around low ledges. Three miles of quickwater and Class I rips bring you to the first of two ME 117 bridges at Turner Center; there is a strong Class II rapid just below this bridge. The second bridge is 1.0 mile below. It is then 3.0 miles more to the dam at Keens Mills, where most paddlers take out rather than go the additional 0.25 mile to the Androscoggin River.

Nezinscot River (West Branch)

The West Branch of the Nezinscot flows from West Sumner to the main river at Buckfield. The dirt River Road that follows and crosses the river may be impassable for all but four-wheel-drive vehicles in the spring (when the river is usually run). The first mile of river below the ME 219 bridge is heavily obstructed by alder and is not recommended.

West Sumner ➤ Nezinscot River	10.75 mi
Description:	Flatwater, quickwater, Class I, II
Date checked:	2000
Navigable:	High water (April)
Scenery:	Forested, rural
Maps:	West Summer, Buckfield; DL 11
Portage:	9.75 mi dam in Buckfield

The best spot to start is the River Road bridge 1.0 mile south of West Sumner. Take Decoster Road south from West Sumner, and after 0.25 mile bear left onto River Road. This road follows the river to North Buckfield.

In a short distance, the rapids begin as Class I with stretches of quickwater between. There is a drop of 1.5 feet, which is run easily. All of the drops are runnable, with no spot more difficult than Class II. There are a few small islands that can be run on either side and an occasional fallen tree, which will not hinder progress. The stream banks are picturesque and the woods mostly hardwood and open.

There is a short stretch of flatwater. Then, as you approach North Buckfield, the gradient becomes steeper and more effort and quickness are required to maneuver around the rocks. The stream is not brisk, and flow rates around 100 to 150 cfs provide the best running. You can take out downstream on the right at the North Buckfield bridge, but parking is limited. A few hundred feet of rapids remain, then the river flattens, flowing through meadows and woods. Approaching Buckfield, the stream becomes quite steep with numerous rocks. The dam in Buckfield spills water, and the pool above it is neither long nor still.

It is awkward to reach the river below the dam. After a short rapid, it runs into a meadow, meandering until it joins the East Branch to form the Nezinscot about 1 mile below Buckfield.

Little Androscoggin

The Little Androscoggin is one of the larger tributaries of the Androscoggin. It rises in Bryant Pond southeast of Bethel, flows southeast to West Paris, and then south through Paris to Oxford. There, it turns easterly to flow through Mechanic Falls and join the Androscoggin at Auburn. The first 4.0 miles below Bryant Pond are too steep and rapid to run. From Tubbs School in Greenwood you can paddle it all the way to the mouth, although there are a number of dams to be carried in some of the towns. Because of the pond at its head, all but the lower part can be run fairly late in the spring; it is apt to be too low in the summer. The scenery away from the towns is attractive but not spectacular.

Third Bridge ➤ South Paris		12.0 mi
Description:	Flatwater, quickwater, Class I, II	
Date checked:	2000	
Navigable:	Medium water (April and May)	
Scenery:	Forested, towns	
Maps:	Greenwood, West Paris; DL 10 and 11	
Portages:	2.0 mi e dam carry across road	
	4.5 mi e Snows Falls 100 yd	
	6.0 mi R Bisco Falls 20 yd	
	(12.0 mi dam)	

Put in at the third ME 219 bridge upstream of West Paris at a stream junction. The Little Androscoggin is small, with easy rapids halfway to West Paris and then quickwater to the dam located below a bridge on a side road in the center of town. Take out upstream of the bridge, and carry across the road.

For 0.5 mile the rapids below the bridge are more difficult than those above. Then the river is smooth until it reaches Snows Falls at a highway rest area on ME 26. Rapids and small ledges extend for 0.25 mile; then there is quickwater leading to Bisco Falls and an 8-foot dam at a natural ledge. Access here is difficult. Rapids continue below the falls, gradually diminishing.

Below there is a long stretch of smoothwater with meanders. It is 5.0 miles to South Paris. You can take out where the river comes close to the road 2.5 miles below the falls, the ME 26 bridge, or 1.0 mile farther down at the ME 117 bridge.

South Paris ➤ Mechanic Falls		20.0 mi
Description:	Flatwater	
Date checked:	2000	
Navigable:	Spring	
Scenery:	Rural, forested	
Maps:	Greenwood, West Paris, Norway 15, Poland 15, Lewiston 15; DL 11	
Portage:	1.0 mi dam	

This section is largely flatwater through meadows and woodlands, with many meanders. Put in just below the ME 117 bridge in South Paris. The stream continues for 2.0 miles in a southwesterly direction to a point below Norway, where the stream from Penneseewassee Lake joins on the right. The river winds for the next 7.0 miles through meadows and woodlands to Oxford; there, it passes under the ME 121 bridge. The stream from Thompson Lake enters on the right, just below the bridge. The river twists and has numerous oxbows for the next 2.0 miles to the dam at Welchville. The following 8.0 miles to Mechanic Falls are mostly through meadows and woodlands, with many meanders and more oxbows. Take out at the ME 11 bridge just west of town. There are several mills and a large dam in Mechanic Falls.

Mechanic Falls ➤ Auburn		13.0 mi
Description:	Flatwater	
Date checked:	2000	
Navigable:	Spring, summer, fall	
Scenery:	Forested, rural, towns	
Maps:	DL 11 and 5	
Portages:	4.0 mi dam	
	5.0 mi dam	

This section is all flatwater. Put in below the dam at Mechanic Falls. From here to the next dam at Hackett Mills are 4.0 miles of river winding through meadows, some of which are overgrown with bushes and trees. From Hackett Mills to the next dam at Minot is 1.0 mile of paddling. The next 7.0 miles to

Auburn are also through meadows, but the river does not wind and twist quite as much as above. There is a gauging station at the bridge 4.0 miles downstream. Take out several miles below this bridge on a side road on the right bank, before entering Auburn. Several dams and an impassable rapid are located before the Little Androscoggin enters the Androscoggin River in the middle of Auburn.

Sabattus River

The Sabattus River drains the Sabattus Pond through Lisbon to the Androscoggin River. It is only 9.0 miles long and flows through pastures and woods for the first 8.0 miles. The Sabattus can be run at any time—water levels vary only slightly. The water is light green in color due to algae. There is little current, and the water quality is good since the mills have ceased operation. The last mile below the dam at Lisbon Center flows through a steep ravine with a technical Class IV rapid that contains an undercut ledge. This last mile is not recommended.

Sabattus ➤ Lisbon Center	8.0 mi
Description:	Flatwater, quickwater below dams
Date checked:	2000
Navigable:	Medium water
Scenery:	Rural, towns
Maps:	USGS Lewiston 15; DL 12 and 6
Portages:	3.5 mi L dam and ledge 50 yd
	(6.5 mi dam)
	(6.75 mi dam)
	(7.75 mi dam)

Sabattus has three dams, so you should put in at the ME 126 bridge that crosses the river below these dams. The river is a quiet, wandering stream that passes under a bridge in 1.0 mile and under the Maine Turnpike 1.0 mile farther. Below are 1.5 miles of large meanders that lead to the dam at Robinson Corner. **Caution!** This dam has been breached, but it needs to be portaged because there are debris and snags in the river just below the old dam. The dam is marked by a low highway bridge; take out on the left before the bridge for the shorter portage. From here, it is 3.0 miles to the first dam in Lisbon, where most people take out. There is another dam 0.25 mile below the first Lisbon dam. Two miles of easy paddling brings you from this dam to the one at Lisbon Center, which marks the end of navigation.

Chapter 3
Kennebec Watershed

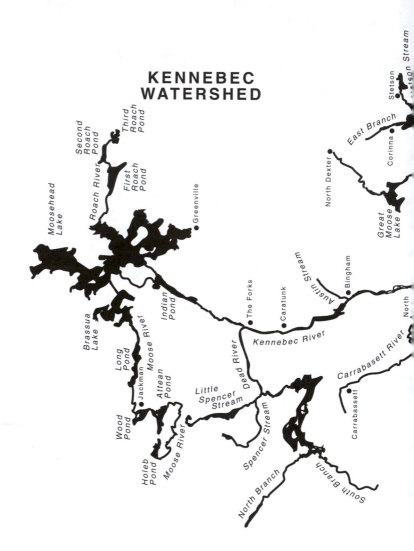

KENNEBEC WATERSHED

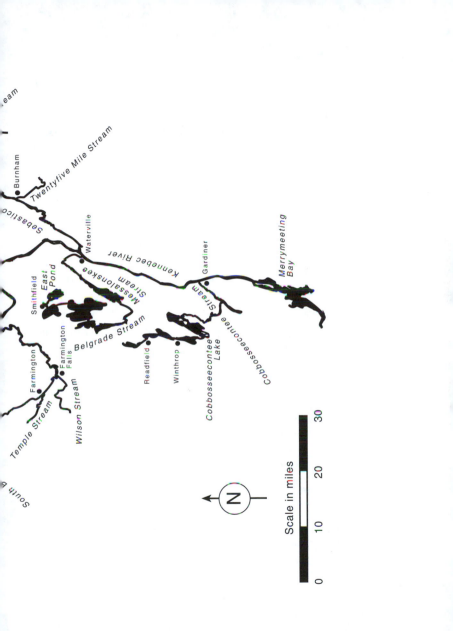

Scale in miles

0   10   20   30

Kennebec River

The Kennebec River is one of the largest rivers in Maine. It flows from Moosehead Lake southwest to the Atlantic below Bath, having received the waters of the Androscoggin River at Merrymeeting Bay just above Bath. Because the river has largely been harnessed for power, most of it is smooth paddling. The upper part above The Forks is rapid and should be run by experienced paddlers only.

This river was the route of Benedict Arnold's abortive invasion of Canada in the fall of 1775. Arnold ascended the river to Carrying Place Stream about 25 miles above the present site of Anson and then crossed through the three Carry Ponds to Bog Brook on the Dead River, a spot now flooded by Flagstaff Lake. From there, he followed the North Branch of that river into Quebec. His tiny force of 1,100 men suffered severely, and many men were lost on the journey.

Moosehead Lake ➤ Harris Station

Moosehead Lake drains by two outlets into Indian Pond; the two outlets provide different types of paddling. The West Outlet, which leaves the lake 2.0 miles below Rockwood (halfway up the lake on the west shore), carries relatively little flow of water and consists almost entirely of a series of ponds. About 9 miles long and followed most of the way by a dirt road, it is passable with some carries. The East Outlet, which leaves the lake at the village of Moosehead one-quarter of the way up the lake on the west shore, is only 3.5 miles long, with heavy and continuous rapids, and is suitable for experts only. Its flow, which is controlled for power generation, is fairly constant and usually very heavy.

West Outlet ➤ Indian Pond   10.0 mi

Description:	Lake, quickwater, Class I
Date checked:	2000
Navigable:	Check Long Pond
Scenery:	Forested
Maps:	Moosehead Lake 15, Brassua Lake 15; DL 40 and 41
Portage:	5.5 mi liftover

When this route has water, it is an easy run through rather wild country. From ME 15, just below the small dam, 1.75 miles down a pond leads to Class I rapids between Long Pond and the next pond. If these are runnable, all of the rapids should be. From here to Churchill Stream each pond is followed by rapids. A dirt road on the right is not obtrusive.

Just beyond a railroad bridge, you will see a very low bridge that you may have to carry on the left. Just beyond Churchill Stream is a slightly harder rapid, followed by a mile of quickwater and another rapid to Round Pond. The outlet is straight across the pond.

After another smooth mile, 0.5 mile of rapids ends in the backwater of Indian Pond. Keep to the left around islands for another mile to the main body of the lake. A boat ramp is 1.0 mile directly across the lake to the south. You may also be able to drive to the lake at a campsite 0.5 mile to the north.

East Outlet ➤ Indian Pond   3.5 mi

Description:	Quickwater, Class II, III, IV
Date checked:	1990
Navigable:	Spring, summer, fall; controlled release
Scenery:	Wild
Maps:	Moosehead Lake 15, Brassua Lake 15; DL 40 and 41

The rapids on this run are separated by sections of quickwater. At low flow (below 2,000 cfs), they are mostly Class II–III; at higher flows, they are Class III–IV.

The dam at the lake is followed by a railroad bridge, and the ME 15 bridge. In 0.5 mile is a narrow chute with a long ramp and cliff on the right. Scout from the left. The next 2.0 miles alternate fast current and rapids, which are usually spread out, but there are a few large boulders. A dirt road, which follows high on the left bank, descends here to river's edge. At 3.0 miles, the flowage from Indian Pond comes into view, but just before reaching the pond there is a heavy drop over a ledge not easily seen from above. Land on the right and scout. The far left has an insignificant drop; the right is all Class

III–IV and can be run in more than one place. Below, you will find a quiet pool and a picnic site on the right.

Indian Pond
9.0 mi

Indian Pond is a nautral body of water that was enlarged by the Harris Dam. This long, narrow lake offers good wildlife-viewing opportunities in the wetland area at the north end, and a scenic forested shoreline with minimal development for much of the remainder of its length. It is 9.0 miles from either approach to a boat ramp at the southern end. Campsites are near the northern end, one on an island at the West Outlet, and one at the East Outlet, both of which are inclined to be insect-infested. Two other campsites are halfway down, one on each side.

Take out at the landing and picnic areas to the left of the 155-foot-high Harris Dam, which is maintained for the public by the Central Maine Power Company.

Harris Station ➤ Carry Brook
3.75 mi

Description:	Class III, IV, V
Date checked:	2000
Navigable:	Spring, summer, fall; controlled release minimum 140 cfs, usually run at 4,800–5,000 cfs
Scenery:	Wild
Maps:	The Forks 15; DL 40

Below Harris Station, the Kennebec flows through a wild gorge that is among the most impressive in size and beauty in New England. Because of its dependable water flow and continuous difficulty, it is the finest decked-boat whitewater run in Maine. However, the canyon walls, rising sheer from the turbulent river, that give the gorge its incomparable attraction make it difficult to navigate. Scouting is difficult, and the most severe drops are not feasible to portage, line, or evade. This run is only for boaters of proven skill. Most people prefer to enjoy the gorge from a commercial raft trip.

The flow in the Kennebec is most inconvenient for paddling this section of river. When the generators at the Harris Station are shut down, there is practically no water in the river. Then it must be run from Carry Brook Eddy by poling or lining down the shallow rapids. When the generators are started up in midmorning on weekdays, the river rises several feet in a few minutes' time. With all three generators operating, the flow is 6,500 to 8,000 cfs. Spring is the best time for high water on weekends.

To get the water release schedule from Harris Station for the day or the following day, call Central Maine Power's flow-information line (800-557-3569). There is also a sign at the put-in that states the amount of flow and approximate duration of the flow for that day.

All boaters must sign a release form at the dam office that says that CMP is not responsible for what might happen to them on the river. The dam attendant will also know the flow. A road leads down to the river to the left of the power station. You must arrive before 9:30 A.M. if you wish to drive to the base of the dam to unload equipment. All vehicles must park at the top of the hill near where the rafting companies have their assembly points. If you arrive after 9:30 A.M., you will have to carry all your equipment from the parking lot to the dam.

For more information, see the *AMC Classic Northeastern Whitewater Guide.*

The river is extremely narrow and because of the cliffs, can be a long, bad swim. The size of the waves varies with the water level, but unpredictably. Wave size also is dependent on whether the river is rising or falling. The river has been run by canoes from 140 cfs to 7,200 cfs. At 140 cfs, it is a very technical Class II–III trip. Keep in mind that there is always the possibility that the river may rise if there is a need for more power. It takes only 5 minutes to increase the level from 140 cfs to 8,000 cfs. If you run the Kennebec at minimum water, take out at Carry Brook; the river is too shallow at this water level to continue to The Forks.

Do not attempt to run the Kennebec unless you have an effective self-rescue if you are a canoeist, or a bomb-proof roll if you are in a decked boat. The swim is long and very unpleasant. If you lose your boat, it is very difficult to hike out.

The rapids begin just as you move out of sight of the dam. The waves build to 3 to 4 feet, and the current gets pushy. The first rapid with a name is Taster, so named because it gives you a taste of what the gorge will be like. The next rapid of any consequence is called Rock Garden. At 2,400 cfs or below, it looks like a rock garden. At 3,800 cfs and up, it is a large curling wave on the right side of the river that is best hit on the left side of the wave for a drier run. There are eddies from the start of the run all the way down, ranging in size from large to small; all take some effort to catch.

Below Rock Garden comes Big Mama, which used to be known as Three Sisters until the flood of 1984 rearranged the rocks—and thus the rapid. At 3,800 cfs, it is a pulsating wave; above 3,800 cfs, it begins to get more constant and continues to build. At 6,500 cfs, it is easily an 8- to 10-foot wave. Big Mama is on the right-hand side of the river and can be run anywhere, although the sides provide better opportunities to catch eddies. In a decked boat, the best ride is to head straight for the wave. If you hit it just right, the ride will be incredibly gentle and smooth.

Below Big Mama, Upper Alley Way starts. Stay to the center as you approach the next two rapids. Goodby Hole is nasty if you run it right and Whitewasher is nasty, too, if you get into it on the left. Below Whitewasher there are some large 6- to 8-foot waves. A good eddy on the left is just below these waves. From here down, it is a nice ride through waves to Cathedral Eddy. There are eddies on both the left and right here, although the left eddy starts to resemble a whirlpool and is difficult to exit at levels above 4,800 cfs. This is a good surfing spot.

Next comes Z-turn, which is another play spot. This bend is followed by 100 yards of Class II. Then Magic Rapid, Class V, begins in another 0.25 mile; it can be seen ahead where the river disappears from sight except for some large exploding waves that appear over the horizon line. The Kennebec drops

25 feet in 250 yards here. A trail on the left makes the mandatory scouting easy. The trail leads to a spot just a few yards from Magic. It is also entertaining to watch the rafts punch Magic, since a fair number of them flip. Prominent features here are two holes. At the beginning, on the left near the shore, is Magic (Rock) Falls. Fifty yards below and just to the right of center is an even worse hole called Maytag. The rest of the drop consists of large waves and smaller holes. Once you pass Maytag, you will find that the right side has fewer holes to avoid.

There are two basic ways to run Magic: the Highway, or Magic Hole itself. The Highway consists of a run that starts just right of Magic and then cuts behind Magic to the left to avoid Maytag farther down. There is a large diagonal wave just after Magic and above Maytag that can be used to push to the left. If you stay left, you will have to contend with Hellhole and Bonecruncher, two holes that you should avoid at low water; to do this, cut back right below Maytag.

You can run Magic itself at levels greater than 4,800 cfs; below this level, it becomes very sticky. Above 4,800 cfs it is more forgiving but still can flip rafts. The foam pile on the left of Magic Falls is another place to avoid.

In another mile, Dead Stream enters on the right, dropping over a series of pretty falls. Carry Brook Rapid starts immediately and ends at Carry Brook Eddy.

Carry Brook ➤ The Forks   8.5 mi

Description:	Quickwater, Class I, II, III, IV
Date checked:	2000
Navigable:	Spring, summer, fall; controlled release
Scenery:	Wild
Maps:	The Forks 15; DL 40

Although most of this section is an easy float, Black Brook rapids are 0.5 mile long and unfeasible to line or portage, so the boater putting in here should be prepared to deal with them directly. At open boat levels under 3,000 cfs, the rapids are Class III; above 3,000 cfs, they are Class IV.

You can reach the put-in at Carry Brook by taking a road that leaves the Indian Pond Road at an old shack 0.5 mile north of the Black Brook Bridge. There is a parking area at the end of the road and CMP has now put in steps from the river up the cliff, which makes this former Class V take-out much easier.

Black Brook Rapids start just below the confluence of Carry Brook with the Kennebec, which is 1.0 mile from the start of Carry Brook Eddy. They are continuous for 0.5 mile, with one easier spot in the middle, and cliffs on each side that prevent lining or portaging. Halfway down, and 100 yards above where the river bends to the right, a wide, dangerous hole exists at levels below 5,000 cfs. It is in the center of the river, so stay to either side.

Around the bend to the left is Stand Up Rips, which is Class III at most levels. There is one good surfing hole called Jacuzzi on river right about two-thirds of the way through the rapid. It is fairly sticky at 4,800 cfs or less, so have a throw rope handy to pull out boaters after they tire. For the next 6.5 miles to The Forks, the current is good and the rapids are nearly continuous but easier (Class I and II).

Take out at the ballpark on the right above the bridge or on the left at the confluence.

The Forks ➤ Caratunk	9.0 mi
Description:	Flatwater, quickwater, Class I
Date checked:	2000
Navigable:	Spring, summer, fall; controlled release
Scenery:	Forested
Maps:	The Forks 15, Bingham 15; DL 40 and 30

Below the confluence with the Dead, the Kennebec becomes more gentle, offering a pleasant, easy paddle, which, though not remote like the rivers above, is attractive and away from the road for most of the distance.

There is a pull-off just at the confluence on the left that makes a good launch spot. The rapids are continuous, but easy. In 3.0 miles, you pass Gilroy Island, with a good channel on either side, and Class II rapids below. You can take out at the Appalachian Trail crossing.

Caratunk ➤ Wyman Dam 12.0 mi

Description:	Flatwater, quickwater, Class I
Date checked:	2000
Navigable:	Spring, summer, fall; controlled release
Scenery:	Forested, rural, towns
Maps:	The Forks 15, Bingham 15; DL 30

The current gradually diminishes somewhere around 5 miles to the backwater from Wyman Dam, an attractive lake with steep, wooded hills rising above it. A public boat landing near the head of the lake offers access. Carry the 140-foot-high Wyman Dam in Moscow on the western end, near the powerhouse.

Wyman Dam ➤ Skowhegan 30.0 mi

Description:	Flatwater, quickwater, Class I
Date checked:	2000
Navigable:	Spring, summer, fall; controlled release
Scenery:	Forested
Maps:	Bingham 15, Anson 15, Norridgewock 15, Skowhegan 15; DL 30, 20, and 21
Portages:	5.0 mi L Solon Dam 200 yd
	18.0 mi R 2 dams in Madison 1.0 mi
	(30.0 mi L 2 dams in Skowhegan 0.5 mi)

At this point the river becomes considerably more settled and the banks more open. One mile below the Wyman Dam you pass Bingham on the left; in another 5.0 miles, you reach Caratunk Falls and Solon Dam. Portage 200 yards on the east bank. Then it is 8.0 miles to the mouth of the Carrabassett River at North Anson. In another 5.0 miles, mostly through open meadowlands, you reach the twin towns of Anson and Madison. Here there are two dams 0.5 mile apart; between them the river loops to the east. The portage is on the west bank. There is a rapid below the lower dam for a short distance and then a short rip 0.5 mile below. It is then 2.0 miles to the confluence with the Sandy River at some open fields on the right bank. The next 4.0 miles to Norridgewock offer no obstructions. Another 5.0 miles largely through open fields bring you to Skowhegan, where there are two dams. Here, the river divides into two channels around an island: the North Channel and the South Channel. The best take-out spot is about 200 yards above the North Channel Dam on the left. Then you can carry along Elm, Russell, and Water streets to the Great Eddy below the gorge. This avoids the difficult scramble down into the gorge below the dams.

This gorge can only be run by experts. If conditions are right, experienced paddlers may take out on the island between the dams and put in below to run the gorge, 1.0 mile (Class III–IV), to the Great Eddy.

Skowhegan ➤ Waterville   20.0 mi

Description:	Flatwater, quickwater
Date checked:	2000
Navigable:	Spring, summer, fall; controlled release
Scenery:	Rural, urban
Maps:	Skowhegan 15, Waterville 15; DL 21
Portages:	13.5 mi R dam at Shawmut
	19.0 mi R dam at Waterville
	(20.0 mi L Ticonic Falls)

This stretch has no obstructions, and the river runs through rolling country with open banks and a fair and pleasant landscape for 13.0 miles to the dam at Shawmut in the town of Fairfield; there, the carry is on the right bank. Below the dam is a bit of quickwater followed by 3.0 miles of pleasant country at least as far as Fairfield (3.0 miles above Waterville, where urbanization starts). There are two dams across the river in Waterville: the first is best carried on the right, or Waterville side; the second, 1.0 mile down at Ticonic Falls, is more easily portaged on the left, or Winslow side.

Waterville ➤ Augusta   20.0 mi

Description:	Flatwater, quickwater
Date checked:	2000
Navigable:	Spring, summer, fall; controlled release
Scenery:	Rural
Maps:	Vassalboro 15, Augusta 15; DL 21, 13 & 12

There are no obstructions in this section of the river. A mile below the dam the Sebasticook River enters on the left, and

1.5 miles farther down Messalonskee Stream enters on the right.

The removal of Edwards Dam completed in the fall of 1999, has transformed this section from a uniform impoundment to a river full of variety. Although there are several rips, the only section requiring some concentration is at Six Mile Falls. You can spot the "falls," a series of small drops, in advance by a wire with orange markers stretching across the river about 9 miles below Waterville. The "falls" can be run easily on either the far right or far left. The Sidney boat launch provides an alternative put-in about 10 miles below Waterville.

Augusta ➤ Bath		30.5 mi
Description:	Tidal	
Date checked:	2000	
Navigable:	Spring, summer, fall; controlled release	
Scenery:	Forested, rural, towns	
Maps:	DL 12 and 6	

This section is freshwater tidal and passes some large towns, most of which have public launching ramps. High tide at Augusta is 3 hours 54 minutes later than Portland; tidal range is 4 to 5 feet. It is 6.0 miles to the Gardiner boat ramp and another 11.0 miles to Richmond and the head of Swan Island.

From the ramp in Richmond it is a 9-mile circuit of Swan Island. At low tide, mud flats extend 0.5 mile south of the island.

From Richmond it is 8.5 miles through Merrymeeting Bay, a freshwater tidal ecosystem where 6 rivers meet, to the Chops into Goose Bay. At the Chops one-third of Maine (the Androscoggin and the Kennebec) drains through a gap less than 0.25 mile wide. Currents can be tricky at certain tides. The eastern side of Lines Island has less current and more scenic interest as well as intriguing water conditions. There is a public ramp on the western side at the northern end of Bath, and a public float above the bridge.

Moose River

Moose River rises in Beattie and Lowell townships just east of the Maine/Canadian border (22 miles ± as the crow flies) west of Jackman, Maine. It runs east into and out of Holeb Pond. (Holeb Stream has a unique propensity: it runs into Holeb Pond when there is more rain to the west on the upper Moose and runs out of Holeb Pond when the water is higher in Holeb than in the Moose.) It picks up water as it makes up and flows through Attean, Big Wood, Long Pond, and Brassua, flowing easterly toward Moosehead Lake. Moose River is the primary water source for Moosehead Lake and thus plays a major role as headwater source of the Kennebec River, which flows southerly to the Atlantic.

The Bow Trip, a favorite for groups, makes the Moose one of Maine's better rivers for canoe or kayak camping, especially if the group wishes to put in and take out at the same spot. The Bow Trip is 34.0 miles of lakes and river; it starts and finishes at the end of the access road to Attean Pond. (The Holdens, who operate Attean Lake Camps and maintain the state landing at the north end of Attean, request that Bow trippers park on the left at the sign-designated space and to offload and upload to the left at the beach site, thus leaving a cleared space to the Holdens' dock.)

The Bow Trip is popular because it can be canoed in three days. The fact that there is a minimum of whitewater appeals to families and new paddlers. Wild game abounds, and there is a dearth of human presence both on the river and lakes. Popularity has its price, however. The river is heavily traveled in the summer and on long weekends in the spring and fall. Weekend traffic can best be circumvented by starting your trip on a Monday. The next best way to beat weekend numbers is to start your trip one day before or one day into the weekend. Good advice to any trip leader is to speak to any and all paddlers along the way to coordinate with them where it is best for each group to camp for the night. Campsites are too few for all groups to head for the same destination each night.

Many paddlers now choose to preclude the 1.25-mile portage

between Attean and Holeb, as well as much of the lake travel. The onerous nature of lake paddling and portaging has to be weighed against the inconvenience of shuttling cars between a new/different put-in site and the Attean take-out site. One can shuttle between Turner Brook Beach (at road's end on the north shore of Holeb Pond); or one can shuttle between a put-in at the old Moose River bridge site (next right off the Beaudry Road, past the RR crossing). If you put in at Turner Brook beach on Holeb Pond, you subtract 7.75 miles of lake paddle and 1.25 miles of portage—thus making your Moose River trip a total of 25.0 miles. If you choose to put in at the old Moose River bridge site, your Moose River trip is all river and 27.0 miles long.

The road to Attean Pond leaves US 201 just south of the junction of US 201 and ME 6/15. Turn left off US 201 and travel to the road's end. For those shuttling to either Holeb Pond or the old Moose River bridge site, turn left off US 201, 3.25 miles north of the bridge over the Moose River in Jackman. Follow the well-traveled dirt road 10.0 miles and make a sharp left-hand turn onto the small, rough dirt road that ends at Turner Brook beach at Holeb Pond. If you wish to put in at the old Moose River bridge site, continue 5.0 miles past the 10-mile turn-off to Holeb Pond to a right-hand turn which ends shortly at the old Moose River bridge site.

Bow Trip	34.0 mi
Description:	Lakes, flatwater, Class I
Date checked:	2000
Navigable:	Spring, summer, fall
Scenery:	Wild
Maps:	USGS 1:24,000—Both Attean and Holeb Pond; DL 39. Contact Bureau of Parks & Lands for its Holeb brochure/map (207-287-3821).
Portages:	4.25 mi from Attean Pond to Holeb Pond 1.25 mi
	19.25 mi L, Holeb Falls
	30.25 mi L, Attean Rips; then R, Attean Falls
	(Each of these rips may be run in high

	water. The first set, Attean Rips, can be taken with a setting pole at low water. Both rips and falls have been blasted and harbor sharp rocks.)
Campsites:	All campsites on the Moose River require fire permits. If the party is guided, the guide can acquire from the Maine Forest Service a blanket permit allowing him and his party to camp at all permit sites. If not guided, stop in Caratunk at the Forest Service station and get your permit or call 800-750-9777 during the planning stage.
Sites:	1.25 mi 1 site—N, Attean Pond
	4.25 mi 1 site—W end of Attean at beginning of portage
	6.0 mi 2 sites—E end of Holeb Pond at end of portage between1 site—N at rocky point
	9.0 mi 2 sites—N, Holeb; sandy beach cove, due east of Turner beach put-in
	12.0 mi 1 site—Barrett Brook outlet on S shore
	14.0 mi 1 site—N shore just before 1st Camel Rips; 1 site—N shore at 1st Camel Rips
	18.5 mi 1 site—beginning of Holeb Falls portage 3 sites—end of portage
	2 log cabins—off the portage trail, one L and one at end L; both cabins are left open for Moose River campers by the owner, Leroy Martin (remember to ask for permission to camp)
	1 site—S shore at the bottom of the last pitch
	2 sites—Mosquito Rips, just around the bend from the Holeb Falls portage put-in. 1 N; 1 S.

22.75 mi: 1 site—Spencer Rips, N shore
30.75mi: 3 sites—Attean Falls
  2 R above falls
  1 L, below falls

After off-loading vehicles and packing boats, you leave the north shore of Attean and paddle west for 4.25 miles down the long arm of Attean Lake to the portage. At least three trails lead westerly from this point. The middle trail, just to the left of the campsite, is the correct one. If you do not cross railroad tracks within 1.0 mile, you are too far south.

There is a 3.25-mile paddle the length of Holeb Pond to the outlet, Holeb Stream (9.25 mi). In 1.0 mile, Holeb Stream meets the Moose River (10.25 mi). From Holeb Stream, it is 3.75 miles to a minor ledge drop at first Camel Rips (14.0 mi). Second Camel Rips is in a 90-degree left turn about 500 yards downriver. As you approach Holeb Falls portage, be on the lookout for a high, rocky ledge on the right and large boulders in the river. At this point, take the smaller left branch and immediately turn right. Follow this branch past two short drops with rock ledges on both banks. At a point 0.5 mile from the last left turn, take another left turn into a narrow streamlet. (A flotsam of old logs can usually be seen just before this last left turn.) Follow this narrow stream to the end, offloading to the left at the beginning of Holeb Falls portage. It is imperative that you take these two left-hand turns off the main river and that you note that, at each turn, the river markedly gets smaller.

The river meanders for 11.0 miles from Holeb Falls to Attean Falls (30.25 mi). Mosquito Rips is a sharp drop (19.75 mi), just around the bend from the put-in from Holeb Falls portage. At Mosquito Rips you can hand line the boats to the right if the water is too low. Be very cautious of slippery ledges underfoot. Spencer Rips (23.25 mi) can be run at high water and poled at lower pitches. Be careful. This drop has been dynamited, leaving sharp, jagged rocks. Attean Rips begins 7.0 miles farther, just above Attean Falls (30.25 mi). Attean

Falls is a misnomer—it is a quick drop laden with sharp rocks and preceded by Attean Rips, the longest set of rapids on the Bow Trip. Each of these pitches has also been dynamited in the past to facilitate long-log passage down the Moose in the late 1800s and early 1900s. The resultant sharp and jagged rocks make each pitch difficult in low water. They both may be run in high water. Attean Rips may be poled at low to medium pitch. There is a portage to the left above Attean Rips which bypasses both the rips and Attean Falls. If you choose to run the rips, there is a portage to the right around Attean Falls. A paddle of 3.5 miles from Attean Falls to and across Attean Pond brings one home to the starting point of the Bow Trip on the north shore of Attean.

Attean Landing ➤ Long Pond		19.0 mi
Description:	Lakes, quickwater	
Date checked:	2000	
Navigable:	Medium water	
Scenery:	Forested	
Maps:	Attean 15, Long Pond 15; DL 39 and 40	

The western shore of Wood Pond at Jackman is built up, but east of US 201 the river and lakes along it are mostly wild. Long Pond has an alder- and willow-lined shore that suggests a dam long since washed out. The shoreline of Brassua Lake typifies that of a flooded lake: dry-ki, a few exposed sand banks, and green trees with dead limbs that died when these trees were within a forest, not along a lake. Both lakes are, for the most part, undeveloped.

From the landing on Attean Pond there is 0.75 mile of flatwater on the river and another 2.5 miles across Wood Pond to the outlet. On the short river segment between Attean and Wood Ponds, the remains of a steamboat and barge rot away on the left. At Wood Pond, there is an excellent campsite on the left. Access at Jackman is from a public landing on Wood Pond or at the US 201 bridge.

Except for the riffle under the bridge, it is 6.5 miles of smooth and somewhat winding river to Long Pond (11.0 mi), an 8-

mile paddle with two narrow guts between the three separate sections. You can reach the river at the outlet by a dirt road leading north off of ME 6/15 just west of the Long Pond-Sandwich town line. At the east end of the clearing by the railroad tracks, follow a well-worn path to the river.

Long Pond ➤ Moosehead Lake	15.5 mi
Description:	Lakes, quickwater, Class I, II, III, IV
Date checked:	2000
Navigable:	Spring, summer, fall
Scenery:	Forested
Maps:	Long Pond 15, Brassua Lake 15; DL 40
Portages:	2.5 mi L ledge/falls 200 yd
	12.5 mi R Brassua Dam 200 yd
Campsite:	5.0 mi L Brassua Lake (on point where lake opens)

Between Long Pond and Brassua Lake, the Moose River drops steadily through wooded hills. Here, there are several miles of challenging rapids when the water is high. Because this is a large river, the rapids are passable in lower water when they are easier to negotiate and when the harder pitches can be lined.

Below Long Pond, the intermittent rapids of Class I and II extend for 2.5 miles to a bridge at the site of the former Long Pond Dam on a well-used logging road that comes in from ME 6/15. **Caution!** Under the bridge is a ledge, which should be scouted. Landing on the left to scout, line, or carry may be difficult as the current is fast. You can also take out here. A short distance below is a low waterfall that you can portage or line on the left.

Below these two ledges are nearly continuous rapids for 1.75 miles. At the start, they are Class III, but soon they moderate to Class II. A half-mile from the bridge is a sharp left turn followed by a short stretch of quickwater. Soon there are more Class II rapids and one more, larger section of quickwater. This is followed by more Class II and another Class III section, which starts just above a quick S-turn that begins to the right. Intermittent Class II rapids continue to slackwater, which soon opens into Brassua Lake (5.0 mi).

It is 7.5 miles across Brassua Lake to the dam (12.5 mi), the road to which may be closed. Portage on the left. Below the dam are Class I rapids and quickwater for 1.0 mile. The last 2.0 miles to Moosehead Lake (15.5 mi) are flat, highly developed, and mostly close to the highway.

Roach River

The headwaters of the Roach River consist of a complex of mountain ponds east of Moosehead Lake, of which it is the largest tributary. It combines a variety of lake and whitewater paddling with good views of mountains that range from 2,500 to 3,500 feet.

Access to Third Roach Pond is public, on the northeast arm reached from a private logging road. Always remember to ask for and obtain permission before crossing property lines.

Third Roach Pond ➤ Kokad-jo		12.5 mi
Description:	Lakes, Class I, II	
Date checked:	2000	
Navigable:	High water (mid-May to mid-June)	
Scenery:	Forested	
Maps:	Jo-Mary Mountain 15, First Roach 15; DL 42 and 41	
Portages:	0.75 mi R dam 50 ft	
	5.75 mi L dam	
	(12.5 mi dam 100 ft)	

Roach River begins 0.75 mile from the road access to Third Roach Pond. It is marked by an old log crib at the western end of the pond. The washed-out dam is full of spikes.

Fallen trees are the major hazard, especially at the start; the river is narrow and fast. Second Roach Pond is 1.5 miles beyond an old bridge abutment.

You may need to line the dam at the outlet of Second Roach Pond (5.75 mi). The next 1.75 miles are continuous, fast, with easy riffles and some mountain views. From the northern inlet of First Roach Pond (7.5 mi), it is a 5-mile paddle down the lake to the outlet at Kokad-jo (12.5 mi).

Kokad-jo ➤ Mooshead Lake		6.5 mi
Description:	Lake, Class II, III	
Date checked:	2000	
Navigable:	High water (May ice must be out on Moosehead)	
	Annual draw-down in October	
Scenery:	Wild	
Maps:	First Roach Pond 15, Moosehead Lake 15; DL 41	
Campsites:	6.5 mi R high bluff MFS	
	6.5 mi L small island MFS	

The most interesting aspect of the Roach, other than the scenery and the continuous Class II rapids, is the shuttle. From Kokad-jo, proceed 2.5 miles toward Greenville. Take a right on a logging road and follow it 4.5 miles to a junction. Take a right and go 1.0 mile to Jewett Cove on Moosehead Lake. This is a MFS campsite.

The rapids are intermittent for 1.0 mile until Lazy Tom Stream enters on the right. From this point, the rapids are continuous. After 2.5 miles of fairly continuous Class II, there is 0.25 mile of quickwater. One mile of slightly harder Class II–III rapids, featuring several easy ledge drops, gives way to Class II to the lake. The total drop is 200 feet. There are no dangerous spots, but there are no sections of flatwater until you reach the lake. You will find your car parked near the first deep cove on the left, after a mile of pleasant lake paddling.

Dead River

The not-so-Dead River flows from Flagstaff Lake to the upper Kennebec River. It is one of New England's most outstanding whitewater rivers, and you can run it from early spring to late autumn. You paddle through nearly continuous rapids for hour after hour along a 15-mile section of wild river where the gradient averages 20 feet per mile.

The river takes its name from the flatwater section that now lies beneath Flagstaff Lake. The main discharge on the Dead is controlled by the dam at Flagstaff Lake. There are seven scheduled high-water (3,500 to 7,000 cfs) releases each summer, and eleven scheduled low-water (1,500) releases. Call Central Maine Power's toll-free river-information line (800-557-3569), and follow the touch-tone menu. For early May releases, the actual river flow tends to be higher than those announced due to additional flow from the Dead River's tributary streams. For more information on the Dead, see the *AMC Classic Northeastern Whitewater Guide*.

You can reach the head of the rapids at the mouth of Spencer Stream via a confusing road network from US 201 at West Forks. For transportation to the Spencer Stream put-in, call Webb's Store (207-663-2214).

Above Grand Falls the Dead River flows slowly through meadows, where there are good views looking back at the Bigelow Range. Below Grand Falls, a spectacular drop of about 30 feet, the narrow river valley is very attractive, although you will spend most of your time looking at the river itself. At a medium water level (1,000 cfs), it takes 2.5 to 3 hours to reach Spencer Stream from Big Eddy, and 3 to 4 to run the rapids to The Forks.

Flagstaff Lake   18.0 mi

Flagstaff Lake is formed by a dam that floods the "dead" part of Dead River and backs up the North and South branches. The lake is 18.0 miles long. The shores are wild, and the views of the jagged peaks of the Bigelow Mountains a half-mile above are spectacular.

The first half has enough points and islands to break the wind, but a strong wind would be troublesome for paddlers on the wide last half. Take the northern channel around the high island a couple of miles east of Jim Eaton Hill.

Over the years, stumps of the old forest have pulled free of the bottom and become stranded in coves and shallows. The end of the southern channel around the island is blocked by thick rafts of stumps from shore to shore.

At Flagstaff Dam, you should land as close to the left as possible. Either drag across the stumps and dam or use a short trail around them. Carry 0.75 mile, much on a good road accessible by a paved road from New Portland.

Big Eddy ➤ Spencer Stream   7.75 mi

Description:	Flatwater, Class I, II
Date checked:	2000
Navigable:	Spring, summer, fall; controlled release
Scenery:	Wild
Maps:	Little Bigelow Mountain 15; DL 29
Portage:	7.0 mi L Grand Falls 0.5 mi
Campsites:	0.5 mi R Big Eddy MFS car
	7.75 mi L Spencer Stream permit car

On the western side of the river at the foot of Long Falls, there is an observation point below the road to Spring Lake. You can lower a boat to the river here for 0.5 mile of easy Class II rapids that extend under the bridge to Big Eddy Campsite.

Below Big Eddy (0.5 mi) there is flatwater for 6.5 miles to Dead River Dam. The portage around Grand Falls begins on the left bank above the washed-out dam, following a dirt road, and turning right onto another in about 0.25 mile. The portage ends at a pool, below and out of sight of the falls.

Below the end of the portage, the current is strong as it passes an island at the mouth of Spencer Stream (7.75 mi).

Spencer Stream ➤ The Forks   16.0 mi

Description:	Class II, III
Date checked:	2000
Navigable:	Spring, summer, fall; controlled release
	Medium water (1,000-1,300 cfs)
Scenery:	Wild
Maps:	Pierce Pond 15, The Forks 15; DL 29,
	30, 39, and 40

This is the classic Dead River run. The river is generally wide and boulder strewn, offering many choices of routes. The first 7.0 miles of the run are a good warm-up. After Enchanted Stream enters on the left just above Elephant Rock Rapid, the rapids are generally steeper and require solid Class III skills. Normally, the water depth is 2 to 3 feet.

Shortly below the put-in at Spencer Stream, the fun begins at Spencer Rips (0.25 mi), the first set of rapids. Stay in the middle of the waves going down the drop and eddy-out on the left. There is a nice pool here to pick up the pieces, should that be necessary. Unless you go with someone who is familiar with the river, it will seem to be an indistinguishable succession of Class II and III rapids, broken occasionally by pools and easier drops.

At 2.0 miles, a long rapid begins and culminates in the section known as the Minefield, which ends at a big, deep pool with an old log chute high on the right (2.75 mi). Hayden's Landing, marked by some log cribwork, is on the right (3.0 mi). Just below is Hayden's Landing Rapid, also known as Humpty-Dumpty. This is a short, intense rapid. The Basin, 3.5 miles from the start, is a long section of quickwater.

At 4.5 miles, you will be able to see the gravel pit put-in on the left if you look carefully. Unless you know it is there, it is difficult to spot. This put-in is an alternative to going all the way to Spencer Stream. It is just above the confluence of Stony Brook Stream and the Dead.

Next you will come to a section of quickwater that lasts about 0.75 mile, then the rapids begin again. Enchanted Stream (7.0 mi) enters on the left and marks the beginning of Elephant Rock Rapid. Elephant Rock is a large rock on the right at the bottom of the rapid. It is a good play spot; the eddy below the rock is often full of boaters waiting for their chance to play in the holes on either side of the rock.

The rapids are fairly continuous from Elephant Rock to a short section of quickwater (8.5 mi), when the river makes a sweeping bend to the left. Shortly below this, Mile Long Rapid begins. This rapid offers many choices, but the best routes are on the left, especially near the bottom, due to a wide pile of boulders on the right.

As the river finishes another sweep to the left at a short rapid, you can look up on the left and see Spruce Ledge. Upper Spruce Ledge Rapid (10.5 mi) is an excellent rapid with a good pool below. Near the bottom, on the left side, is a hole that can keep boats and boaters for a period of time. Shortly, Lower Spruce Ledge Rapid begins and carries the boater around a bend to the left.

At 11.5 miles, Little Poplar Hill Falls begins. This rapid is tough in low water because it is very rocky. In higher water, waves and holes form, giving the river a very turbulent look. At the bottom of the rapid on the left is a hole formed by a basket of rocks. Stay away from this spot. There is a big pool at the bottom to make rescues, if necessary, but be aware that Poplar Hill Falls (12.0 mi) begins immediately below the pool. These rapids may be scouted on the right. The most difficult section is at the top. There are a variety of routes through the rocks and holes. The left side is the most difficult. There are three or four large waves and drops in the first third of the rapid that happen fast, one after the other. You don't have time to think, only time to react. The middle is easier and still fun; the right is rocky, but the current is slower. Old bridge abutments on both shores mark the end of the difficult rapids. Class I rapids continue until the Dead reaches The Forks.

There is a public parking lot on the left, north of The Forks. This take-out has been provided to relieve some of the traffic congestion in The Forks.

Spencer Stream ➤ The Forks		16.0 mi
Description:	Class III, IV, V	
Date checked:	2000	
Navigable:	Spring (high-water releases)	
	High water (3,500–5,500 cfs)	
Scenery:	Wild	
Maps:	Pierce Pond 15, The Forks 15; DL 29, 30, and 40	

At high-water levels, the Dead changes its character from a boulder-strewn Class II–III run to a strong Class IV, with a few rapids approaching Class V. The river is characterized by waves of up to six feet, and there are innumerable holes. The water is brown, and at times it can be difficult to differentiate waves from holes.

Because the water is up to the alders, paddlers may have some problems eddying out. The current is strong and quick, and when you do catch an eddy, it can be difficult to stay in it. Therefore, a swim at this high level can be very long and dangerous. **Caution!** Canoeists should have a good self-rescue skills, and decked boaters should have a strong roll; a strong party of boaters is a must. The river at high water is for properly equipped experts only. If you doubt your abilities, do not do the run, or leave a car at the gravel pit as a backup. If you have had any trouble from Spencer Stream down to the gravel pit, take out. The run from Elephant Rock to Poplar Hill Falls is much heavier than the first 4.5 miles to the pit.

Another aspect of high-water days on the Dead River is that the releases have been set up for the rafting industry. You will be sharing the river with a very large number of rafts. The put-in gets crowded, so be prepared to wait your turn to get on the river. You also might wait and put in after the rafts have launched. Remember, too, that rafts move more slowly than canoes and kayaks, that they hamper visibility, and that they often go into large holes that individual boaters would choose to avoid.

You will notice right away that Spencer Rips looks very different. At this level, you can run it on the left, but the best ride is still on the right-hand side, right down the wave train. Catch the eddy on the left, and you will be able to go back up and play in the wave train.

At 1.25 miles, a good surfing spot can be found on the right side of the river. There is a good series of standing waves which decked boaters can surf to their hearts' content. The best play spots at high water tend to be above Elephant Rock; just remember to save some energy for the end of the run.

A fairly long rapid starts 0.75 mile below the surfing spot. The rapid culminates in a section called the Minefield, just above a big pool. There are two dangerous holes to avoid here. One is left of center near where the river turns to the left and the big pool becomes visible for the first time; the other is on the right, near the right banks just above the pool.

Hayden's Landing (3.25 mi), the next major rapid, contains several large holes than can recirculate boats and boaters. The one on the left at the bottom is particularly notorious. The route here is down the center through the wave trains.

The gravel-pit put-in/take-out is 4.5 miles from the Spencer Stream put-in. If you are planning to take out here, it is a good idea to tie a flag to the trees to mark the spot. On high-water days, this take-out has a festive air from the many brightly colored markers that blow in the wind.

Elephant Rock is the next big rapid. At high water, there is a large hole at the top, just a bit right of center. Holes pepper the right side all the way down. The best run is to enter a little left of center and then move over to catch the wave train at the bottom just left of Elephant Rock. Do not catch the eddy below Elephant Rock. At this level, there is a large hole behind the rock, and there is a very large whirlpool that will suck you back up into the hole.

Mile Long Rapid is full of holes and big waves. If you are in a canoe, you will want to run this dry, if possible. The rapid is very long and can be tiring, but there are several places to eddy out behind rocks in the center of the river. When you can see the pool below the rapid, the best route to get there is not obvious because the entire end of the rapid is a huge wall of waves. A run left of center (about halfway between left and center) will take you through safely. Catch the eddy on the left and take a breather.

Upper Spruce Ledge has a nice series of waves, and the hole that is bad at lower water becomes a big wave here. Little Poplar is turbulent, with many large waves and several holes to avoid. A run just a bit right of center is a conservative route. Remember that a swim here could mean a swim through Big Poplar because the pool at the bottom of Little Poplar has a quick current and does not leave much time for a rescue.

Poplar Hill Falls is a Class IV–V rapid, depending upon the water level and where you run it. The left side is the most difficult because of its 6-foot waves and a number of very large holes. The middle is less arduous but is still quite thrilling. If you run the middle, be aware that it is the easier run for the first third of the rapid; then it becomes quite difficult. At this point, it is best to move toward the left. The far right-hand side also can be run at this level because most of the rocks are covered. Do not relax until you have reached the old bridge abutments, because even the last section of Poplar has holes, cross-currents, and barely submerged rocks waiting to catch boaters who let their guard down too early.

Once you have run Poplar, you will realize that you are smiling. It's been a great run, you've made it, and you are already looking forward to the next high-water release.

Dead River (South Branch)

The South Branch of the Dead River flows out of Saddleback Lake on the northern side of Saddleback Mountain northward for some miles and then turns northeast. The river then travels through an open valley with many farms to Flagstaff Lake, which it reaches at its southwestern corner near the town of Stratton. South Branch offers a fine variety of paddling; a steep and difficult gorge, a long stretch of mostly smoothwater, and a great whitewater run. All of these are in a beautiful setting between the Saddleback Range on the one side and East Kennebago Mountain on the other, much of it through green farming country that offers fine views to the river traveler. It is a small river, and the water runs off quickly once the snow is gone. Most of the rapids, therefore, are very shallow after the middle of May.

Dallas School ➤ Langtown Mill		5.75 mi
Description:	Class II, II, IV	
Date checked:	2000	
Navigable:	Spring (April)	
Scenery:	Forested	
Maps:	Kennebago Lake 15, Rangeley 15, Quill Hill, Tim Mountain, Stratton 15; DL 28 and 29	

Put in at the ME 16 bridge in Dallas and paddle 2.0 miles of smoothwater to a few small rapids near a state picnic area. Below this, the river enters a deep gorge, a portion of which you can see from the highway. An alternate put-in is available about 0.5 mile above the entrance to the gorge. A short dirt road (75 yd) leads right down to the river's edge. There is also a wide shoulder for parking vehicles where the dirt road turns off ME 16. The gorge is difficult to scout, but you can see much of it by walking through the woods and peering down into the gorge.

There are four ledge drops in the gorge. Each has a break in the ledge that allows a defined, but tricky, passage. Depending on water level, these rapids are Class III or IV. At lower water, there are a lot of rocks; at higher water, more rocks are covered but the current can be pushy. If you catch an eddy before each drop and you are a solid Class III boater, you should be able to read the drops and run them. The last drop is best run on the left. As you approach it, catch the large eddy on the left above it; you will drop over a small ledge on your way to the eddy. Once in the eddy, you can see the rooster tail and wave train clearly. If you line up with them when you leave the eddy, you will have a good run.

After 1.0 mile in the gorge, the river comes near the road, where paddlers who wish to avoid the difficulties of the gorge above will probably choose to put in. The rapids for the next 3.0 miles to Langtown Mill gradually become easier (Class II). The take-out is on river right about 50 yards before a green iron bridge across the river. The bridge is posted as private property. Ask for and obtain permission to take out here.

Langtown Mill ➤ Green Farm Bridge	6.5 mi
Description:	Flatwater, quickwater
Date checked:	2000
Navigable:	High water (April)
Scenery:	Forested, rural
Maps:	Kennebago Lake 15; DL 29

Below Langtown Mill the river flows slowly, with many meanders and views of Bigelow and East Kennebago mountains. A thin veil of trees lines the banks.

Green Farm Bridge ➤ Flagstaff Lake (ME 27)	7.5 mi
Description:	Lake, quickwater, Class II, III
Date checked:	2000
Navigable:	High water (May)

Scenery:	Forested, rural
Maps:	Quill Hill, Stratton 15; DL 29

This bridge is about 1 mile off ME 16 on a gravel road that leaves the highway at Green Farm; it makes a good put-in spot for the lower section of the river. The first 4.0 miles below the bridge are quickwater with frequent Class I rapids. Most of the boulders in the riverbed were dynamited years ago for log runs. About 1 mile above Lutton Brook, the rapids begin abruptly; for the next 1.5 miles to Nash Stream, they are continuous and difficult (Class III).

As the river burrows into the bedrock, the scenery becomes outstanding: ragged cliffs, rocky portals, and sunlight slanting through the hemlocks. The riverbed is mostly shallow ledge with a few deep pools. The last 1.5 miles of rapids below Nash Stream are not as difficult. About 0.3 mile below Nash Stream, the river doubles around a rock spine with a little beach shelving into a deep pool.

As the river nears Flagstaff Lake, the current tapers off. After entering Flagstaff Lake, a dirt road on the right is passable to four-wheel-drive vehicles. In the last mile, you can see Bigelow Mountain. When the lake is full, the ME 27 bridge is too low to pass under, but boats can slide through a culvert on the right. Stratton is another mile.

Dead River (North Branch)

Much of the waterway that Benedict Arnold and his men struggled with on their way to Canada in the fall of 1775 has been flooded, and little remains of the wilderness through which they traveled. It was on the North Branch of the Dead River that Arnold's party was beset by floods late in October 1775.

Today, this river still flows relatively freely in a rugged setting. The river is followed by ME 27, but only occasionally is the highway close enough to be visible from the water. Except for a few cabins, there is hardly a building above Eustis. From the head of Chain Lakes, the narrow valley frames a view of the Bigelow Range.

The North Branch has some challenging rapids, but most of it is flat; more than 17 miles of the route described here is runnable in all but low water.

Chain Lake ➤ Eustis	19.0 mi
Description:	Lake, flatwater, quickwater, Class II, III
Date checked:	2000
Navigable:	High and medium water (mid-May through June)
Scenery:	Forested
Maps:	Chain of Ponds, Jim Pond, Tim Mountain, Stratton 15; DL 38, 28, and 29
Portages:	5.0 mi L Chain Lakes Dam 10 yd
	7.25 mi R Sarampus Falls 15 yd
	(19.0 mi Dam at Eustis)
Campsites:	0 mi Chain Lakes (NW end) car
	13.5 mi R Alder Stream (upstream 0.5 mi) MFS car
	21.5 mi R Cathedral Pines private $ car

Portage the dam (5.0 mi) at the outlet of Chain Lakes on the left. The North Branch begins with 0.75 mile of quickwater, which slackens at an abrupt left turn just above the ME 27 bridge (5.75 mi). Then there are 1.5 miles of good current to Sarampus Falls (7.25 mi), which is a short ledge drop beside a roadside picnic area. Usually, it must be lifted around.

Little Sarampus Falls, just around the next right turn, is a shorter drop. It is followed by 4.25 miles of flatwater to Shadagee Falls (11.75 mi), which is flanked on both banks by low ledges; Shadagee Falls should be scouted. Beyond, flatwater continues for another 4.25 miles to Upper Ledge Falls Dam.

The washed-out log-driving dam (16.0 mi) is usually run on the left, and it is followed by 150 yards of Class II rapids. After about 300 yards of flatwater, you reach Ledge Falls, a Class III set of rapids (roughly 300 yards long) that begin with a sharp drop by a large boulder on the left. These rapids should be scouted before running. Flatwater continues for 2.25 miles to the dam at Eustis (19.0 mi).

When the water level in Flagstaff Lake is low, there are a few riffles below the dam, and the river banks are exposed for several miles. There is a bridge and a causeway 2.0 miles south of Eustis. At the northeastern end of the lake, the Dead River begins below Long Falls Dam (40.0 mi).

Spencer Stream

Spencer Stream rises on the slopes of Kibby Mountain just west of Spencer Lake and flows south and west to the Dead River below Flagstaff Lake. It passes through some beautiful and wild country. The stream is usually too low for paddling by the end of June, but it does comes up after heavy rains. It is difficult to reach the headwaters of the river. The old access road to Baker Pond is at times flooded by beavers. Flying in may be most sensible option.

Baker Pond ➤ Logging Bridge	13.75 mi
Description:	Lake, quickwater, Class I
Date checked:	2000
Navigable:	High water
Scenery:	Wild
Maps:	Spencer Lake 15, Pierce Pond 15; DL 39 and 29

From the inlet, it is a 1.5-mile paddle down the point to the outlet at the south end and then 1.5 miles down Baker Stream to Spencer Stream. Baker Stream is small, with many shallow rapids, which may have to be lifted over. From the mouth of Baker Stream there are 2.0 miles of pleasant quickwater in Spencer Stream. Three miles of slackwater follow to Spencer Dam (7.25 mi), a logging dam of which only the foundation remains. Below the dam are 4.5 miles of continuous rapids to a logging road bridge that offers access on weekdays but is gated on weekends.

Logging Bridge ➤ Dead River	7.5 mi
Description:	Class I, II, III
Date checked:	2000
Navigable:	High water

Scenery:	Wild
Maps:	Pierce Pond 15; DL 29
Portage:	4.5 mi L falls

Below the bridge are more Class I rapids to Spencer Gut (4.25 mi), which is a 0.5-mile gorge with high rock walls. From these walls, the stream plunges in a series of falls and pools. The portage is on the left bank over a high ridge. On the right is the grave of a logger who drowned in the Gut in 1905. Below the Gut you will see sporty rapids past smaller cliffs. Heavy rapids continue for 1.0 mile to the mouth of Little Spencer Stream (5.25 mi); below, there are 2.0 miles of Class I rapids to the Dead River.

Little Spencer Stream

Little Spencer Stream flows out of Spencer Lake south to Spencer Stream about 2 miles from its confluence with the Dead River. It provides an alternate route to Spencer Stream and the Dead River. In high water, Little Spencer is a pretty stream to pole down, but usually it is low and you will have to lift over the shallow places.

Whipple Pond ➤ Fish Pond	5.5 mi

This is a chain of wilderness ponds just to the north of Spencer Lake, separated by short pitches that are too small and steep to run. The scenery, especially on Hall Pond, is outstanding.

Put in from the jeep road from US 201 to Spencer Rips on Moose River, at the eastern end of Whipple Pond. Follow the narrow arm west to the rocky outlet, where an old trail is blazed to Hall Pond. The glacier dropped great boulders in clumps and rows, nearly blocking the pond at one point. The remains of an old logging dam mark the start of a short, rocky pitch to the next pond. Drag and paddle through several more ponds to the marsh above Fish Pond.

Fish Pond ➤ Spencer Stream		12.75 mi
Description:	Lake, quickwater, Class I, II	
Date checked:	2000	

Navigable:	High water, medium water (scratchy)
Scenery:	Wild
Maps:	Spencer Lake 15, Pierce Pond 15; DL 39 and 29

The Spencer Lake–Rock Pond road crosses Clark Stream, the inlet to Fish Pond, which is 1.0 mile of narrow, winding stream above the pond. With a high-clearance vehicle, you can drive to Fish Pond, passing through a beautiful stand of white pine 0.25 mile before the inlet. It is 1.5 miles down Fish Pond to the narrows, 400 feet into Spencer Lake, which is 5.25 miles to the southern end. The old dam (7.75 mi) at the outlet was burned; lift over.

Little Spencer Stream is a delightful paddle, with intermittent rapids in a narrow stream for the 5.0 miles to the confluence with Spencer Stream. Because Spencer Stream is wider, it will be too low when it is still possible to paddle Little Spencer Stream; in that case you can take out at the confluence.

Austin Stream

Austin Stream drains a number of small swamps and ponds northeast of Bingham. There is some easy paddling where the stream follows Dead Water Road north of the falls. The real attraction, though, is the continuous rapids between the pool below the falls and the Kennebec River. The gradient is unusually uniform—it has no steep ledge drops but rather has many short, steep rapids.

Falls Pool ➤ Side Road Bridge	5.25 mi
Description:	Class II, III, IV
Date checked:	2000
Navigable:	Medium-high water (April or after heavy rain)
Scenery:	Wild
Maps:	Bingham 15; DL 30

The stream drops 360 feet in the first 4.0 miles below the falls pool. Short, steep, boulder-strewn rapids alternate with gentler, gravelly rapids, but there is no slackwater in which to catch your breath. Stopping requires catching shore eddies; the ability to do this is critical, as there always seems to be at least one tree blocking the river somewhere in this upper part. Strainers formed by trees are normally the greatest hazard on this stream. However, in high water, a capsized boat could result in a long and bruising swim, as rescue would be very difficult.

The take-out is under a side-road bridge about 1.25 miles from US 201. Take the first left heading north on Route 16 to get to the take-out.

You can find the put-in by heading north on ME 16 another 0.25 mile to the Dead Water Road on the left. About 6 miles up the road, the stream comes right beside the road and is nearly at road level. This is just above the falls. Turn around and head back down the road about 0.3 mile (about 100 yards below where the old road comes in). About 200 yards into the woods and 150 feet down the side of the hill is a small pool a few hundred yards below the falls, which is the best place to launch boats. There is no trail, but the woods are quite open. The pool is near the 820-foot contour line on the topographical map. If you have any doubts about running the stream, remember that taking out anywhere before the bridge will require pulling boats through the woods and up similar (or worse) hills.

There could be trees in the river here, and extra caution is advised. Constant maneuvering is required to thread a path down the riverbed. After several miles of naturally formed rapids, the riverbed becomes channelized just above where Chase Stream enters on the right (4.0 mi). From this point down, the riverbed is gravel and the rapids are Class I, II. When the water is high, an interesting trip might be to put in at the side-road bridge over Chase Stream and run the rock-free waves down to the Kennebec.

Side Road Bridge ➤ Kennebec River Boat Landing   1.75 mi
Description: Class I, II
Date checked: 2000
Navigable: Medium-high water (April)

| Scenery: | Rural, towns |
| Maps: | Bingham 15; DL 30 |

Put in at the side-road bridge on Austin Stream (or about 1.25 miles farther up on the Stream Road bridge over Chase Stream) and enjoy some rock-free rapids. In higher water there may be some Class III waves and eddy lines. Take out at the boat landing on the Kennebec behind the mill in Bingham (Lander Street).

Carrabassett River

The Carrabassett River rises in the mountains of northwestern Maine on the northern side of Sugarloaf Mountain. It is a wild and tumultuous mountain brook above Carrabassett Village, but from there down it offers fine whitewater paddling and in its lower stretches some smoothwater travel. The valley is sparsely settled, and the stream is rocky and clear. After rain, the river rises and falls quickly. The best time for running is probably early in May, when the snows are still melting on Sugarloaf.

Sugarloaf Entrance ➤ Carrabassett		6.0 mi
Description:	Class II, III, IV, V	
Date checked:	2000	
Navigable:	Low water (April and after heavy rain)	
Scenery:	Forested	
Maps:	Stratton 15, Little Bigelow Mountain 15; DL 29	
Portages:	1 or more	

This section of the river can be run by a team of experts at the right water levels. Several drops must be scouted, lined, or portaged. Boats should have full flotation, and rescue lines should be set up below the more difficult drops. Several of the most difficult drops are visible from ME 27 in the 2-mile stretch of river that starts 1.5 miles north of Valley Crossing.

Put in where the river is close to the road, a little south of the Sugarloaf Mountain Ski Area entrance. The river should be somewhat scratchy Class II–III near the start if the water level is right for the gorge below.

The first 2.0 miles are generally Class I, II, and III, with a few more difficult spots. Then the rapids become progressively harder, and the number of big drops increases as you approach the start of the gorge.

In the gorge, the river is very rocky, the current very pushy, the eddies very small, and the area in which to maneuver minimal. The gorge is definitely a Class IV–V section. Three drops in the gorge stand out from the rest. The first, which is visible from the road, falls 15 feet in three stages, with the last stage being about 8 feet straight down. The second big drop is just out of sight of the road, behind some camps. The river forms a 13-foot-wide chute between two rock walls and drops about 10 feet into a river-wide hole, which is a keeper. The third, The Pinnacles, is beside a high rock island at the end of the gorge, where there is a complicated approach to a 10-foot slanted drop. Below this drop, the rapids are Class I–II for the last 1.5 miles to the ledges just above the Valley Crossing bridge. Take out on the left above the bridge or the right, just below the bridge.

Carrabassett ➤ Kingfield	10.0 mi
Description:	Class I, II, III
Date checked:	2000
Navigable:	High and medium water (April, early May, after heavy rain)
Scenery:	Forested, towns
Maps:	Little Bigelow Mountain 15; DL 29 and 30
Portage:	10.0 mi R dam

Generally, the put-in is at the Valley Crossing bridge where the gauge is on the upstream side of the right bridge abutment. Minimum level is 0 on the gauge, but more water is definitely better. The river is Class II at the start and continues steadily to a left turn away from the road. The rapids on the corner where the river bends back to the right (0.5 mi) can be tricky, especially in low water; there, the riverbed is very rocky and there are few channels.

At 1.0 mile, you will reach the bridge above Packard's Pool. This should be scouted since a change in water level affects the rapid. For the next 2.5 miles, the river is mostly Class I with occasional Class II sections.

At 3.5 miles, the river again turns away from the road. Then you arrive at the Elbow, which is a Class II–III rapid ending in a pool by a log cabin. The river continues with stretches of Class II water and bends to the right to parallel the road again. At about 5 miles, the river sweeps to the left, with a Class III drop above a small island. Either side can be run, but the left is better in low water. There is a nice pool at the bottom of the rapid. Rock Garden (5.5 mi) starts just after the pool and continues for about 1 mile. The river is filled with rocks that appear to offer many routes but some are dead ends, so paddlers should choose carefully. From here to the take-out at the State Highway Garage on the right, the river continues as a Class II with occasional quickwater sections.

This section of the Carrabassett has been run at flood stage when no rocks were showing. A run at this level is for experts only. A swim at this level can be long and dangerous. If the water is too high, do not run it.

Kingfield ➤ New Portland	6.5 mi
Description:	Class I, II
Date checked:	2000
Navigable:	High water (early May)
Scenery:	Forested
Maps:	Little Bigelow Mountain 15, Kingfield 15; DL 30 and 20

This is an attractive stretch; the river is wider and the rapids are not as difficult as the section above. The valley is more open. Take out at the wire bridge in New Portland.

New Portland ➤ North Anson	13.5 mi
Description:	Flatwater, quickwater
Date checked:	2000
Navigable:	Spring, wet summers
Scenery:	Forested, rural, towns

Maps:	Kingfield 15; DL 20
Portages:	5.5 mi ledge
	9.5 mi L Cleveland Rips
	(13.5 mi falls)

The views improve as you reach East New Portland. Take out above town, as there is an impassable drop under the bridge.

Put in on the right bank below the drop. This section is mostly quickwater, but halfway down is Cleveland Rips. There is some open pastureland, but it is mostly wooded until you get close to North Anson. Take out above the village of North Anson, as there is an impassable falls in town. It is then 1.0 mile to the Kennebec River.

Sandy River

The Sandy River rises in the Sandy River Ponds a few miles south of Rangeley and flows east to the Kennebec River, which it reaches a few miles south of Anson. Its upper reaches are a tumultuous mountain torrent and unrunnable until Smalls Falls, about 4 miles above Madrid. In the 52.0 miles from here to the junction with the Kennebec, the river drops 700 feet and offers a variety of runs for all tastes. Because of the many dams, paddling on weekdays will be better, for there will be more water in the river and the season will be prolonged, lasting even into the summer. For weekend paddling, the spring will be better, when the snows are still providing water from the melting on Saddleback and Mount Abraham.

Smalls Falls ➤ South Branch		5.5 mi
Description:	Class II, III, IV	
Date checked:	2000	
Navigable:	High and medium water	
Scenery:	Forested, towns	
Maps:	Rangeley 15; DL 19	
Portages:	3 mi R ledges	
	3.5 mi R ledge	
	4.25 mi e falls	
	4.75 mi e falls	

The Sandy river is small here, but it can rise quickly when the snows are melting in the mountains. Then the rapids become very heavy. In high water, it is an interesting kayak run; in medium water, it can be run by open canoes. Four ledges are particularly difficult. The action you take at them depends on the water level.

Put in below Smalls Falls from a track on the left bank. The first mile is continuously difficult, with some fallen trees, especially at a sharp S-curve. Below the first US 4 bridge, the going is easy away from the road. As the river turns back toward the road, and just below a long island, a series of four ledges starts, with the last one being the highest. These are best scouted/lined on the right and run on the left and are more ledgy compared to the rounded boulders above. The rapids become easier as they follow the road to the bridge in Madrid (3.5 mi).

The second ledge below the bridge should be scouted as it is full of sharp rocks. The river swings away from the road and 0.25 mile above the second US 4 bridge there is a small gorge, which should be inspected in advance. Below the second US 4 bridge is another falls (the steepest) with a large boulder below, which makes an island in the gorge. The rapids gradually ease to the third ME 4 bridge, just above the confluence with the South Branch.

South Branch ➤ Phillips		5.75 mi
Description:	Class II, III	
Date checked:	2000	
Navigable:	High water (early May)	
Scenery:	Forested, rural	
Maps:	Phillips 15; DL 19	

This run is somewhat less difficult than the section above, but only experienced paddlers should attempt it, as there are a number of Class III rapids. From the ME 4 bridge 2.0 miles south of Madrid, it is only 200 yards to the confluence of the South Branch. About 1 mile below here, Orbeton Stream (which flows out of Redington Pond on the east flank of Saddleback) enters on the left. The junction is a fine lunch spot. You will leave the brawling mountain stream behind at this point and travel on a wide river, with open pastures providing many fine views of the mountains to the north and west. The rapids are nearly continuous although not difficult, but at almost every bend there are heavy waves, which must be avoided. Take out on the left a mile upstream of Phillips at Davenport Flats where the road comes close to the river.

If, for any reason, you are considering running through Phillips, be aware that both the ME 142 and the ME 149 bridges have unrunnable gorges above them. Paddlers attempting the gorge above ME 142 should scout carefully from above and below, as the height is deceptive. The best approach is from directly upstream through a 3-foot-wide chute on the left of the rock island. You can take out at a railroad park on the left bank, 1.0 mile above the next waterfall.

Phillips ➤ Fairbanks Bridge — 17.25 mi

Description:	Class I, II
Date checked:	2000
Navigable:	High and medium water
Scenery:	Forested, rural
Maps:	Phillips 15, Kingfield 15; DL 19 and 20

Below the ME 149 bridge, put in on the left to run the Class III rapid within sight downstream and another Class III rapid 0.25 mile downstream, where the river makes a sharp turn to the right. You can also put in on the left below these. The remainder of the 8.0 miles to Strong is quickwater and riffles, with lovely mountain views.

A half-mile above Strong is a Class II rapid that runs for 0.25 mile. A ballpark on the right below the bridge in Strong offers good access.

At Strong, the river turns south; several Class II rapids occur. The river is constantly changing in depth from shoal water to deep pools. One mile above the Fairbanks Bridge, ME 4, an easy ledge drop can make things sporty. Access is downstream on the right.

Fairbanks Bridge ➤ Farmington Falls   10.25 mi
Description: Quickwater, Class I, II
Date checked: 2000
Navigable: Medium and low water
Scenery: Rural, towns
Maps: Kingfield 15, Farmington; DL 19 and 20

The river is smooth for the remaining 3.5 miles to Farmington. At 0.5 mile below, Farmington Temple Stream enters on the right. Another 0.5 mile brings an interesting ledge drop; then the river is smooth and winding for the next 6.0 miles to Farmington Falls. Just above the ME 156 bridge Wilson Stream enters on the right. Paddlers wishing to avoid whitewater should take out well above the bridge or a mile farther upstream, where the river comes close to the road on the right.

Farmington Falls ➤ New Sharon   6.0 mi
Description: Class I, II, III
Date checked: 2000
Navigable: Medium water
Scenery: Rural
Maps: Farmington, New Sharon, Farmington
                           Falls; DL 20

The remains of a washed-out dam are visible above the bridge as the river begins to pitch for 200 yards of Class I–II water. Then the river smoothes out and winds through farm country to the town of New Sharon. Here the river turns sharply to the left and under the US 2 bridge.

Rapids start well above the bridge, increasing in intensity to a sharp right-hand turn that generates 5-foot waves. These should be avoided except by experts in high water and scouted carefully in medium water. The rapids end in 0.75 mile; there is a campground on the left bank.

New Sharon ➤ Kennebec River   20.25 mi
Description: Flatwater, quickwater
Date checked: 2000
Navigable: Medium and low water
Scenery: Forested, rural

Maps:	New Sharon, Norridgewock 15, Anson
	15; DL 20
Portage:	16.0 mi dam

The river flows smoothly with good current below the rapids in New Sharon. There is a USGS gauging station near Mercer and in 5.0 miles there is a dam below Sandy River. Below the dam are 3.5 miles of winding river to the junction with the Kennebec River. Take out 1.0 mile downstream on the left bank or 5.75 miles downstream at Norridgewock, where there is a boat ramp.

Sandy River (South Branch)

The South Branch is a very small stream that can be run in medium water as an alternate start to the Sandy River. It has been run from above the confluence of the branches 2.7 miles above ME 4 on Number Six Road, but this is too small and obstructed to be recommended. A better start is after 1.5 miles, where the river comes close to the road. It is a fast Class II to an abutment on a private road 1.0 mile above ME 4, where the difficulty gradually diminishes.

Temple Stream

Temple Stream rises in Avon and flows southeast to the Sandy River at West Farmington. It is small, there are several dams, and the running is mixed smoothwater and rapids.

Drury Pond ➤ Sandy River		8.5 mi
Description:	Class I, II, III	
Date checked:	2000	
Navigable:	High water (early spring)	
Scenery:	Forested, rural, towns	
Maps:	Farmington; DL 19	
Portages:	1.5 mi dam at Temple	
	7.5 mi dam at West Farmington	

If the water level is high enough, you can put in just below the outlet of Drury Pond north of Temple. The first 2.0 miles to the dam are all smooth. The next 2.5 miles below the dam to the first bridge have Class II rapids. In the next 1.5 miles to the millpond the rapids become steeper, Class III. Then it is 1.5 miles down the pond to the dam at West Farmington. Below the dam the river is mostly smooth for the remaining mile to the Sandy River, 1.0 mile below Farmington.

Wilson Stream

Wilson Stream rises on the northern side of Saddleback Mountain but does not become runnable until Wilson Pond in Wilton. The 15.0 miles from there to the junction with Sandy River at Farmington Falls offer a variety of rapid and smoothwater with only two dams to carry.

There is a sharp rapid through the town for 0.75 mile to the lower dam, so it is well to put in below this dam. In another 0.75 mile, there is a fall that requires a carry, so most paddlers will decide to put in below this fall.

Wilton ➤ East Wilton		3.5 mi
Description:	Class II	
Date checked:	1990	
Navigable:	High water (early spring)	
Scenery:	Forested, rural, towns	
Maps:	Farmington; DL 19	
Portage:	(3.5 mi dam East Wilton)	

Put in below the lower dam in a parking lot on the right just below the bridge, 1.5 miles below Wilton. From here to East Wilton the river is mostly Class II rapids. In East Wilton, take out on the left above a broken dam. Carry on the road across the bridge, and put in on the right.

East Wilton ➤ North Chesterville		10.0 mi
Description:	Quickwater	
Date checked:	2000	
Navigable:	Medium water (May)	
Scenery:	Forested, towns	
Maps:	Wilton, Farmington Falls; DL 19 and 20	
Portages:	1.0 mi low dam	
	(11.0 mi broken dam North Chesterville)	

After a short Class II rapid below the dam, it is mostly quick-water to the dam at North Chesterville. A small dam 1.0 mile below the start may be lifted over.

North Chesterville ➤ Farmington Falls   4.0 mi
Description:	Smoothwater, Class II
Date checked:	2000
Navigable:	Medium water (May)
Scenery:	Forested, towns
Map:	DL 20

There is a short rapid below the dam. The following 4.0 miles to Farmington Falls and the junction with the Sandy River at Farmington Falls are all smoothwater.

Sebasticook River

The Sebasticook River rises in North Dexter and flows south for a long distance, paralleling the Kennebec before finally joining that river at Winslow, opposite Waterville. Because most of the drops have been dammed for power purposes, you can experience a long river run, even in the summer, through a section of rural Maine in which urbanization has hardly begun. The upper section should probably be run in the spring, when there is plenty of water.

North Dexter ➤ Great Moose Pond   22.0 mi
Description:	Flatwater, some rapids
Date checked:	2000
Navigable:	High water (early spring)
Scenery:	Forested, rural
Maps:	DL 31

Put in at North Dexter from ME 23, or if the water is low, from a side road that leaves the main road south of North Dexter and reaches the river 0.5 mile lower down, where it is somewhat larger. This section of river is still somewhat small and best run at high water. It is mostly smooth and is the only rapid that can be lined or carried. The river runs through mountainous country that has fine views in all directions. For 13.0 miles from the start, the river runs through marshes in a general southwesterly direction to Mainstream Pond. There are then 3.0 miles of paddling to its southwestern end and the town of Mainstream. Below the town there is 0.5 mile of rapids followed by 1.0 mile of easy river to Lake Como. The outlet leaves the lake at its southwestern corner; in 0.25 mile there is a sharp rapid, after which the river is easy for 2.0 miles to Great Moose Pond. One can take out at Castle Harmony just before entering the lake or continue southwest across the lake 3.0 miles to the boat launch on Great Moose Drive on the west side of the outlet.

Great Moose Pond ➤ Pittsfield	10.0 mi
Date checked:	2001
Navigable:	Spring, summer
Scenery:	Forested, rural, towns
Maps:	DL 31 and 21
Portages:	2.0 mi dam at Hartland 0.5 mi
	9.0 mi dam at Waverley Ave. (Pittsfield)
	10.0 mi dam at Mill Pond (Pittsfield)

From the boat launch upstream of the outlet of Great Moose Pond it is only 2.0 miles to the dam at Hartland. It is best to make the 0.5-mile carry around this dam, the remains of a lower dam, and a very rocky set of rapids that is difficult to traverse in low water. Below this point the river transitions to flatwater at the upstream end of Douglas Pond, upstream of the ME 2 bridge. Douglas Pond is a large impoundment fringed by vast wetlands that is an important nesting area for black terns. A 2.0-mile paddle south on Douglas Pond brings you to the dam at Waverly Avenue in Pittsfield. A boat launch sits just upstream of the dam and the Waverly Avenue bridge, on river right. Below this dam is a 1.0-mile stretch of flatwater through the Mill Pond to a second Pittsfield dam, just downstream of Main Street.

Pittsfield ➤ Burnham	9.0 mi
Description:	Quickwater, Class I, II, III
Date checked:	2000
Navigable:	Spring, most summers
Scenery:	Forested, rural, towns

Maps:	DL 21
Portages:	9.0 mi dam

Access below the second Pittsfield dam, downstream of Main Street, is somewhat difficult. Most paddlers launch in Manson Park which is less than 1 mile downstream of the dam. From Manson Park it is 2.5 miles to the confluence with the East Branch of the Sebasticook River, and another 1.0 mile to the small boat launch just downstream of the Peltoma Avenue (Horseback Road) bridge on river right. You can take out here or continue for another 2.5 miles of mostly flatwater paddling to the Eel Weir Road bridge. Just upstream of the bridge, a small rapids marks the upstream influence of the backwater from the dam near the Pittsfield–Burnham line. The large impoundment of this dam is 2.0 miles long. A small take-out area beside ME 100, on river right, sits just upstream of this dam.

Burnham ➤ Clinton   10.0 mi

Description:	Some rapids, Class I and II, and long pools
Date checked:	2001
Navigable:	Spring and most summers. Flows subject to hydropower regulation.
Scenery:	Forested, rural, towns
Maps:	DL 21

Presently there is no convenient access immediately below the dam near the Pittsfield–Burnham line. Eventually, federal relicensing of the dam will require a boat portage, and access below the dam. Flows can be highly variable in this stretch, depending on operation of the dam. Most paddlers choose to skip the 2.0-mile stretch below the dam and put in near the intersection of Troy Road and ME 100 in Burnham Junction, just downstream of the confluence with Twenty-five Mile Stream. From here it is 8.0 miles downstream to Clinton, where there is an unimproved boat access area on Main Street (river right) at the site where an old woolen mill was torn down.

Clinton ➤ Winslow   10.0 mi

Description:	Flatwater, Class I, II, III
Date checked:	2001
Navigable:	Spring and most summers. Flows subject to hydropower regulation.
Scenery:	Forested, rural, towns
Maps:	DL 21
Portages:	5.0 mi dam at Benton Falls
	10.0 mi dam at Winslow

Below the boat access area in Clinton, at the site of the former woolen mill, is a steep rapid that some paddlers may choose to portage around. From here it is mostly gently rapids and pools to the impoundment at the Benton Falls dam. There is a boat launch upstream of the dam, on river left, or you can portage around the dam. Below the dam tailwater, with its ledge out-croppings, is the upstream end of the backwater influence of the dam in Winslow. The dam in Winslow has an impound-ment that is approximately 5 miles long. There is a boat launch just upstream of the dam on river left where most pad-dlers take out. Below the dam it is less than 0.5 mile to the Kennebec River in Winslow.

Sebasticook River (East Branch)

The East Branch of the Sebasticook River rises in Martin Bog in the southern part of Dexter, but is hardly runnable until it reaches Corinna. From here, it provides an alternative and some-what shorter start for the trip down the main Sebasticook River. It flows though open, rolling country in which the banks are largely wooded. The East Branch has a number of spots for access, so the trip can be matched to the stage of water. Below Corinna it can probably be run in any but a dry summer.

Moody ➤ Newport   11.0 mi

Description:	Lake, quickwater
Date checked:	2000
Navigable:	Spring (high water)
Scenery:	Forested, towns
Maps:	DL 32 and 22

Portages:	6.0 mi dam at Corinna
	6.25 mi second dam at Corinna
	6.75 mi third dam at Corinna

When there is sufficient water, you should be able to put in at the bridge on the side road off ME 7 in the northern part of the town of Corinna. This bridge is just west of Moody and below a dam on the river. The river is small for a few hundred yards. Then it opens up to a wider stream for the 3.0 miles to the millpond above Corinna, passing a bridge at Lincoln Mills, 2.0 miles down (an alternative starting point). There is then 1.0 mile of deadwater to the upper dam at Corinna. Below the upper dam there is 0.25 mile of millpond to the middle dam, then 0.5 mile of millpond to the lower dam.

The area between the upper and lower dams is a federal Superfund site, due to groundwater contamination by an old woolen mill. This stretch of river may not be navigable for many years on account of the extensive cleanup and the physical relocation of a stretch of the East Branch. You should take out above the upper dam and put in below the lower dam, thereby avoiding the Superfund site in downtown Corinna. Once river restoration is completed, you will be able to paddle through Corinna again.

There are 3.0 miles of river below the lower dam to the entrance to Sebasticook Lake. Then there are 3.0 additional miles across the lake to the town of Newport at the southwestern corner, where the river flows out, and where there is a small park and boat launch.

Newport ➤ Sebasticook River   9.0 mi

Description:	Quickwater
Date checked:	2000
Navigable:	Spring, summer
Scenery:	Forested, towns
Maps:	DL 22 and 21

Two dams are located at Newport: the first at the lake and the second 0.5 mile below, across the millpond. The second dam eventually will be removed to allow fish passage. If you start here, put in below these dams. There are then 9.0 miles of good current, the last half though a large bog to the main Sebasticook River 3.0 miles below Pittsfield. Those not wishing to go farther can take out 1.0 mile down that river at the Peltoma Bridge on Horseback Road. Beware of woody debris jams which sometimes create obstructions on the East Branch.

Stetson Stream

Maps: Stetson 15, Pittsfield 15

Stetson Stream is the outlet of Pleasant Lake in Stetson and flows west to Sebasticook Lake, thus providing an alternate means of access to the East Branch of the Sebasticook River. It runs largely through swamps and is sluggish, losing most of its altitude at the dam at Stetson. It may be run in the summer if not too low, but is better in the spring.

Pleasant Lake ➤ Newport   12.0 mi

You can put in at the east end of Pleasant Lake from a side road off ME 222. It is then 2.0 miles west across the lake to the outlet, which is located in a bay on the north side near the western end. Some 1.5 miles of travel down the river through a swamp bring you to the ME 143 bridge and the dam at Stetson. Then there are 2.5 miles of river, again largely through swamp, to Sebasticook Lake. One mile down the arm of Sebasticook Lake, you pass under Durham Bridge into the main lake. Some may wish to take out here. It is then 5.0 miles across the lake to the town of Newport at the southwest corner, where the East Branch of the Sebasticook flows out, and where there is a small park and boat launch.

Martin Stream

Martin Stream rises in Troy and Thorndike and flows north and west into the East Branch of the Sebasticook 1.0 mile below Newport. It becomes runnable in Dixmont and is a pleasant trip on a small stream with good current through relatively wild country.

The spring migration of suckers up Martin Stream is most impressive, sometimes carpeting the bottom with masses of fish.

Dixmont ➤ Newport	16.0 mi
Description:	Lake, flatwater, quickwater, Class I, II
Date checked:	1986
Navigable:	High water (spring)
Scenery:	Wild, forested, rural
Maps:	Dixmont, Plymouth, Newport; DL 22
Portages:	1.5 mi R Dixmont Falls 20 yd
	9.75 mi R Plymouth dam 150 yd

Put in at Mitchell Road just west of ME 7 between Dixmont and North Dixmont. The stream is small. It is 1.5 miles to Dixmont Falls, then 150 yards to the ME 7 bridge in North Dixmont. After 0.5 mile, the river enters an alder jungle thick enough to impede all but the most determined paddlers.

At 7.0 miles you reach the backwater from the dam in Plymouth. Paddle down the lake to the dam and falls in Plymouth (9.75 mi). Just below is a nice Class II rapid.

At 13 miles there is a sharp ledge drop to look over. The bridge at Ridge Road in Newport is 14.5 miles, the last before the confluence with the East Branch (16.0 mi).

Twenty-five Mile Stream

	8.0 mi
Description:	Flatwater, mild rapids
Navigable:	Spring (high water)
Scenery:	Forested, rural, wetlands
Maps:	DL 21
Portages:	Beaver dams, woody debris jams

Twenty-five Mile Stream flows from the outlet of Unity Pond 8.0 miles before joining the Sebasticook River in Burnham Junction. The stream is mostly slow-moving water through wetlands, with beaver dams and woody debris jams that may shift from year to year, making passage difficult. The stream can be accessed from the outlet of Unity Pond on the Horseback Road, or 2.0 miles farther downstream at ME 139 by dragging boat 50 yards down Bog Brook. Just upstream of the confluence with the Sebasticook is a curving section of rapids that flows past an old dam site. If you wish to avoid the rapids, you can take out at the Troy Road bridge in Burnham Junction.

Belgrade Lakes Trip

Maps:	Norridgewock 15, Augusta 15, Waterville 15; DL 12 & 20

The Belgrade Lakes offer a variety of trips. The usual trip is a circular one starting from East Pond and ending at Messalonskee Lake only 3.0 miles from the starting place. You can then return to the start or descend Messalonskee Stream to the Kennebec River at Waterville.

East Pond	2.5 mi

This is the highest of the chain and the usual starting point. There is access at a public picnic spot off East Pond Road, just south of Alden's Camp.

The Serpentine	2.0 mi

This is the outlet of East Pond. It is wide and smooth, and in 1.5 miles there is a sharp left turn. The channel to the right can be explored but is only the outlet of Sucker Brook. Just beyond on the right is a picnic site. In another 0.5 mile, the dam at Smithfield is reached. This can either be carried, if there is enough water in the brook below, or you can put in 300 yards farther at the beach on North Pond.

North Pond	2.0 mi

From Smithfield on the eastern shore it is only 2.0 miles to the outlet, Great Meadow Stream, which takes off at the center of the southern shore. But there are many more miles of lake to explore, including a trip into Little Pond through the Narrows at the southern end of the western shore.

Great Meadow Stream	4.0 mi

Great Meadow Stream is the outlet of North Pond, and it leaves that pond near the center of the southern shore. It twists and turns for 4.0 miles to Great Pond, marking the boundary between Rome on the right and Smithfield and Belgrade on the left.

Great Pond   5.0 mi

This is located in Belgrade, although the northern and part of the western shores are in Rome. It is a very large lake, and one should be on the alert for sudden squalls. There are public campsites on Crooked and Oak islands. It is only 5.0 miles southwesterly across the lake to the outlet at Belgrade Lakes on the western shore, but there are many bays and inlets to explore. The outlet is really only an extension of the lake for 0.5 mile to the dam. Take out at the cement bridge and carry 50 yards around the dam and into Long Pond.

Long Pond   6.0 mi

Although the northern end of the pond in Rome is worth exploring, the usual route crosses the pond to the western shore, where it turns south and passes under the bridge at Castle Island in 2.0 miles. Paddle another 4.0 miles south on a constantly narrowing pond to the outlet, Belgrade Stream. About 1.0 mile above the outlet, Ingham Stream enters on the right.

Belgrade Stream   9.0 mi

It is 2.0 miles down the stream to Wings Mills. After going under the bridge, keep to the right to avoid the sluiceway on the left. Boats can be hauled over the old fish ladder on the right. It is then only 6.0 miles more to Belgrade and another 1.0 mile to Messalonskee Lake.

Messalonskee Lake   8.0 mi

This is an Abenaki name meaning Snow Pond. The lake is long and narrow and provides an 8-mile paddle to its northern end, where at Oakland you are only 3.0 miles from the starting place at East Pond. You can terminate the trip here or continue down Messalonskee Stream to the Kennebec River.

Messalonskee Stream   9.0 mi

This is the outlet from the Belgrade Lakes; consequently, the water level holds up well and the stream can be run in the summer. The banks are a mixture of wooded and open land, and the river flows in a pleasant valley. There are three dams and an impassable cascade in Oakland, so that you cannot go directly into the river from Messalonskee Lake. It is best to make a 2-mile carry around all these obstructions and put in at the pond below town. Below Oakland 1.5 miles is a dam and a 0.5 mile carry on the right. It is then 4.0 miles to the first dam in Waterville and then 1.0 mile of backwater to the second dam. From this last dam it is 1.0 mile to the Kennebec River.

Cobbosseecontee Stream

The upper Cobbosseecontee Stream is a series of lakes and streams, starting with Torsey Lake in Mount Vernon and descending through Maranacook Lake and Lake Annabessacook to Cobbosseecontee Lake, from which Cobbosseecontee Stream flows to the Kennebec River at Gardiner. The trip can be made in either direction as most of the way is lakes or backwater from dams, with easy paddling through gentle, rolling country. Only the 0.8 mile of rapids between the dams below Cobbossee Dam requires high water. The trip can be extended for many miles of additional paddling on the lakes.

Torsey Lake ➤ Gardiner	40.5 mi
Description:	Lakes, flatwater
Date checked:	2000
Navigable:	Spring, summer, fall
Scenery:	Forested
Maps:	Augusta 15, Gardiner; DL 12
Portages:	Numerous on connecting streams; see text below

Torsey Lake	3.5 mi

You can put in at the north end of the lake from a side road about 1 mile off Cobbs Hills Road, or at the southern end at the very tip of the lake, where there is a public boat launch. The lake is long and narrow, twisting about in its course southward.

Torsey Lake Outlet 2.0 mi; 3 dams

There is a dam at the outlet and then 1.0 mile of millpond to Readfield, where there are two dams. Carry these both together. The final mile to Maranacook Lake is meandering meadow brook. If the water in this stream is too low, the entire 2.0 miles can be easily carried by road.

Maranacook Lake 5.5 mi

From the inlet stream, crossed by ME 41 almost at the lake shore, it is 5.0 miles down the lake. You pass the town of Maranacook halfway to Winthrop, where there is a public launch area at Norcross Point with toilets and water. At Winthrop the outlet is Mill Stream.

Mill Stream 0.75 mi; 1 dam

This provides the connection from Maranacook Lake to Lake Annabessacook or vice versa. At the Maranacook Lake end, enter the stream under Memorial Drive, lift over the small dam at the other side of the bridge, and descend to the Main Street bridge. Here, you must portage across the street 100 yards to the water just beyond the Carlson Woolen Mill building. Then you can paddle the remainder of the distance and enter Lake Annabessacook through a large culvert under US 202.

Lake Annabessacook 4.0 mi

It is 4.0 miles down this lake to the outlet stream and about 2 miles to the narrows. From here, you should head for the southeastern corner, where the outlet is located.

If the season is not too dry you can paddle up the outlet stream to Lower Narrows Pond, passing under a road and through a culvert.

Juggernot Stream 1.25 mi; 1 dam

This stream, the outlet of Lake Annabessacook, provides unobstructed travel to Cobbosseecontee Lake, except for a short carry over the outlet dam.

Cobbosseecontee Lake   6.5 mi

Cobbosseecontee means Sturgeon Lake in the Abenaki language ("contee" meaning "lake"). Rightfully, the word "lake" should not be repeated, but as so few people know the Indian languages, the usage will probably continue. The dam at the outlet raised the level of the lake 9 feet, enlarging the lake area but reducing the size of some of the islands. Although it is only 6.0 miles north up Cobbosseecontee Lake to the outlet, Cobbosseecontee Stream, on the eastern side, there are another 3.0 miles to the head of the lake at East Winthrop, and 2.0 miles from the inlet to the southern end of the lake at Dismal Swamp in Monmouth. Many islands here invite exploration.

Cobbosseecontee Stream   11.0 mi; 2 dams

It is only 0.25 mile from the bridge near the lake shore to the outlet dam, which must be carried on the western end. There is an 0.8-mile set of Class II rapids at high water, but they must be carried in low water, on the western side. The Collins Mill Dam is another short portage (on the west) 2.25 miles below Cobbossee Outlet dam. Some 6.0 miles below the dam Oxbow Pond is reached, and in another mile Horseshoe Pond. The river is wide all the way to Pleasant Pond, after the Collins Mill Dam.

Pleasant Pond   2.0 mi

Although it is only 2.0 miles down Pleasant Pond from the inlet to the outlet (Cobbosseecontee Stream) at the northern end, one can paddle 4.0 miles to the south into Upper Pleasant Pond and enjoy considerable mileage of lake travel.

Cobbosseecontee Stream ➤ Gardiner   4.0 mi

From Pleasant Pond it is an easy paddle for the 4.0 miles to Gardiner. Take out above the first dam, because in the last 1.5 miles to the Kennebec River there are three more dams and some difficult Class III–IV rapids.

Chapter 4
Penobscot Watershed

PENOBSCOT WATERSHED

N

Scale in miles

0	10	20	30	40

Penobscot River (Headwaters)

The Penobscot River has two major tributaries, the East Branch and the West Branch, which offer a variety of paddling trips through a vast semiwilderness area of Maine. The West Branch is itself formed by the confluence of the North Branch and the South branch, two small streams that drain a wild and densely forested area that is accessible only by private logging roads.

The North Branch was formerly the principal means of access to the headwaters of the Saint John River. Carry trails to Fifth Saint John Pond and Baker Lake were popular routes before modern logging roads and airplanes.

The West Branch from Seboomook Lake to Millinocket is a large river with good paddling throughout the summer. However, during spring runoff, the high water can cause dangerous conditions in some places. The West Branch is one of the most scenic sections of the Penobscot. Its banks are heavily forested, with little evidence of civilization, and the spectacular views of Mount Katahdin along the lower section add to its wilderness character. Roads from Greenville and Millinocket allow easy access at several points along the river.

The East Branch of the Penobscot flows from Grand Lake Matagamon at the northeastern corner of Baxter State Park to Medway, where it joins the West Branch, forming the main river. The East Branch, although not as large as the West Branch, offers good paddling throughout most of the season and, like its western sister, affords good views of the mountains of Baxter State Park. Webster Stream, a tributary of the East Branch, flows from Telos Lake to Grand Lake.

Penobscot River

This is a large river paralleled by highways, often on both sides, and bordered by a mixture of forests, farms, cities, and towns. It is quite different from the East and West branches, which join it downstream.

Because most of the drops have been harnessed for power, this river consists primarily of smoothwater, with some quickwater. In many sections, it is more like a long, thin lake than a river.

Medway ➤ Bangor	70.0 mi
Description:	Flatwater, quickwater, Class I, II
Date checked:	2000
Navigable:	Spring, summer, fall; controlled release
Scenery:	Forested, rural, towns
Maps:	Millinocket 15, Mattawamkeag 15, Winn 15, Lincoln 15, Passadumkeag 15, Orono 15, Bangor 15; DL 43, 44, 33, and 23
Portages:	7.0 mi L Mattaseunk dam
	36.0 mi R West Enfield dam
	60.0 mi L Old Town dam
	61.0 mi L Veazie dam
	(70.0 mi R Bangor dam)

From Nicatou Island at the confluence of the East and West branches, the Penobscot River flows for 7.0 miles to Mattaseunk Dam, carried left. From there, it is 4.5 miles to the mouth of the Mattawamkeag River (11.5 mi) at Mattawamkeag. In another 1.75 miles is the beginning of Five Island Rapids, which are 0.5 mile long. They are easy Class II, and the principal drop (frequently bony in low water) is at the end of the islands as you approach Winn. Flatwater predominates for the next 16.0 miles past the North Lincoln bridge (20.0 mi) to Mohawk Rapids, a 0.75-mile section with some rocks and a good current. In another 5.5 miles the West Enfield Dam is reached and carried right.

Below the West Enfield Dam (36.0 mi) the Penobscot passes the mouth of the Piscataquis River (37.0 mi) on the right, the ME 6/155 bridge (37.25 mi), and the Passadumkeag River (41.25 mi) on the left. In the next 18.75 miles to Old Town, the river flows through somewhat wider bottomlands and spreads into several channels with many islands.

About 2 miles above the first dam at Old Town, you should take the left channel if you wish the most direct route. On the right, the Stillwater River (actually a western channel of the Penobscot) leaves, headed northwesterly.

The first dam at Old Town (60.0 mi) is located upstream of the highway bridge connecting Old Town with Milford. It is carried left. One mile of flatwater brings you to (61.0 mi) the second dam at Old Town, also carried left. There is a Class II rapid below this dam. Two miles downstream, where the Stillwater rejoins the Penobscot, there is a Class III rapid, the most difficult on the lower river. Scouting from the right side may be warranted for those with loaded boats. On the right there is an easier passage. Four miles below (all Class I) you come to the Veazie Dam (67.0 mi), carried left. Three miles downstream you encounter the remains of the Bangor Dam (70.0 mi). If the tide at Bangor is high or nearly high, you can paddle through this breach. Otherwise, avoid its powerful currents.

Bangor ➤ Bucksport		21.0 mi
Description:	Tidal	
Date checked:	2000	
Navigable:	Spring, summer, fall	
Scenery:	Forested, rural, towns	
Maps:	DL 23	

The Penobscot is tidal below Bangor and a large river. Take note of tide and weather. A number of launching ramps are available.

The section below the breached Bangor Dam, 1.5 miles upstream of the mouth of the Kenduskeag River, is very urban and has strong currents when the water level in the river is high. From East Hampton to South Orrington, the river generally is scenic and flat except when wind and tide are opposed. The river then opens up and becomes over a mile wide in places.

It is possible for experienced paddlers to go down the main (western) channel from Bucksport and then back up East Channel for an 11-mile circuit of Verona Island. The combination of ebbing tide and upstream wind can create large rolling waves in the main channel. Current patterns near the northern end of the island can also be confusing.

The tidal range at Bangor is 13 feet; high water is 4 minutes later than at Portland.

Penobscot River (West Branch)

The West Branch of the Penobscot is formed by the junction of the North and the South branches at the western end of

Seboomook Lake. It flows generally east for 108.0 miles through well-wooded valleys and unpopulated lakes to Medway, where it joins the East Branch.

Its upper waters were formerly the most traveled waterways in Maine because they were the access not only to the West Branch itself, but also to the East Branch, the Allagash, and the Saint John. Today, private logging roads provide easy access to many points along the river. Remember to ask for and obtain permission before crossing property lines.

The river is large enough to be run at any season, but some of the more difficult rapids must be carried at high water.

Pittston Farm ➤ Seboomook Dam	12.5 mi
Description:	Lake, flatwater, Class I
Date checked:	2001
Navigable:	Spring, summer, fall
Scenery:	Wild
Maps:	Seboomook Lake 15, North East Carry 15; DL 48 and 49
Portage:	(12.5 mi L Seboomook Dam)
Campsites:	12.0 mi R Seboomook Dam $ car, MFS permit

Put in at the Ranger Station at Pittston Farm at the western end of Seboomook Lake. It is a 12.5-mile paddle across the lake to Seboomook Dam. Take out on the left. If you have a loaded boat, you will want to skip the run from below Seboomook Dam to Roll Dam Campsite. You can start your trip again at the campsite, which is right beside the last drop.

Seboomook Dam ➤ Roll Dam Campsite	3.5 mi
Description:	Class III, IV
Date checked:	2001
Navigable:	Spring, summer, fall; controlled release
Scenery:	Wild
Maps:	Seboomook Lake 15, North East Carry 15; DL 49
Campsites:	0 mi R Seboomook Dam $ car, MFS permit
	4.0 mi R Roll Dam $ car, MFS permit

Put in on the left below the dam. The gauge is chiseled into a large rock on the left just downstream from the put-in. This is a fun run with a reading from 1 to 3. It can be run lower (a 0 reading corresponds to 300 cfs), but some of the ledges may be scratchy. At levels higher than 3, some of the hydraulics will be keepers.

There is flatwater for 0.75 mile below the dam. The first ledge, Double Hydraulic, sets the mood for the more difficult section below. At a reading of 3, this rapid has a keeper in the middle. The best run is on the extreme right.

Another 0.5 mile of flatwater leads to a more continuous section of ledges. The ledges range in height up to 5 feet with a clean chute through each one. Generally, the ledges can be scouted on the right side, if desired. The exception to the scout-right rule is a line of rocks that seems to block the river. The best route here at low water is on the extreme left, while higher water opens up a route on the extreme right.

The maze section follows. It features huge rocks in the center and a choice of routes, with the most exciting surfing and ender possibilities on the left. A pool leads to the last ledge in this section, which features a pour-over in the center. Go right. The take-out is just below on the right, either before or after a final small ledge.

At low water, the ledges may look intimidating, but there is a good rescue pool below each one. The run is considered Class III at low levels. Higher levels result in more powerful holes and cross-currents and are considered Class IV.

Roll Dam Campsite ➤ Ripogenus Dam	43.5 mi
Description:	Lakes, flatwater, Class I
Date checked:	2001
Navigable:	Spring, summer, fall
Scenery:	Wild
Maps:	North East Carry 15, Caucomgomoc Lake 15, Chesuncook 15, Ragged Lake 15, Harrington Lake 15; DL 49 and 50
Portage:	43.5 mi R Ripogenus Dam 2.5 mi by car
Campsites:	8 sites between Roll Dam and Pine Stream BPR

21.0 mi R Pine Stream
24.0 mi R Boom House
8 sites on Chesuncook Lake
41.5 mi R Chesuncook Dam $ car

This is the smoothwater section of the West Branch. Below Roll Dam Campsite the river continues with moderate current to North Easy Carry (4.25 mi).

Lobster Stream enters on the right in 2.5 miles. Sometimes it flows backwards into Lobster Lake when the West Branch is rising.

Lobster Lake, which has several attractive campsites, makes a good side trip. The lake is an easy 2-mile paddle via Lobster Stream. The bridge for the private road from North Easy Carry crosses Lobster Stream just above the confluence with the West Branch.

In the remaining 17.25 miles there are a variety of campsites, some of which are listed above. The current slows, becoming flowage from the lake for the last several miles. The bridge on the Ragmuff/Caucogomoc private road crosses at 11.0 miles. At Boom House campsite (24.0 mi), the river opens up into Chesuncook Lake.

Chesuncook Dam (41.5 mi) near the southeastern end is a convenient take-out point. There is no dam there; it is just the site of a dam flooded out by the present Ripogenus Dam (43.5 mi) 3.0 miles to the east at the end of Ripogenus Lake.

If you are continuing down the West Branch, you must portage 2.5 miles along the road on the southern bank from Rip Dam to Big Eddy because Ripogenus Gorge is impassable to loaded canoes. See the *AMC Classic Northeastern Whitewater Guide* for further information.

Ripogenus Gorge ➤ McKay Station		1.5 mi
Description:	Class III, IV	
Date checked:	2001	
Navigable:	Spring, summer, fall; controlled release recommended level 800 to 2,000 cfs only	
Scenery:	Wild	
Maps:	Harrington Lake 15; DL 50	

This run begins just below the dam with a short but exceedingly difficult portage. This is a run for experienced decked boaters only after thorough and complete scouting. The most difficult drop is the last one.

McKay Station ➤ Big Eddy		2.5 mi
Description:	Class IV, V	
Date checked:	2001	
Navigable:	Spring, summer, fall; controlled release	
	cfs below 1,000 is dangerous	
	cfs from 1,500 to 2,300 is	
	recommended	
	cfs above 2,300 becomes very pushy	
	cfs above 4,500 approaches Class VI	
Scenery:	Wild	
Maps:	Harrington Lake 15; DL 50	

This is a difficult whitewater run and is only for expert boaters. The access road to the river is now gated, and a fee is being charged per vehicle. The fee includes camping, too, unless you choose to camp in a privately owned campground.

The gorge is about 220 yards long and is a series of 30-foot standing waves, which ends in Exterminator, a Class IV set of very large waves ending in a hole. You can run the left side of the gorge and avoid most of the waves and Exterminator (a good idea). But even on the left side, you must cross a number of small diagonal holes that tend to draw you toward the center of the river. There is an eddy on the left opposite Exterminator and another eddy farther down on the left, right before the drop into Staircase Rapid. Staircase is a Class IV+ rapid that consists of a series of four very large holes. It is important to note that the character of Staircase changes dramatically with a change of water level.

Just after Staircase is an eddy that will give you a chance to catch your breath. Here you can decide whether you want to run Little Heater, a Class IV cascade that is 7 feet high, on the right of the island, or Big Heater, a Class III rapid on the left. Shortly afterward, you leave the gorge and enter Little Eddy which can be a take-out or a put-in on the left.

Below Little Eddy is a Class II–III rapid about 220 yards long. There is also an excellent view of the Katahdin skyline. In about 330 yards, you come to Troublemaker Rapid (Class IV), which contains several small holes and a very strong breaking standing wave. Next, there are 220 yards of Class II rapid before the last eddy ahead of Cribwork Rapid. You will see Telos Bridge. Take out before the bridge on the right to portage Cribwork; take out on the left to scout Cribwork before deciding whether to run it.

Cribwork Rapid is long (about 660 yards). It is a very heavy Class V rapid with no way to stop in the middle. It must be scouted. (Watch someone else run it first if possible.) As you pass under the bridge, pass Telos Hole, which guards the rapid. From here, it is a wild and rocky rapid, dropping more than 25 feet. Do not underestimate the difficulty of the entrance to the rapid: If you get off your line at the top, the rest of the run could easily become disastrous. **Caution!** If you feel any hesitation, do not run it! Remember that better paddlers than you have walked this rapid!

You will barely have time to recover after Cribwork before you enter Bone Cruncher (2.0 mi), a Class IV rapid with large holes and waves. The remaining distance is Class I to Big Eddy Rapid, Class III.

Big Eddy ➤ Spencer Cove	22.25 mi
Description:	Class II, III, IV, V
Date checked:	2001
Navigable:	Spring, summer, fall; controlled release up to 3,000 cfs recommended
Scenery:	Forested
Maps:	Harrington Lake 15, Katahdin 15, Norcross 15; DL 50 and 42
Portages:	2.25 mi R Big Ambejackmockamus Falls
	6.0 mi L Nesourdnahunk Falls
	11.0 mi R Pockwockomus Falls
	13.75 mi R Debsconeag Falls
Campsites:	0 mi Big Eddy private $ car
	Many additional campsites

This section is one of the most scenic along the Penobscot's many branches. It also contains some heavy rapids which are separated by considerable lengths of deadwater. Many paddlers set up mini-shuttles along the river to cut out the flatwater stretches.

The regular text is for boaters who wish to run rapids up to Class III. The text in italics is for experts in whitewater boats.

It is 1.0 mile to Little Ambejackmockamus Falls, a Class II or III drop, depending on the water level. One mile beyond and past some rapids, take out on the right where the road is close to the river at a sharp left turn (2.25 mi) in order to carry around Big Ambejackmockamus Falls (Big A).

Big A is 0.25 mile of standing waves leading to a Class IV drop with a very large, dangerous keeper in the center. At the second drop, run right or left because there is another hole in the center. The third drop has a large wave with a pool at the bottom. Each drop should be scouted on the right.

A short distance below Big A, the Horserace begins, a long rocky Class II–III rapid. If the water level is not right, or if you are inexperienced, carry 1.5 miles around both Big Ambejackmockamus Falls and the Horserace to Nesourdnahunk Deadwater.

After 2.0 miles of deadwater, take out above the ledge on the left and carry Sourdnahunk Falls (6.0 mi).

Nesourdnahunk Falls is another Class IV. As you turn left in Class III rapids, the river goes over a falls with an 11-foot drop. The right is rocky, although at the correct water level the water covers a smooth rock that can be used as a slide to make the drop. The left is a very heavy run over the drop into a large hole with about ten standing waves below, followed by 330 yards of Class II rapids. You can carry back up and do the drop several times.

At the end of the carry around Nesourdnahunk Falls is the 3-mile Abol Deadwater, which extends to some Class I rips under the Abol bridge (0.5 mile above Abol Falls). There is an easy Class II above Abol Falls (10.0 mi). Stay along the right bank; the portage begins at a small beach right after a large one, and close to the falls. Follow the roads and take a left. A cabin faces the falls, which is visible from above.

Abol Falls is another Class IV rapid. It is 275 yards long and full of very large rocks and waves. The right has smaller waves and many rocks. The center has bigger waves and holes and fewer rocks. The run behind the island on the right is very narrow with large rocks.

Quickwater continues for 0.5 mile; then there are easy Class II rapids to a cabin on the right marking Pockwockamus Falls (11.0 mi). Portage along the road on the right, then take the third left to the bottom of the falls. A shorter trail begins close to the top of Pockwockamus Falls.

Big Pockwockamus Falls (Class IV) is characterized by large rocks and many standing waves. Scout from the right, and locate the large hole on the right about 100 yards into the rapids. Find a good marker on short so that you will have something to sight from in order to miss this hole.

Pockwockamus deadwater extends for 2.5 miles to Debsconeag Falls (13.75 mi), which can be portaged on either side. The portage on the left begins 100 yards above the falls in a small cove and is about 0.5 mile long. The portage on the right is below a large island in a tiny clearing where the bank is steep but only 3 feet high. The portage is 620 yards up a hill and down to the end of the falls.

Debsconeag Falls is a very dangerous Class V rapid that starts off with two huge holes (keepers) at the top. It is necessary to make the move around these holes. There are several other large holes before the rapid ends. This is the hardest rapid in this section of the river; if you attempt to run it, scout on the left and run it in several sections.

There is a drop with a big wave; then it is a 3-mile paddle across Debsconeag Deadwater to Passamagamet Falls (17.0 mi), a Class III rocky drop with two chutes. In 1.75 miles, you reach Ambejejus Falls, although high water in the lake below may flood them out. The river soon opens into Ambejejus Lake (19.0 mi).

In Spencer Cove, 3.25 miles to the east, the road to Baxter State Park comes close to the lake (22.25 mi).

Spencer Cove ➤ ME 11 (Quakish Lake)   11.0 mi

Description: Lakes
Date checked: 2001
Navigable: Spring, summer, fall
Scenery: Forested
Maps: Norcross 15, Millinocket 15; DL 43

From Spencer Cove it is 4.0 miles across Ambejejus Lake and the end of Pemadumcook Lake to Nicks Gut, where you pass into North Twin Lake, and an additional 5.0 miles down that to Elbow Lake. You can make a detour here into South Twin Lake, which is about the same size. It is 1.0 mile across Elbow Lake to the dam, which must be carried. There is then 1.0 mile of river, passing under ME 11 halfway down, to Quakish Lake.

ME 11 ➤ Shad Pond, via West Branch   6.5 mi

Description: Flatwater, Class III, IV
Date checked: 2001
Navigable: Spring (sometimes)
Scenery: Forested, towns
Maps: Millinocket 15; DL 43
Portage: 1.0 mi Quakish Dam

The distance from the boat-launching ramp at ME 11 to Quakish Dam is 2.0 miles. The dam diverts most of the water to power plants, but during spring runoff this stretch is sometimes possible. This historic stretch contains Blue Rock Pitch and Grand Falls, 3.0 miles below the dam, and runs into Shad Pond.

Quakish Dam ➤ Shad Pond   3.5 mi

(alternate route via Millinocket Stream)
Description: Lakes, quickwater
Date checked: 2001
Navigable: Spring, summer, fall
Scenery: Towns, forested
Maps: Norcross 15, Millinocket 15; DL 43

When there is no water in the West Branch, through travelers may be able to paddle the mile to the outlet of Ferguson Pond and portage through the Great Northern Paper Company mill to Millinocket Stream, Millinocket is followed for 2.25 miles to Shad Pond.

Shad Pond ➤ East Branch Penobscot   5.5 mi

(alternate route via Millinocket Stream)

Description:	Flatwater, quickwater
Date checked:	2001
Navigable:	Spring, summer, fall
Scenery:	Towns
Maps:	Millinocket 15, DL 43
Portages:	1.75 mi 60-foot dam
	3.5 mi dam at East Millinocket
	5.0 mi dam at Bethel Church

You can put in or take out at Rice Farm on the left, at the entrance to Dolby Flowage. At the end of this is a 60-foot-high dam. In another 1.5 miles you reach the somewhat lower dam at East Millinocket. It is then only 1.5 miles more to the last dam at Bethel Church; 0.5 mile below, the West Branch meets the East Branch to form the main Penobscot River.

Penobscot River (South Branch)

The South Branch flows from the border mountains northwest of Jackman to Seboomook Lake. Its upper part is too steep and too small for paddling even in high water. The lower part, below Canada Falls Dam, has a series of ledges so that a portage along the road to Pittston Farm is recommended. Although the middle section provides a fast run in high water, it is not worth the effort of getting to the put-in point, especially since there are better and more accessible rivers in the same general area. The upper part of the watershed contains only a few ponds, so the water level drops rapidly after spring runoff.

Bridge ➤ Canada Falls Dam   17.5 mi

Description:	Lake, Class I, II
Date checked:	2000
Navigable:	High water (May)
Scenery:	Wild
Maps:	Andy Bay, Penobscot Lake 15,
	Seboomook Lake 15; DL 47 and 48
Portage:	(17.5 mi ledges 3.0 mi (by car))
Campsite:	17.5 mi L Canada Falls Dam MFS $ car

A private road from US 201 about 12.0 miles northwest of Jackman follows the southern bank of the South Branch for 8.0 miles until it crosses the river 3.0 miles downstream from Little Canada Falls. The bridge is out, however.

There are shallow rapids for about 2.0 miles to Kellher Falls, a sharp ledge drop that cannot be run and is difficult to line. This section can be carried on the left. Always remember to ask for and obtain permission before crossing property lines.

The next 9.5 miles to Canada Falls Lake (11.5 mi) are mostly good current with shallow rapids. It is 6.0 miles across the lake to Canada Falls Dam (17.5 mi) at the end of the northeastern arm.

The remaining 3.5 miles to Seboomook Lake contain several severe ledge drops that cannot be run or lined through. It is recommended that this section be portaged using the road to Pittston Farm on Seboomook Lake.

Canada Falls Dam ➤ Seboomook Lake		3.5 mi
Description:	Class IV, V	
Date checked:	2000	
Navigable:	Spring (May–early June)	
Scenery:	Wild	
Maps:	Seboomook Lake 15; DL 48	
Portage:	1.0 mi R 20-foot waterfall 150 yd	
Campsite:	Canada Falls Dam MFS $ car	

Put in below Canada Falls Dam at the campground there. There is a gauge painted on a rock at the put-in. High water is over 1 on the gauge, medium is 0 to 0.75, and low is below 0. **Caution!** If the water is over 1 do not run it! If you cannot easily handle Class IV rapids do not run at any level. This is a Class IV+ run at medium water and a III+ at low water, with some shallow spots. There is one mandatory carry around a 20-foot waterfall and five difficult Class IV+ drops that are very difficult to portage.

The first 0.25 mile is quickwater, followed by a Class III drop. Another 0.25 mile below this is a Class IV gorge about 400 yards long. Another 0.5 mile (1.0 mi) below this gorge is a small island in the river. Be extremely careful here because the waterfall is just 20 feet below the island. Take the channel on the right side of the island and portage to the bottom of the falls.

The next 0.75 mile contains two Class II rapids. After this, watch carefully at every river bend for a rocky cliff on the right shore and a cabin across from it on the left bank. As soon as you can see the cabin, eddy out immediately; this is the start of Cabin Rapid, a Class III+ with very heavy current that flows into a nasty souse hole. Scout and/or carry on the left. Most boaters catch the eddy on the right just yards above the hole, then ferry to an eddy on the left from where they can take the left channel. If you have had any problems getting downriver to this point, take out at the cabin. This is the closest the road comes to the river; the rapids below are much more difficult and dangerous.

After Cabin Rapid, you will enter a gorge with sheer rock cliffs. A quarter-mile into the gorge is the first of three Class IV+, V drops within a 40-yard distance. The first drop is marked by a large rock outcropping in the middle of the river. It has been run on both sides; take a long, hard look at both sides because a swim here means a swim through the next two drops. There is a carry trail on the left from which you can also scout the next two drops. The second drop is just like the first—a large rock outcropping in the middle of the river that can be run on either side. The third drop is marked by a near river-wide hydraulic which is a keeper. The only soft spot is on the left side of the hole, but it requires a very difficult approach only a few feet from a drop into the reversal.

After the gorge, there is a short Class III+ S-turn, then a Class II+, III and finally there is flatwater to the bridge and the take-out.

Penobscot River (North Branch)

The North Branch flows from Little Bog south to Seboomook Lake where it joins the South Branch to form the West Branch. Since there are few lakes and swamps to provide headwater storage, this section can only be run during early spring runoff. The lower position contains broad sandbars; usually after May low water makes paddling impossible.

Access to Little Bog is by private logging road. The trip can also begin at Big Bog. There are several bridges out on the private logging roads in this area, but it is usually possible to ford the river.

Big Bog Dam ➤ Pittston Farm		20.75 mi
Description:	Class II, III	
Date checked:	2000	
Navigable:	High water (May)	
Scenery:	Wild	
Maps:	Norris Brook 15, Penobscot Lake 15, Seboomook Lake 15; DL 48	

Most of this river has good current with shallow rapids. There is a bridge 4.5 miles below the put-in point at Big Bog Dam, and in 4.25 miles you reach the mouth of Dole Brook (8.75 mi). There are easy rapids and smoothwater for the 7.25 miles to Leadbetter Falls (16.0 mi). This is a short rapid under a bridge, which can be run in medium water but which is difficult in high water. In 4.0 miles, the river opens into a bay at the end of Seboomook Lake (20.0 mi), with Pittston Farm beyond on the right (20.75 mi).

It is a 12.75-mile paddle down Seboomook Lake from the mouth of the North Branch to Seboomook Dam (32.75 mi).

Nesowadnehunk Stream

Nesowadnehunk Stream (locally spelled Sourdnahunk and pronounced "sourdihunk") originates in Little Nesowadnehunk Lake on the Penobscot side of the divide south of Telos Lake and in a steep mile of travel runs into Nesowadnehunk Lake. Below this lake, enlarged by the lumbermen to run logs down the river below, the stream flows south for 17.0 miles to the West Branch of the Penobscot about 0.5 mile below the Sourdnahunk Falls, in the Abol Deadwater. Because the water level is controlled at the dam, it can be run almost anytime down to the Daicey Pond Brook (about 13.0 miles), but Baxter State Park authorities discourage running more than the first 5.0 miles down to Campground 5 at Sourdnahunk Field. The lower end of the stream is a tumultuous descent over falls and cascades to the

Penobscot; unrunnable, but well worth a visit on foot.

Nesowadnehunk Lake ➤ Campground 5		5.0 mi
Description:	Class I, II	
Date checked:	2000	
Navigable:	Medium water	
Scenery:	Wild	
Maps:	Telos Lake 15; DL 50	

Nesowadnehunk Lake is a large body of water 5.0 miles long and 1.5 miles wide. The Sourdnahunk Tote Road from Baxter Park reaches the lake at the outlet dam. You can put in below the dam and enjoy a fine 5-mile run down easy water (mostly Class I and II rapids with numerous pools in between) to Sourdnahunk Fields where the road from Ripogenus Dam crosses. This is a delightful and easy run that offers fine views of Mounts Veto and Doubletop on the right and Katahdin with its subsidiary peaks on the left.

Campground 5 ➤ Daicey Pond Brook		8.0 mi
Description:	Class I, II, III	
Date checked:	2000	
Navigable:	Spring, summer, fall	
Scenery:	Wild	
Maps:	Harrington Lake 15; DL 50	
Portage:	2.0 mi L Ledge Falls 100 yd	
	Lower river impassable	

This is a considerably more difficult section and should be undertaken by experts only, as the river drops sharply with pools in between the drops. Ledge Falls is a natural rock falls. Then it is Class I–II for 1.75 miles to the washed-out Slide Dam, with 250 yards of Class III below; scout from the left. The river is then easier for the 2.0 miles to the road crossing for the Kidney Pond Camps. This is an easy spot to take out. About 2 miles below here is the Appalachian Trail crossing, about 0.25 mile above the Daicey Pond Brook. You can take out here and carry a short distance to the Daicey Pond Camp road. River travel is possible for another 1.0 mile, but there is no way to take out except by poling back upstream. The old toll dam there marks the beginning of the wild plunge down to the Penobscot.

Nahmakanta Stream (via Debsconeag Lakes)

Nahmakanta Stream is a tributary of the Penobscot River (West Branch) at Pemadumcook Lake. It flows from Mahmakanta Lake, a medium-sized lake situated among the low mountains southwest of Baxter State Park. The beginning of this stream can be reached from Debsconeag Deadwater on the West Branch via the Debsconeag Lakes.

A circuit trip from Spencer Cove on Ambejejus Lake, up the West Branch, through the Debsconeag Lakes, and down Nahmakanta Stream to Pemadumcook Lake is a three- or four-day trip through relatively isolated country. The Debsconeag Lakes are clear and in rugged settings, but there are several long portages on this approach to Nahmakanta Lake. Nahmakanta Stream provides a short but enjoyable run in May.

Penobscot River (West Branch) ➤ Nahmakanta Lake 10.25 mi	
Description:	Lakes
Date checked:	2000
Navigable:	Spring, summer, fall
Scenery:	Wild
Maps:	Katahdin 15, Harrington Lake 15, Jo-Mary Mountain 15; DL 42 and 50
Portages:	2.5 mi L into Second Debsconeag Lake 0.75 mi
	4.75 L toward Third Debsconeag Lake 400 yd
	5.0 mi into Third Debsconeag Lake
	7.5 mi R into Fourth Debsconeag Lake 0.5 mi
	9.0 mi R into Nahmakanta Lake 1.25 mi
Campsite:	0.5 mi R First Debsconeag Lake (beach at eastern end) permit

Keep to the west of the island that encloses the northern end of Debseconeag Deadwater and follow the short passage westward into First Debsconeag Lake. The latter is 2.0 miles long. At the western end (2.5 mi), a 0.75-mile portage leads to Second Debsconeag Lake. (The portage trail forks near the middle; go right.)

On the southern shore of Second Debsconeag Lake near the west end, a small brook enters the lake. The portage (4.75 mi) begins just east of this brook and ends at a small pool above an abandoned driving dam. A 100-yard paddle leads to the third portage, a 30-yard scramble into Third Debsconeag Lake.

Third Debsconeag Lake (5.0 mi) is the largest of these lakes and is roughly horseshoe-shaped. The portage to Fourth Debsconeag Lake leaves a short distance before the end of a narrow western arm.

The portage to Nahmakanta Stream follows a dirt road to a bridge over the stream just below Nahmakanta lake. Begin this portage at a landing on the western shore a short distance from the southwestern end of the lake.

Nahmakanta Stream

Nahmakanta Lake ➤ Pemadumcook Lake		5.25 mi
Description:	Quickwater, Class I, II	
Date checked:	2000	
Navigable:	High water (May)	
Scenery:	Wild	
Maps:	Harrington Lake 15, Jo-Mary Mountain 15, Norcross 15; DL 50, 42, and 43	
Campsites:	9.0 mi R Shelter on Appalachian Trail	
	5.0 mi R	
	7.75 mi L 2 sites	
	9.5 mi R	
	12.0 mi R Pemadumcook Lake car	

Nahmakanta Stream begins at the southeastern end of Nahmakanta Lake. At the right-hand bend below the bridge is a narrow 200-yard Class III rapid that can be scouted or portaged most easily on the right bank. Following a 0.25-mile deadwater, there is a succession of short, easy Class I and II rapids, which are all separated by pools. These extend for about 1 mile.

Then you reach a second 0.25-mile section of flatwater (1.5 mi), followed by more short rapids and a nice 0.5-mile Class II rapid that extends through about a half-dozen bends in the river before it ends at a pool (2.75 mi). There is then another mile of short, easy Class I and II rapids with pools or quickwater between them. The last 1.5 miles are mostly quickwater with a few easy rapids.

From the mouth of Nahmakanta Stream (5.25 mi), it is 10.25 miles down Pemadumcook Lake and across Ambejejus Lake to Spencer Cover (15.5 mi) on the road from Millinocket to Baxter State Park.

Millinocket Stream

Millinocket Stream is the outlet of the Millinocket Lake north of Baxter State Park and a tributary of the Aroostook River. It should not be confused with another Millinocket Stream, which is the outlet of another Millinocket Lake and a tributary of the West Branch of the Penobscot. Millinocket Lake can be reached by a short portage from a branch road from the Grand Lake Road. Inquire locally for directions.

Millinocket Lake ➤ Libby Camp		6.0 mi
Description:	Lakes, flatwater, Class I, II	
Date checked:	2000	
Navigable:	Spring, summer, fall; controlled releases	
Scenery:	Wild	
Maps:	Millinocket Lake 15; DL 57	

Portage the dam at Millinocket Lake. It is a short distance to Round Pond, with an old logging dam at the outlet. Just below is Millinocket Falls, a short Class I–II rapid, which should be scouted from the left bank. This is followed by 1.5 miles of Class II rapids to Millimagassett Stream. It is possible to ascend 0.5 mile of stream and 0.5 mile of log sluice to Millimagassett Lake, which features beautiful islands and a view of Baxter Park mountains.

Below are 1.5 miles of deadwater and 0.5 mile of Class I water to the bridge at Mooshorn Crossing. This is followed by 1.0 mile of quickwater to Devils Elbow, a 0.5-mile series of Class II ledge drops. It is then 0.5 mile to Libby Camp, where Munsungan Stream joins up to form the Aroostook River.

Mooseleuk Stream

The swift Mooseleuk Stream, which rises in Mooseleuk Lake just off the American Realty Road in T10 R9, is one of the major tributaries of the upper Aroostook River. The trip can make an excellent weekend in the wild. Beware of being swept into the bushes in the many bends.

Mooseleuk Lake ➤ Old Fire Warden's Camp	18.0 mi
Description:	Lake, quickwater, Class I
Date checked:	2000
Navigable:	High water (spring)
Scenery:	Wild
Maps:	Mooseleuk Lake 15, Millinocket Lake 15, Grand Lake Seboeis 15; DL 56 and 57

It is a very pretty 2-mile paddle down Mooseleuk Lake to the outlet and the remains of an old logging dam. At once you enter a swift stream (Class I) with many sharp bends. At 10.0 miles the large, heavily used bridge from Ashland crosses just above Chandler Stream. In 2.0 more miles, there is a sharp right bend in the stream to Boars Head Falls, where the river narrows into Class II rapids. Boars Head Falls is an excellent camping spot. It is only 3.0 more miles to the Aroostook River, in a large deadwater just below the privately owned (old) fire warden's camp.

Saint Croix Stream

The Saint Croix Stream rises in Saint Croix Lake in T8 R4 and flows north to the Aroostook River at Masardis. Although the Bangor and Aroostook Railroad parallels the stream, it is a very wild area full of history of past logging days. The stream is a large one and drains a large swamp above the Saint Croix River, so it makes good paddling in all but the lowest-water season. The stream varies from smooth to very rough water in the middle section.

Howe Brook ➤ Aroostook River	18.0 mi
Description:	Lake, quickwater, Class II, III+
Date checked:	2000

Navigable:	High water (difficult)
	Medium water (excellent)
	Low water (scratchy)
Scenery:	Wild
Maps:	Howe Brook 15, Oxbow 15; DL 58

There is about 1 mile of lakelike river below the lake before you enter Saint Croix Stream. From here, it is 5.0 miles of slow swampy paddling to a bridge where the water quickens, with several sets of Class II rapids and a falls, which is a Class III+ stretch of water with ledges. This can be run, lined, or carried on the right side. In 0.5 mile, you reach Pride; then there are 4.0 miles of Class II whitewater from Pride to Griswold (9.5 mi). In Griswold are the remains of an old mill site with a very nice chute (Class II+). Below Griswold are 7.0 miles of flat swampy stream, until the Blackwater River enters on the right (16.5 mi). Below, there is a section filled with rocks, which can be hard going in low water. In another 1.5 miles, you reach Masardis and the US 1 bridge, below which is the confluence with the Aroostook River.

Squa Pan Stream

Squa Pan Lake, south of Castle Hill, is a dogleg-shaped lake about 15 miles long and 1 mile wide, for the most part wild and unspoiled. The lake is used to hold water by the WPS New England Generation. The outlet stream is short but swift and flows into the Aroostook River above Ashland.

Squa Pan Lake ➤ Aroostook River		3.0 mi
Description:	Flatwater, quickwater, Class I, II
Date checked:	2000
Navigable:	Whenever dam is open; call WPS New
	England (207-493-4589) for informtion.
Scenery:	Wild, rural
Maps:	Ashland 15, Presque Isle 15; DL 58

When the water is low, you can see the remains of the original dam a few miles up the lake.

The dam and bridge at the outlet must be carried about 100 yards on either side. Below the bridge are continuous Class II rapids for 2.5 miles. In this distance, the river drops 63 feet through wild, wooded country. Then you go under several railroad bridges and, finally, the ME 11 bridge into a deadwater for the last 0.5 mile to the Aroostook River.

Sandy Stream

Millinocket Lake has one major tributary: Sandy Stream. It drains the southeastern flank of Mount Katahdin. The upper sections of Sandy Stream are too steep to paddle, but the lower part, reachable by Togue Stream, is runnable. These streams are remote, and they are only occasionally run. Access to Togue Stream is possible only after the ice has gone out of Lower Togue Pond; that usually occurs in early May.

The first mile of Togue Stream is the hardest. Where there are drops in elevation—you cannot really call them rapids— there is a combination of large rocks, overhanging trees, and jackstrawed logs that requires you to line the boat. Portaging is not an easy alternative, so you must resign yourself to working the boat slowly downstream, snaking around some obstructions here and sawing some logs there. Improvements made one year are likely to be undone in the high water of the next. Patience, determination, and about two hours will bring you to a large beaver pond. From that point, the river is virtually unobstructed, and for the next 2.0 miles you will find yourself in a very wild section of Baxter State Park.

The flow in Sandy Stream is subject to rapid fluctuations because of the steepness of the upper watershed. There are only a few ponds and swamps in its headwater, so the water level is responsive to a heavy rain fall or a rapid melting of the snow.

Lower Togue Pond ➤ Millinocket Lake	10.5 mi
Description:	Lakes, quickwater, Class I, II
Date checked:	2000
Navigable:	High water (heavy rain or rapid snowmelt)
	Medium water (May)
Scenery:	Wild
Maps:	Katahdin 15, Norcross 15, Millinocket 15; DL 51
Campsite:	10.5 mi L mouth of Sandy Stream, permit

Lower Togue Pond lies just inside of the southern boundary of Baxter State Park, and the road from Millinocket to the park goes along the western shore. The entrance of Togue Stream (1.25 mi) is on the northeastern shore of the pond, but the exact location is difficult to see unless you are close to it.

In the first 100 yards of Togue Stream is a short, lineable drop; in the middle of the drop is an old, rotting bridge that you can just sneak under in medium water. For most of the next mile, short navigable sections alternate with others where lining and some clearing is necessary. After a couple of hours of slow progress, you reach a large beaver pond (2.25 mi) that is several hundred yards long. It is located along the northernmost portion of the stream.

For the next 2.75 miles, there is a mixture of flatwater, quickwater, and Class I rapids. Then there is a 50-yard, Class II rapid immediately above the confluence with Sandy Stream (5.0 mi).

Sandy Stream is much larger than Togue Stream. The first half consists mostly of quickwater over small stones with gravel bars and wide, sweeping turns. An occasional overhanging tree constitutes Sandy Stream's primary hazard.

In 3.0 miles, you reach a 50-yard, Class II rapid that begins at a washed-out driving dam (8.0 mi). After 1.0 mile of flatwater, you come to Red Pine Rapids (9.0 mi), a 0.25-mile pitch that is Class II in medium water and Class III in high water. It extends through an S-turn, and it may be easily scouted from or portaged along the left bank. The final 1.25 miles to Millinocket Lake (10.5 mi) are smooth.

Take out at the dike between Millinocket Lake and Spencer Cove on Ambejejus Lake (15.0 mi).

Penobscot River (East Branch)

The East Branch drains the region north and northeast of Mount Katahdin. It has also been the recipient of part of the Allagash drainage since the construction of Telos Dam in 1841. In that year, three other dams were constructed along the Allagash, making it possible to drive logs from the upper

Allagash region down the East Branch rather than north to the Saint John River. Today, Telos and Grand Lake Matagamom Dams are used to store water for use in power generation farther downstream.

Generally there is sufficient water in Webster Stream through early June. The East Branch is navigable for much of the season. The lakes are usually drawn down from mid-September to mid-October, providing a good flow at that time.

You can travel by canoe or kayak from the West Branch to the East Branch using the two access routes described in Chapter 5, "Allagash Wilderness Waterway."

Grand Lake Dam ➤ Medway		47.5 mi
Description:	Class I, II, III	
Date checked:	2001	
Navigable:	Spring, summer, fall; controlled release	
	High water difficult, medium water recommended, low water passable but thin	
Scenery:	Wild	
Maps:	Traveler Mountain 15, Shin Pond 15, Stacyville 15, Millinocket 15; DL 51 and 43	
Portages:	Many, depending on water level	
Campsites:	0.75 mi L Grand Lake Road (bridge) private $ car	
	9.75 mi L Grand Pitch permit	
	23.5 mi L Lunksoos Camp MFS car	
	27.25 mi L Whetstone Falls (between rapids) MFS car	

From just below Grand Lake Road bridge, where there are a few rapids, there is smoothwater for 4.5 miles to Stair Falls (5.25 mi), a series of shallow ledges. They are best run on the left if water level permits; if it does not, there is also a portage on the left. Then for 1.25 miles, there is quickwater to Haskell Deadwater, below which is Haskell Rock Pitch (7.0 mi), the first of four falls on the East Branch. (The USGS Traveler Mountain Sheet shows Haskell Rock Pitch in the wrong location.) There is a 0.5-mile portage on the right. In the next mile to Pond Pitch (7.75 mi), the second falls, there are three sets of rapids. There is a portage on the left.

Below Pond Pitch, in 0.75 mile, you reach Grand Pitch (9.75 mi), the third and most spectacular of the Grand Falls of the East Branch. The portage is on the left. About 0.5 mile beyond is Hulling Machine Pitch, the fourth falls. Stop above the rapids just above the falls, and portage on the right. Less than 1.0 mile below these falls is Bowline Falls, a short Class II rapid. If you run it, starting on the far right is recommended. Mostly smoothwater continues for the remaining 9.0 miles to the mouth of Sebeois River (21.0 mi).

Flatwater continues for the next 6.0 miles to Whetstone Falls (27.0 mi). These consist of two sets of rapids separated by fastwater. The upper section, Class III, can be run by experienced paddlers in medium water. The lower part is easier in medium water, but it should be scouted first. It may be difficult in high water. At Lunkssos Camp (23.5 mi), as well as above the bridge at Lower Whetstone Falls, the MFS campsites offer good access to the river.

The next rapids are in 9.0 miles at Crowfoot Falls, Class II or III, depending on the water level. After another 2.25 miles, below a railroad bridge, is Grindstone Falls. This is a Class III–IV rapid, which should be run empty. The first drop is best run on the left, the remainder (about 0.5 mile of heavy rapids even at medium water) is runnable between the shore and the main current.

The last 9.0 miles to the confluence with the West Branch (47.5 mi) in Medway are mostly smooth, except for Meadowbrook Rips (40.5 mi) and Ledge Falls (45.0 mi). The latter are difficult in high water. You pass under the ME 157 bridge (47.0 mi) 0.5 mile before reaching the West Branch.

Webster Stream

Webster Stream flows from Telos Lake through a human-made canal to Webster Lake and then on to Grand Lake Matagamon. Because most of the stream and much of Grand Lake lie within the boundaries of Baxter State Park, campsites must be arranged and paid for in advance with the park office.

Telos Landing ➤ Grand Lake Dam		24.0 mi
Description:	Class I, II, III	
Date checked:	2000	
Navigable:	Spring, summer, fall; controlled release	
	High water (over 600 cfs) difficult, dangerous	
	Medium water (300-500 cfs) recommened	
	Low water (100-150 cfs) skinny but runnable	
Scenery:	Wild	
Maps:	Telos Lake 15, Traveler Mountain 15; DL 50, 56, 57, and 51	
Portages:	2.0 mi R Telos Dam 25 yd	
	14.5 mi R Grand Pitch 0.5 mi	
Campsites:	0 mi Telos Landing AWW $ car	
	4.5 mi R Webster Stream lean-to	
	8.0 mi R Little East Branch Grand Lake (5 sites)	
	24.75 mi L Grand Lake Road (below dam) private $ car	

From the end of the Allagash Wilderness Waterway access road at Telos Landing, it is 2.0 miles to Telos Dam. Below the dam, a 1-mile canal leads to Webster Lake. The flow is controlled at the dam, and you can often arrange for water to be let through for paddling. It is a fast run in medium water. From the end of the canal, it is 3.0 miles across the lake to the outlet (6.0 mi).

The first 6.5 miles from Webster Lake to Indian Carry (12.5 mi) are mostly shallow rapids and fast current. Indian Carry in medium water is a Class III rapid that can be run by experts. However, it requires very difficult maneuvering, and it is recommended that this drop be carried on the right bank.

The next 2.0 miles to Grand Pitch (14.5 mi) contain several very difficult Class III ledge drops, which can be run by experts in medium water. At Grand Pitch, obscure portage trails on each side of the stream require considerable effort to carry this falls. A 0.5-mile alternative on the right bank follows a trail that leads to a logging road. It bypasses the main falls as well as two more severe ledge drops 0.5 mile below these falls.

You reach Grand Lake Matagamon (15.75 mi) 0.5 mile below the last drop, and 8.25 miles down the lake is the dam (24.0 mi), which you portage on the right.

Seboeis River

Seboeis River flows from Grand Lake Seboeis south to the East Branch of the Penobscot, joining the latter 21.0 miles below the Grand Lake Matagamon Dam. It offers a good alternative to the upper section of the East Branch. Because there are no difficult rapids and only one short carry around a pretty, though impassable falls, it is particularly suitable for inexperienced paddlers. It has a continuous, moderate current to its junction with the East Branch and flows through an unspoiled valley.

The usual starting point is the MFS campground on the Grand Lake Matagamon Road and ME 159 from Patten. Above there, the river has very steep and difficult rapids with poor access and is not recommended for paddling. The first place to take out on the East Branch is at the MFS campsite at Lunksoos Deadwater, 2.5 miles below the mouth of Seboeis River.

The flow drops fast after the spring runoff, and the trip should not be attempted after the second week in June. Good campsites can be found along most of the river, although with good water the river can be run easily in one day.

Grand Lake Road ➤ East Branch		17.25 mi
Description:	Class I, II	
Date checked:	2000	
Navigable:	Spring	
Scenery:	Wild	
Maps:	Shin Pond 15, Stacyville 15; DL 57 and 51	
Portage:	0.25 mi L Grand Pitch 100 yd	
Campsite:	0 mi L Grand Lake Road MFS car	

There are 1.25 miles of Class II rapids to Grand Pitch, an unrunnable drop with a 100-yard portage on the left. The approach to the falls is marked first by a small ledge drop and then by a very large, high ledge on the left bank of the river. The remaining 16.0 miles to the East Branch (17.25 mi) contain fairly continuous Class I rapids.

Mattawamkeag River

The Mattawamkeag River is a large tributary of the Penobscot that flows through a big area southwest of Houlton. The West Branch drains two large lakes in addition to extensive swamps; in late spring or early summer, its water level is more dependable than that of the East Branch. Below Island Falls, the river is apt to be runnable after other rivers in northern Maine have become too low.

The Mattawamkeag flows through several small towns, a factor that calls into question the drinkability of the water.

The longest trip on the Mattawamkeag described in this book—some 90 miles—begins in Patten on Fish Stream. Unfortunately, there are few established campsites.

Haynesville ➤ Kingman	34.25 mi
Description:	Flatwater, quickwater, Class I, II
Date checked:	2000
Navigable:	Spring, summer, fall
Scenery:	Forested, rural, towns
Maps:	Amity 15, Danforth 15, Wytopitlock 15; DL 53, 54, and 55
Campsite:	28.25 mi L Meadow Brook permit, permission

There are two large deadwaters, one below Haynesville and the other beginning at Wytopitlock. They total 19.0 miles in length. The balance is a mixture of smooth and quickwater with some rapids.

In two places, local highways more or less parallel the river for a total of 15.5 miles. Although not a wild river in these sections, it is attractive. Below the ME 171 bridge in Wytopitlock, the river flows slowly for 9.75 miles through a large hardwood swamp with almost no evidence of humans.

Rock cribs in the river at Wytopitlock are all that remain from the days of the log drives, which ended about 1950.

Below the US 2A bridge in Haynesville there are 7.5 miles of deadwater. The deadwater ends 1.0 mile below the Ferry Bridge, where the current picks up to Ledge Falls (9.5 mi), which is wide and about 100 yards long (shallow, but passable in medium water). As its name implies, it is all ledge. A short distance beyond is a brief, easy rapid.

There is a good current most of the way from Ledge Falls to Wytopitlock. Occasionally, there are sections that are Class I. Below the falls 4.75 miles Baskahegan Stream enters left (14.25 mi), and 4.25 miles farther is the Bancroft railroad bridge (18.5 mi).

The easy traveling ends 1.0 mile above Wytopitlock; after 2.0 miles deadwater the river flows under the ME 171 bridge (23.25 mi). The Wytopitlock Deadwater continues for another 9.75 miles and ends at a series of Class I–II rapids that last for 1.25 miles and end at the ME 170 bridge in Kingman (34.25 mi).

Kingman ➤ Mattawamkeag	12.5 mi
Description:	Flatwater, quickwater, Class II, III, IV, V
Date checked:	2000
Navigable:	Passable at most water levels
Scenery:	Wild, forested
Maps:	Wytopitlock 15, Winn 15, Mattawamkeag 15; DL 44
Portages:	7.25 mi L Heater 300 yd
	8.25 mi L Upper Gordon Falls 50 yd
Campsites:	4.0 mi R First Pitch permit, permission
	4.75 mi L Third Pitch $ car

The Mattawamkeag is one of central Maine's outstanding rivers. The best whitewater is found in this section, with five distinct rapids, ranging from Class II to Class IV–V. The Heater involves a difficult 300-yard portage; the portage around Upper Gordon Falls is an easy 50 yards. The description that follows is for springtime levels; the vast watershed of the Mattawamkeag ensures adequate levels for less-intense boating in most summers The Heater and Upper Gordon always demand respect.

Mattawamkeag Wilderness Park (RL 2, Box 5 Mattawamkeag, ME 04459, 888-724-2465 or 207-736-24650) abuts the southern bank of the river for 1.0 mile from Scatterack Rapid down. The park offers camping and hiking trails. You can also cut out the flatwater at the beginning and end of the trip by putting in at the park above Scatterack and taking out below Lower Gordon Falls. You will miss only Ram's Head Falls. The park road opens in the middle of May. The best 3.0 miles with the easiest shuttle involves putting in at the park gate, above the Heater, and taking out below Lower Gordon Falls.

Put in at the bridge in Kingman or downstream, river left. It is possible to drive a short distance down a gravel road on the left in order to cut out some flatwater. You will find Ram's Head Falls (Class II–III) after 4.0 miles of paddling. The start is a small gorge with heavy waves. A short pool leads to the second half of Ram's Head.

Scatterack (Class II–III) begins after 0.75 mile of flatwater. The heaviest waves are on the left. A sand beach follows, marking the Mattawamkeag Wilderness Park camping area. Slewgundy Heater (Class III–IV at spring levels) follows.

The entrance to the Heater is a series of standing waves. Eddy out left before entering the gorge. The Mattawamkeag is a large river that is narrowed down tremendously at this point. High water finds large exploding waves. You can portage 300 yards on the left, but this is difficult. Medium water finds more manageable waves in the gorge. Eddy right at the end of the gorge and avoid the left side, which contains large holes. A succession of ledges and holes follow, best run on the right side.

Below the Heater 0.75 mile is Upper Gordon Falls (8.25 mi). The easiest portage is on the left bank. Upper Gordon Falls is a difficult Class IV–V drop. It is a classic horseshoe-shaped drop of about 11 feet, with a good rescue pool below. Scout either side. The center run hits the huge waves at the bottom. You can sometimes sneak on the left side. Large holes and abrupt drops await if you fall off your line.

Around the corner to the left is Lower Gordon Falls, Class II–III. Enter left and move to the center, through the heavy waves. Quickwater continues to the US 2 bridge in Mattawamkeag (12.5 mi). You can take out on River Road on the right, avoiding a portion of this section. The Penobscot is 0.5 mile below.

Wassataquoik Stream

The stream flows from Baxter State Park to the East Branch of the Penobscot River.

Katahdin Stream ➤ Whetstone Falls		8.5 mi
Description:	Class III	
Date checked:	2000	
Navigable:	High or medium water (after heavy rain)	
Scenery:	Wild	
Maps:	Stacyville 15; DL 51	

Take the unmarked road to Katahdin Stream. Put in on Katahdin Stream and paddle 100 yards to Wassataquoik Stream. This is a wild river flowing out of the heart of Baxter State Park into the East Branch of the Penobscot River.

There are three alternate take-outs: the first is 4.0 miles downstream at the bridge before the confluence with the East Branch; the second is at Lunksoos Pool on the East Branch at 5.5 miles; and the third is at 8.5 miles at the Whetstone Falls Campground. This take-out allows you to run Whetstone Falls, Class III, III+.

Mattawamkeag River (West Branch)

Below Mattawamkeag Lake, the West Branch, already a large river, is mostly rapids and quickwater for 12.5 miles. It is a pleasant and easy paddle in medium or high water, and it is similar to the lower Allagash. Like the latter, there are places that are scratchy in low water, requiring you to walk your boat down. It is wild, although there are about a dozen cabins along the river.

The West Branch above Island Falls is passable in high water, except in a few places, from ME 11 in the township of Moro. No information, however, is given here.

Island Falls ➤ Haynesville		24.5 mi
Description:	Lakes, flatwater, quickwater, Class I, II	
Date checked:	2000	
Navigable:	High and medium water (mid-May to July)	
Scenery:	Wild	
Maps:	Island Falls 15, Sherman 15, Mattawamkeag Lake 15, Amity 15; DL 52 and 53	

Portage:	0 mi R
Campsite:	11.25 mi L Mattawamkeag Lake (small) MFS

Anyone approaching the US 2 bridge in Island Falls should land above or under it, right bank, and lift around the ledges at the old broken dam. Below, right of the island, there is a short pitch followed by 6.5 miles of flatwater to Upper Mattawamkeag Lake. Upon entering the latter, turn right and southeast through a thoroughfare for 1.5 miles.

It is 3.5 miles southeast across Mattawamkeag Lake to the outlet (11.5 mi), after which there are 0.5 mile of Class II and 1.5 miles of Class I rapids. The remaining 10.5 miles are mostly quickwater, with some easy rapids in the last 0.5 mile before the confluence with the East Branch (24.0 mi).

One-half mile beyond is the US 2A bridge in Haynesville (24.5 mi).

Fish Stream

Fish Stream flows eastward to the West Branch of the Mattawamkeag River at Island Falls. It is an easy paddle through wild country, where there is also good fishing.

Patten ➤ Island Falls	16.5 mi
Description:	Flatwater, quickwater
Date checked:	2000
Navigable:	High and medium water (May–June)
Scenery:	Wild
Maps:	Sherman 15, Island Falls 15; DL 52

A side road reaches Fish Stream from ME 159 about 1 mile east of Patten and downstream from a lumber mill. The upper part is all flat, with a few fallen trees blocking the way. After 6.75 miles there is a ledge, passable in high water, 0.25 mile before the stream swings around the southern end of an esker, a prominent ridge of glacial material that extends north for several miles. The rest of the way to the ME 159 bridge (13.5 mi) is mostly flat, but there are a few riffles that are scratchy in low water. In the remaining 2.25 miles to the West Branch (15.75 mi), there is quick- and flatwater.

Below the confluence 0.75 mile, and past the ME 159 bridge, is the US 2 bridge (16.5 mi). Take out on the right at or above it; beyond it, at the old dam site, there are some ledges that are not passable.

Mattawamkeag River (East Branch)

The East Branch is seldom run in comparison to the West Branch. The rapids in the upper part have to be run in high water, and there is no convenient access at the end of the rapids to run the quickwater of the lower end.

Smyrna Mills ➤ Red Bridge	7.0 mi
Description:	Flatwater, quickwater, rapids
Date checked:	2000
Navigable:	High water
Scenery:	Rural, towns
Maps:	Smyrna Mills 15, Mattawamkeag Lake 15, Amity 15; DL 52

This section is small and is runnable only at high water. Both the beginning and end can be reached from US 2. The river is mixed rapid and smooth and offers an interesting run early in the season.

Red Bridge ➤ Haynesville	20.0 mi
Description:	Class II and more difficult rapids
Date checked:	2000
Navigable:	High water
Scenery:	Wild
Maps:	Mattawamkeag Lake 15, Amity 15; DL 52 and 53

Below Red Bridge are intermittent Class II rapids to the outlet from Pleasant Lake. Below here, around the foot of Outlet Mountain, the going becomes very rough. Paddling becomes easier after that. The remaining distance is open going with a slow current. Local people commonly motor up to Nickerson Brook when fishing.

Baskahegan Stream

Baskahegan Stream, a tributary of the Mattawamkeag River, drains a flat region in eastern Maine. It consists almost entirely of flatwater and large lakes. The shorelines are predominantly lined with hardwood forests, and, except near Danforth, there are few cabins or houses. The water is very dark.

Route 6 ➤ Mattawamkeag River	39.5 mi
Description:	Lakes, flatwater, Class I, II
Date checked:	2000
Navigable:	High or medium water (first 5.75 mi)
	Passable at most levels below 5.75 mi
Scenery:	Wild, town
Maps:	Scraggly Lake 15, Danforth 15; DL 45
Portages:	0.5 mi R dam at Danforth 50 yd
	39.0 mi R ledges in South Bancroft 150 yd
Campsite:	17.75 mi R Baskahegan Lake Dam
	(poor) permit

Begin on ME 6 at Lindsey Brook. There have been beaver dams in the 1.25 miles before the Lindsey Brook enters Toman Deadwater on Baskahegan Stream. At the end of this deadwater, there is 1.0 mile of easy Class I–II rapids that end with a short narrow Class II drop. There is a bridge at the beginning of Middle Deadwater (3.25 mi).

Middle Deadwater is 1.75 miles long, and at its end (5.0 mi) is 0.75 mile of rapids that begin as Class I–II. **Caution!** About 0.5 mile after leaving Middle Deadwater, the river widens somewhat where there is quickwater. Then there is a blind right turn before a narrow sluice, where there is a series of sharp drops between sloping ledges. A short distance beyond, a dirt road on the right provides a better starting point in low water.

Below the dirt road (5.75 mi), the river meanders for 7.75 miles to Baskahegan Lake (13.5 mi). The river is passable at low water, but some wading may be necessary.

The washed-out dam on Baskahegan Lake (17.75 mi) is runnable. The next 9.25 miles to Crooked Brook Flowage are flatwater, with the current being stronger in the last 4.0 miles.

There is a 3.5-mile paddle on Crooked Brook Flowage north-wards to the dam in Danforth.

Below Danforth (30.5 mi), Baskahegan Stream has flatwater for 8.5 miles. Past a bridge near South Danforth, land on the right and portage along the edge of a field past a series of ledges. Easy rapids continue to the Mattawamkeag River (39.5 mi). There is a highway bridge over the Mattawamkeag just above the mouth of Baskahegan Stream.

Wytopitlock Stream

Wytopitlock Stream rises in Wytopitlock Lake in Glenwood and flows south to the Mattawamkeag River at Wytopitlock. It is a relatively small stream but navigable in high water from the lake down. It is mixed rapid and smooth, but most of the rapids are runnable. Wytopitlock Lake can be reached from US 2A at Glenwood.

Wytopitlock Lake ➤ US 2A	9.25 mi
Description:	Flatwater, quickwater, Class I, II
Date checked:	2000
Navigable:	Medium water (late spring)
Scenery:	Wild
Maps:	Mattawamkeag Lake 15, Wytopitlock 15; DL 44 and 52

The stream leaves Wytopitlock Lake just to the east of the launching ramp. There are rapids past the bridge, a short deadwater rapids, another deadwater above the third bridge, and then 0.5 mile of rapids to Thompson Deadwater. There, the river is wide and deep through an open marsh, with much wildlife visible.

The deadwater ends at an old dam site (6.25 mi) and rapids continue the next 3.0 miles to the US 2A bridge.

US 2A ➤ Mattawamkeag River	8.5 mi
Description:	Flatwater, quickwater, Class I, II
Date checked:	2000
Navigable:	Medium water (late spring)
Scenery:	Wild
Maps:	Mattawamkeag Lake 15, Wytopitlock 15; DL 44

The remaining distance to the junction with the Mattawamkeag River is similar.

Molunkus Stream

Molunkus Stream rises in Thousand Acre Bog in Crystal just west of Patten and flows south through Sherman Mills and Macwahoc to the Mattawamkeag River just below Kingman. It is navigable from Sherman Mills, or with good water from Sherman Station. The upper part is best run with high to medium water, but much of the stream can be run at any time. It is entirely through woods, and there are no public campgrounds.

Sherman Station ➤ Sherman Mills		3.0 mi
Description:	Quickwater	
Date checked:	2000	
Navigable:	High and medium water	
Scenery:	Towns	
Maps:	Sherman 15, Mattawamkeag Lake 15, Wytopitlock 15; DL 52	

You can put in at the crossing of the West Branch just below Sherman Station. Then you can run 1.0 mile down to the main stream and 2.0 miles down that stream to Sherman Mills. This is largely through swamp with a good current but no rapids.

Sherman Mills ➤ Macwahoc		20.0 mi
Description:	Flatwater, quickwater, rapids	
Date checked:	2000	
Navigable:	High and medium water	
Scenery:	Wild	
Maps:	Sherman 15, Mattawamkeag Lake 15, Wytopitlock 15; DL 52 and 44	

Just below the put-in spot there is a short rapid down to a deadwater and then another rapid below the deadwater, 1.0 mile in all. The next 6.0 miles to the road crossing 1.0 mile south of Monarda are mostly smoothwater. This spot may be a better place to put in if the water is low up above. Below here are 2.0 miles of mixed rapid and smoothwater and then mostly smoothwater with a fast current for the next 10.0 miles to Macwahoc. For much of this latter part of the run, the river is paralleled by nearby US 2. At Macwahoc US 2 crosses the river.

Macwahoc ➤ Mattawamkeag River	10.0 mi
Description:	Flatwater, quickwater
Date checked:	2000
Navigable:	Medium water
Scenery:	Wild
Maps:	Wytopitlock 15; DL 44

Just 100 yards below the US 2 bridge Macwahoc Stream enters on the left. There is a short rapid for 0.5 mile below the start. Then the river meanders through a swamp for the rest of the way to the Mattawamkeag River, which it enters 2.0 miles below Kingman, where the only convenient take-out spot is located.

Alternatively, you can paddle downstream through the rapids on the Mattawamkeag to Mattawamkeag Wilderness Park.

Macwahoc Stream

Macwahoc Stream starts in Macwahoc Lake in Sherman and flows first southeast, then south and slightly west to join the Molunkus Stream at Macwahoc. You can paddle from its headwaters at Macwahoc Lake all the way to the mouth, but high- to medium-stage water would be best for the upper portions. Macwahoc Lake can be reached easily from US 2 in Sherman, and, if the water is low, Lower Macwahoc Lake, which would provide a better starting place, can also be reached from this road in Silver Ridge.

Macwahoc Lake ➤ Lower Macwahoc Lake	6.0 mi
Description:	Lakes, rapids
Date checked:	2000
Navigable:	High and medium water
Scenery:	Wild
Maps:	Sherman 15, Mattawamkeag Lake 15, Wytopitlock 15, Mattawamkeag 15; DL 52

There are several possibilities for the start of this trip. If the water is high, you can put in from a road off US 2 two miles north of Woodbridge Corner on the inlet stream to Macwahoc Lake and run down the stream 0.5 mile to the lake, 1.5 miles south down the lake to its outlet, and then 0.5 mile down the outlet, Macwahoc Stream. Here, a bridge crosses where a road comes in from US 2 closer to Woodbridge Corner. In somewhat lower water, this would be a better put-in spot. The next 4.0 miles to Lower Macwahoc Lake are largely rapids with small ponds or backwaters between them. The inlet to Macwahoc Lake enters at the center of the northern shore; from here, it is 0.5 mile east to the landing on the eastern shore.

Lower Macwahoc Lake ➤ Macwahoc		20.0 mi
Description:	Quickwater, rapids	
Date checked:	2000	
Navigable:	High, medium, and low water	
Scenery:	Wild	
Maps:	Sherman 15, Mattawamkeag Lake 15, Wytopitlock 15, Mattawamkeag 15; DL 52 and 44	

You can put in at the landing on the eastern shore of Lower Macwahoc Lake reached by a dirt road from the southeast. After about 1 mile down the lake, you enter Macwahoc Stream, which descends with a good current for the next 3.0 miles. Then steep rapids begin for 1.0 mile to a swampy area. After about 0.5 mile of easy going, rapids start again and continue for 1.0 mile to a long swampy area, Reed Deadwater. This continues for nearly 8 miles to the mouth of Reed Stream, where fastwater recommences and continues for the next 5.5 miles to the junction with Molunkus Stream at Macwahoc.

Piscataquis River

The Piscataquis River is one of the major tributaries of the Penobscot. Both of its two branches, the East Branch and the West Branch, rise south of Moosehead Lake and join at Blanchard to form the main stream, which then flows eastward to the Penobscot River at Howland. The West Branch has some miles of good paddling below the crossing of the Shirley Mills–Lake Moxie road. But this is followed by a deep and very difficult gorge north of

Breakneck Ridge with no way to leave the river. The East Branch has some easy paddling above Shirley Mills, but there is no good way to reach it. Below, it is too steep and rapid for some distance; then it is a good run, but inaccessible. In effect the river is runnable only below the junction of the two branches or from Blanchard on down, except for a team of expert paddlers. From Blanchard, the river is mixed rapid and smooth, with some sections practically all smoothwater. Above Dover-Foxcroft, it is usually too low for summer travel, although usable until late in the spring.

Piscataquis River (West Branch)

The West Branch of the Piscataquis is a very difficult but rewarding river to explore. There is no access to the river except for two logging-road bridges. Paddlers who wish to explore the wild flatwater areas must line and portage many difficult rapids and ledge drops, while expert whitewater paddlers must paddle several miles of slow water on each end in order to challenge the ledge drops and rapids. **Caution!** The difficulty of the ledge drops, combined with the isolation of the river, means that extreme caution must be used when running the river.

Shirley Mills Road ➤ Oakes Bog	2.75 mi
Description:	Flatwater, Class I, II, III
Date checked:	2000
Navigable:	Medium to high water (May)
Scenery:	Wild
Maps:	Greenville 15; DL 31 and 41
Portages:	Ledges

Put in at the bridge at the outlet of West Shirley Bog. Most of this section is long stretches of quickwater, separated by short, steep ledge drops or rapids. Several of these will have to be scouted, and one ledge drop will need to be portaged, as there is an undercut ledge sticking out from the right side at the bottom of the drop. There is one unique spot where the river seems to end, but there is a wide slot through a ledge. Take out just above Oakes Bog, where the logging road crosses. This upper section is much easier than the section below Oakes Bog.

Oakes Bog ➤ Blanchard 8.75 mi

Description:	Flatwater, Class I, II, III, IV, V
Date checked:	2000
Navigable:	Medium to high water (May or after heavy rains)
Scenery:	Wild
Maps:	Greenville 15; DL 31
Portage:	5.25 mi L 15-foot falls 100 yd

This section of the river is recommended for experts only. Once you put in the river, you must be prepared to face Breakneck Ridge Gorge. This gorge is Class IV at low to medium-water levels, and Class V at high-water levels, with one falls that is normally portaged.

Put in at the bridge just above Oakes Bog. It is about 1 mile down the bog to the old dam remains, which now form an easy rapid. Hatch Falls (2.25 mi) is the first major landmark after the bog. When you see the river fall out of sight through granite ledges and pine trees, you should land on the right shore and scout. This is a four-stage ledge drop, which is of Class III–IV difficulty, depending on the water level. One hundred yards below Hatch Falls is another sharp 4-foot drop that can take you by surprise. Below this, there is a 2.5-foot ledge and a 5-foot ledge (2.75 mi). The 5-foot ledge is below a cabin on the right and should be scouted.

Once Bald Mountain stream enters on the right (5.0 mi), the rapids build from Class I to continuous Class II–III, with occasional small ledge drops. The walls of the gorge also start to rise. The river will drop 320 feet in the next 3.0 miles. You can recognize the beginning of the most difficult section by a Class III rapid leading into a 100-foot-long sloping ledge (5.0 mi) that forms a tricky Class III–IV drop. Both river banks are all ledge at this point, as the walls steepen. (This point is just above "neck" in "Breakneck" on the topographical map.) It is critical to scout and set up rescue bags at this rapid, as a 15-foot falls is just around the corner. The easiest portage is to the left side of the falls. Below the falls is a pool. Around the next corner are Class II–III rapids leading into a 10-foot sloping ledge, followed by a 7-foot straight drop. The straight drop has a bad hole at the bottom at certain water levels. The next mile is a very tight, rocky Class III–IV rapid. This is followed by a mile of quickwater, through an island maze in which you should generally stay left. The last mile is on the Piscataquis River formed by the junction of the East and West branches. Take out at the bridge in Blanchard.

Piscataquis River (East Branch)

Blanchard ➤ Upper Abbott   8.0 mi
Description: Class II, III, IV
Date checked: 2000
Navigable: High water (spring or after heavy rains)
Scenery: Forested
Maps: Greenville 15, Kingsbury 15, Guilford
                          15; DL 31
Portage: 3.0 mi e Barrows Falls (optional)

Put in above the bridge in Blanchard, where there is a Class II–III rapid. Rapids continue for 100 yards below the bridge. The remaining distance to the bridge above Barrows Falls is largely flatwater.

The bridge makes an alternate put-in, but Barrows Falls starts immediately. Barrows Falls is a beautiful slate gorge that is normally rated heavy Class III. High water results in violent deflection waves and a Class IV rating. Scout right, and carry either side.

Class II rapids follow almost continuously to Upper Abbott. There are some slightly harder rapids, but the difficulty never exceeds Class III. The final rapid is located under the old bridge in Upper Abbott. Run on the left side of the right chute.

Upper Abbott ➤ Dover-Foxcroft   13.0 mi
Description: Quickwater, Class I
Date checked: 2000
Navigable: Spring or unusually wet summer
Scenery: Rural
Maps: Guilford 15, Dover-Foxcroft 15; DL 31 and 32
Portages: 5.0 mi R Guilford 1.25 mi
                          (13.0 mi R Dover-Foxcroft 2 dams 0.75 mi)

There is a shallow riffle from the old to the new bridge at Upper Abbott. The riffles and current diminish and disappear as you draw nearer to the dam in Guilford. There is no convenient take-out at the dam in town; take out at the senior citizens' housing where the river nears ME 6/15 less than a mile upstream on the left.

From the town athletic field below the mills on the left bank there is quickwater and occasional Class I rips for about 3.75 miles to Lowe's covered bridge. This bridge marks the beginning of Class I–II rapids that are rocky in low water and consist of wide expanses of low, choppy waves in high water. The first two rapids are easier than the rest. Rapids 50 to 100 yards long alternate with longer, smooth stretches until you reach a washed out dam marked by the remains of a masonry millhouse on the left. This drop is usually run on the left, but varying water levels may allow other routes. You can carry on the right if you wish. The current is almost gone below the railroad trestle, and from there it is 1.0 mile of flatwater to the handy take-out and parking spot at "the cove." There are two dams in Dover-Foxcroft, each about 20 feet high. Portage by car 0.75 mile from the cove to Brown's Mill (also called the Tannery).

Dover-Foxcroft ➤ Derby		18.5 mi
Description:	Flatwater, quickwater, Class I, II, III	
Date checked:	2000	
Navigable:	Spring, summer	
Scenery:	Rural	
Maps:	Dover-Foxcroft 15, Boyd Lake 15, Schoodic 15; DL 32	

Below Brown's Mill there are two ledges, each 1- to 1.5-feet, followed by a rocky rapid around a long left turn. Both the ledges and rapid are Class II at moderately high water. There is a good current and easy rapids for 3.0 miles to the bridge at East Dover, below which there is a 100-yard-long rapid, which is a fast, wavy, Class I on the left and a mild Class II on the right at most water levels. Seven more miles of smooth river bring you to the bridge at South Sebec, and 8.5 miles farther is the confluence of the Sebec River and the bridge near Derby.

Just above the confluence with the Sebec is a railroad bridge.

Under the bridge is a steep and rocky rapid 100 yards long, Class II at low runnable level and potentially heavy when the river is high. A quarter-mile downstream is the ME 11 bridge, which has a shorter and easier rapid under it.

Derby ➤ Howland		24.5 mi
Description:	Flatwater, quickwater, Class I, II, III	
Date checked:	2000	
Navigable:	Medium water	
Scenery:	Forested, towns	
Maps:	Schoodic 15, Lincoln 15, Passadumkeag 15; DL 32 and 33	
Portage:	(24.5 mi L dam)	

The beginning and end of this section is smooth, broken in the middle by 5.0 miles of rapids, which can be portaged by car. This is a large river, and the rapids generate heavy waves even in medium water.

Downstream from the ME 6/11/16 bridge 4.0 miles, the Pleasant River enters on the left. It flows over several easy rapids and then drops over a steep Class II rapid. Occasional easy rapids continue to the high former railroad bridge (9.0 mi). If you wish not to run the heavier rapids below, take out at a dirt road just above, on the left. This is the last reasonable access, as the banks become steep and high.

Easy rapids start immediately and run to Schoodic Point (10.75 mi), where the Schoodic River enters left in an impressive rapid. The Piscataquis River turns sharply right and begins dropping more steeply, creating large waves (Class III in medium water). The rapids decrease in difficulty for the next couple of miles. If you portaged the long rapids, you can start again 3.5 miles from Schoodic Point, where the river comes close to the road near the Medford-Maxfield town line.

Seboeis Stream enters left 0.5 mile above the I-95 bridge (21.75 mi). The river gradually slows to flatwater. Take out at a launching ramp above the dam at Howland. The confluence with the Penobscot is just below.

Kingsbury Stream

Kingsbury Stream drops 600 feet in the 16.0 miles between Kingsbury Pond and Abbott Village with only one unrunnable waterfall. Although it is small at the outlet of Kingsbury Pond, the stream picks up over a dozen small feeder streams from the large east-west ridge along ME 16, between the pond and where Thorn Brook enters. The two major tributaries, Thorn Brook and Carlton Stream, each carry nearly as much water as Kingsbury Stream just above Cole's Corner. This additional flow makes the waves much bigger and current more powerful below Cole's Corner. The water is best on warm days during the last of the snow melt, as the land it drains is quite steep and water levels drop quickly once the snow is gone.

Kingsbury Pond ➤ Thorn Brook	8.5 mi
Description:	Class I, II, III
Date checked:	2000
Navigable:	High water (mid-April)
Scenery:	Wild
Maps:	Kingsbury 15; DL 31
Portage:	3.75 mi L 30-ft waterfall 100 yd

The upper part of Kingsbury is an interesting run of short, steep rapids, followed by stretches of quickwater when the water level is high. Unfortunately, the water level is right only a few days each year. You are committed to do the entire section once you put in, as the stream does not come near the road again until just before the normal take-out. Put in just below the outlet of Kingsbury Pond on river right. After going under the bridge, you will come to a narrow Class I rapid. If this rapid is scratchy, there will not be enough water in the wider rapids for the next 4.0 miles, and they will require wading.

The stream flows through a peaceful swampy area for about a mile and then starts its descent to the Piscataquis River. There are occasional trees blocking the river, but no ledge drops until the falls (3.75 mi). The falls are located near the word "Stream" on the topographical map. There is a quick current up to the lip of the falls, but no difficult rapids. Pull out on the left bank well above the falls where there is a rough portage trail. The portage trail ends at a 20-foot slanting cliff over which the boats must be lowered. The falls cannot be safely run as the water makes a 90-degree turn off a ledge halfway down the falls.

Kingsbury Stream takes on the character of a larger stream below the falls, as it has picked up a number of small feeder streams by this point. In high water, some moderate-sized waves and holes can develop in several of the tougher spots. Take out where Kingsbury Stream comes beside ME 16 and Thorn Brook enters.

Thorn Brook ➤ Cole's Corner Road Bridge		2.25 mi
Description:	Class II, III, IV	
Date checked:	2000	
Navigable:	Medium-high water (April)	
Scenery:	Forested	
Maps:	Kingsbury 15, Guilford 15; DL 31	
Portage:	0.10 mi e ledge	

This section of Kingsbury Stream makes a nice ending to the upper part of the stream, or a good start to the lower part of this stream if you have planned a medium-length day of paddling. Just below where Thorn Brook enters Kingsbury Stream, there is a Class III–IV ledge drop that can be run at the right water levels. This ledge drop can be scouted quite easily from ME 16 by walking downstream about 150 yards from the bridge across Thorn Brook and then going into the woods about 100 feet.

The portage is normally over the rocks on the right shore. The rest of the run down to the Cole's Corner Road bridge is almost continuous Class II–III. The waves are bigger and the current more powerful than above Thorn Brook, as the stream has nearly doubled its drainage area. Just above Cole's Corner Road bridge, the river narrows into a short, more difficult stretch, with a rock wall on the right bank. This is best scouted from the left bank. Take out at the bridge or about 0.25 mile downstream from the bridge on river right.

Cole's Corner Road Bridge ➤ Abbott Village		5.25 mi
Description:	Quickwater, Class II, III	
Date checked:	2000	
Navigable:	Medium-high water (April)	
Scenery:	Forested	

| Maps: | Guilford 15; DL 31 |
| Portage: | 3.75 mi L 30-ft waterfall 100 yd |

The Class II rapids below Cole's Corner Road bridge quickly mellow to Class I and quickwater once the river swings away from the road. Carlton Stream enters on the right (1.0 mi) in the middle of a swampy area. About 0.75 mile below this is a Class II–III rapid (1.75 mi) where the river makes a wide, sweeping turn to the right. In another 0.75 mile, there are pine trees and granite ledges on river left (3.5 mi). Just around the corner is the most difficult rapid in this section. This double ledge drop should be scouted from the left. Watch out for the holes on the bottom drop. About 1.25 miles farther down is the last big drop (4.75 miles). This is a steep U-shaped rapid than can be run on the left after scouting. Take out about 0.5 mile downstream on the left, where a dirt road comes in from ME 16. **Caution!** Do not run down to the ME 16 bridge in Abbott, as the ledges under the bridge are very dangerous.

Pleasant River

The Pleasant River rises east of Greenville and Moosehead Lake. The West Branch flows out of Gulf Hagas to Katahdin Iron Works to Brownville Junction; there, it joins the East Branch, which flows out of lower Ebecmee Lake, northwest of Seboeis Lake. The combined river then flows south to Brownville, where it turns southeast to meet the Piscataquis east of Derby. The upper part is steep and should be run in moderately high water. The lower river is broad and shallow but can usually be run in the summer. The stream is clear and the banks wooded and attractive.

Brownville Junction ➤ Brownville		5.5 mi
Description:	Flatwater, quickwater	
Date checked:	2000	
Navigable:	High and medium water	
Scenery:	Forested	
Maps:	Sebec 15, Schoodic 15, Boyd Lake 15; DL 42 and 32	

This section would primarily be paddled at the end of a trip on the East or West Branch. There is a "water level" put-in on the left bank of the East Branch a mile above the confluence with the West Branch.

From the confluence it is 1.5 miles of easy paddling to Brownville Junction and another 4.0 miles to the dam in Brownville

Brownville ➤ Piscataquis River		11.0 mi
Description:	Quickwater, Class I	
Date checked:	2000	
Navigable:	Medium water	
Scenery:	Forested	
Maps:	Sebec 15, Schoodic 15, Boyd Lake 15; DL 32	

There is a ledge just below the dam in Brownville. The remainder of the distance is very pleasant with easy rapids and quickwater for 5.0 miles to the ME 16 bridge north of Milo and then another 6.0 miles to the Piscataquis River, which is reached about 5.0 miles below the bridge at Derby. There is no road near the river at this point, but 1.0 mile downstream at the Upper Ferry you can take out on either side of the river.

Pleasant River (West Branch)

Long Pond Road ➤ Katahdin Iron Works		4.0 mi
Description:	Quickwater, Class I	
Date checked:	2000	
Navigable:	Medium water (mid-May to mid-June)	
Scenery:	Wild	
Maps:	Sebec 15; DL 41 and 42	

Put in near where Long Pond Road first comes near the river after crossing the log bridge. This is near "X609" on the topographical map. The river is narrow with good current. It is generally shallow with gravel riffles, downed trees, and forest debris forming Class I obstacles. The stream becomes broader, deeper, and slower in the last mile above Silver Lake. You can take out at the bridge on Long Pond Road or continue 0.75 mile down Silver Lake to Katahdin Iron (K.I.) Works. The old dam at K.I. is completely gone, leaving a swift, shallow, and rocky rapid down past the bridge at K.I.

Katahdin Iron Works ➤ Brownville Junction   9.0 mi
Description: Flatwater, quickwater, Class II, III
Date checked: 1990
Navigable: High water (April)
Scenery: Forested
Maps: Sebec 15; DL 42

Put in at the bridge at Katahdin Iron Works or upstream at Silver Lake. The upstream put-in allows the running of 200 yards of Class III rapids to the bridge. Class II rapids continue to a more difficult spot. Billy Jack Rip (also known as Mud Cut) can be scouted either side (1.5 mi). The best route through this Class III rapid goes down the middle, threading the needle between a pour-over and a hole, through the large waves at the bottom. Other routes are possible.

Class II rapids continue for 3.0 miles, followed by quickwater and flatwater for the remaining 4.5 miles to the ME 11 bridge, where there is a good take-out on the left below the bridge.

Pleasant River (East Branch)

Lower Ebeemee Lake ➤ West Branch   3.5 mi
Description: Class I, II
Date checked: 2000
Navigable: Medium water (May)
Scenery: Forested
Maps: Sebec 15; DL 42
Portage: Near start R 100 ft

Put in at the bridge at the foot of Lower Ebeemee Lake. The 2-foot drop just above this bridge would be runnable (Class II–III) in medium or high water if it were not blocked by a partially detached bridge timber. Drift down 50 yards to where a jumble of small boulders marks the site of an old dam. In high water, the extreme left might be runnable in decked boats (Class III–IV). Most paddlers will carry 100 feet on the right. A 50-yard-long pool leads into a Class II rapid that quickly splits into two channels; 75 percent of the flow goes left. The first 50 feet of this channel are tight and fast, possibly Class III at some levels; the remaining 100 feet are technical

Class II at medium water. You now come to a series of mild (Class I–II) rapids alternating with short stretches of quickwater.

The river suddenly kinks to the right 1.5 miles below the put-in. At the apex of the kink, a 1-foot ledge divides the stream into two chutes. The left chute has most of the flow and forms an irregular souse hole of significant dimensions. The right chute is shallow and contains two 90-degree turns. Between the two chutes is dry ledge at medium or lower water. Just below this drop, which is the last one that should take your mind off the scenery, the river divides into multiple channels, with most of the water going to the left again. The extreme right channel comes close to a gravel pit just north of "the prairie," which makes an acceptable put-in for those wishing to avoid the rapids above. The remaining 2.0 miles to the high ME 11 bridge are very scenic, and the rapids are less frequent and diminish from easy Class II to Class I and then disappear.

The smaller Middle Branch enters a short distance below the bridge. A short side road comes near the left bank, making an easier take-out than the steep climb up to ME 11. The river is smooth for the remaining mile to the West Branch.

Sebec River

The Sebec River drains Sebec Lake, located in Willimantic and Bowerbank, and flows east and south to the Piscataquis River at Derby. Together with the lake it provides an easy 20-mile trip on smoothwater during most seasons of the year.

Earley's Landing ➤ Derby	22.75 mi
Description:	Lake, flatwater
Date checked:	2000
Navigable:	Spring, summer
Scenery:	Forested, rural
Maps:	Sebec Lake 15, Sebec 15; DL 32
Portages:	12.5 mi Sebec Lake Dam
	20.5 mi Milo Dam

Put in at Peaks-Kenny State Park on Sebec Lake or at the outlet, in Sebec. From the state park it is 4.0 miles to the Narrows, where the lake narrows to less than 0.25 mile. For the next

7.5 miles to Sebec the lake is generally less than 1.0 mile wide. At Sebec, there is a dam with a short rapids below. Approximately 4.0 miles farther along there are about 100 yards of rocky Class II rips.

The dam in Milo is right in the middle of town, and the river splits into two channels just below it. The left channel has a small powerhouse put on-line in 1982. Choice of channel and portage route will vary with day of week and amount of water in the river. The rapids for the next 0.5 mile will be bony Class I–II if one gate is open, heavy with more water. The confluence with the Piscataquis is 0.25 mile above the ME 11 bridge, which has an easy Class II rip under it.

Big Wilson Stream

Big Wilson Stream rises in Wilson Pond near the Kennebec-Piscataquis divide south of Moosehead Lake. It is a major inlet to Sebec Lake.

Bodfish Crossing ➤ Willimantic		5.0 mi
Description:	Quickwater, Class I, II, III	
Date checked:	2000	
Navigable:	High water (April, early May)	
Scenery:	Wild, forested	
Maps:	Sebec Lake 15; DL 44 and 31	
Portages:	3.5 mi L 10-foot waterfall	
	3.6 mi L 12-foot waterfall	

Just below the bridge near Bodfish Crossing is a formidable series of cascades. The easiest put-in is slightly below, on the right. Parking is limited. About 1.5 miles of quickwater leads to a Class III rapid caused by three ledges. The first is best run right, with a quick move back left to set up for the center chute in the second. The third is easier with routes on the left and center.

The next 2.0 miles are quickwater. Large boulders on the left, into which the river seems to disappear, mark the beginning of the best part of the run. The main flow turns left into a Class III rapid. A 4- or 5-foot drop over a ledge follows in 75 yards. Scouting reveals a good route on the right. Flatwater leads to the brink of the first falls. Carry the 10-foot, down-right scary, drop on the left.

The outflow of the first falls is a Class III rapid, which drops into a pool. Take out on the left after the pool, or run the Class II rapid that follows and eddy out left at the lip of a 12-foot falls. This drop is not as intimidating as the first, but most paddlers will portage.

Class II rapids lead to some easy, 2-foot ledges in a small gorge. The 2-foot drop in the gorge is easily run left of center. Take out below the bridge on the left.

Willimantic ➤ Sebec Lake		4.0 mi
Description:	Class I	
Date checked:	2000	
Navigable:	Spring, summer	
Scenery:	Wild, forested	
Maps:	Sebec Lake 15; DL 31	
Portage:	4.0 mi Falls at Earley's Landing	

Below the Willimantic bridge the river is Class I with fast, shallow riffles in mid-June. This section is passable almost anytime. From the bridge in Willimantic it is 4.0 miles to Earley's Landing on Sebec Lake. Portage around two waterfalls at Earley's.

Ship Pond Stream

Ship Pond Stream is the outlet of Onawa Lake and flows to Sebec Lake at Bucks Cove, from which point it is 2.0 miles of lake paddling to a road access.

During early spring the road access to the start is impassable, and the lake may also be frozen.

Cow Yard Falls ➤ Sebec Lake		3.0 mi
Description:	Flatwater, quickwater, Class I	
Date checked:	2000	
Navigable:	Medium water (May–June, after heavy rains)	
Scenery:	Wild	
Maps:	Sebec Lake 15; DL 41, 31 and 32	
Portage:	2.75 mi e waterfall 50 yd	

Cow Yard Falls can be reached by a private road (gate) that leaves ME 150 at Earley's Landing at Willimantic. Remember to ask for and obtain permission before crossing property lines. Cow Yard falls is an 8-foot ledge. Put in below the falls or below the Class II ledges, if you prefer. After a few Class I rips, the stream flows quickly over a gravel bed for 0.5 mile. After a mile of meandering river, it spreads out over a shallow stretch, which may have to be waded for 0.25 mile at low water at summer levels. A short piece of deep flatwater leads to the falls at Bucks Cove.

The falls is about 5 feet in several quick steps followed by a rocky pool and a 2-foot ledge drop at the apex of a bend to the right. The rocky out-run leads into Bucks Cove, an isolated arm of Sebec Lake, which contains three wooded islands and many glacial boulders.

It is a mile southeast to the mouth of the cove and another mile west to Packard's Landing. Three miles south across the lake is Peaks-Kenny State Park, and a public landing. To the west of Bucks Cove 0.5 mile is the lower of the two falls at Early's on Big Wilson Stream.

It is not unduly strenuous to paddle Ship Pond Stream in the upstream direction as the finish of a trip on Big Wilson Stream or Sebec Lake.

Passadumkeag River

The Passadumkeag River rises in Lee, flows south for some miles, then southwest, and finally west to the Penobscot River at Passadumkeag. It has many miles of good paddling on it, but the upper part is best done at moderately high water.

Weir Pond ➤ Pistol Green	18.0 mi
Description:	Flatwater, quickwater, marsh
Date checked:	2000
Navigable:	Spring, summer, fall
Scenery:	Wild
Maps:	Springfield 15, Nicatous Lake 15, Saponac 15; DL 44 and 34

Campsites:	9.0 mi R Brown Brook
	12.75 mi L Cold Spring
	18.0 mi L Pistol Green

The stream is fairly small. The described put-in is at the bridge below Weir Pond.

You can put in at Weir Pond or at a road crossing just below the pond, both reachable by the same road off ME 6 west of Springfield. If you put in at Weir Pond, there is 0.5 mile of pond and 0.5 mile of swampy stream to the lower put-in spot. The next 17.0 miles are all smoothwater, with the river meandering through swampy areas all the way to the mouth of Nicatous Stream at Pistol Green.

An alternative start, which may miss some fallen trees, is via the West Branch (Passadumkeag) starting at Number 3 Pond. In this case, there are 2.0 miles of lake and a mile of river to the Passadumkeag reached 1.25 miles below the bridge.

Rand Brook (3.75 mi) marks the start of the old portage across to Upper Sysladobsis and the St. Croix drainage.

Pistol Green ➤ Passadumkeag	32.25 mi
Description:	Lake, flatwater, quickwater, Class I, II
Date checked:	2000
Navigable:	Spring, summer, fall
Scenery:	Wild, forested, rural
Maps:	Saponac 15, Passadumkeag 15; DL 34 and 33
Portages:	4.5 mi L Grand Falls 0.75 mi
	18.5 mi R then L Lowell Dam
	(32.0 mi L dam at Passadumkeag)
Campsites:	5.0 mi L Grand Fall
	13.0 mi L Saponac Pond

The river is smooth for the first 4.0 miles. Grand Falls is a wild rapid in which the river drops 100 feet in a mile and should be carried. There is a good carry road. Also, there is good road access here from ME 188.

The river winds through flat bottomlands to Saponac Pond (12.25 mi). In high water, the river is hard to find in the maple swamp before the pond. A campsite is on the south shore; it is somewhat buggy. There is a mile of river beyond the pond to Pond Rips and White Horse Rips, which some paddlers may wish to line or carry.

The river is smooth again for 3.0 miles to the broken dam at Lowell (18.5 mi). Portage right through a field, cross the river on the bridge, and take the trail along the left bank. The ledges make fearsome waves in high water. Except for Rocky Rips (25.5 mi), the river is smooth all the way to Passadumkeag.

The usual take-out is at an iron bridge 2.0 miles upstream of Passadumkeag.

Nicatous Stream

Nicatous Stream drains Nicatous Lake and flows northwest to the Passadumkeag River at Pistol Green. It is part of a major Indian canoe route.

Nicatous means "Little Fork" and applies to the junction of this stream and the Passadumkeag. At that point, a canoeist ascending the Passadumkeag has a choice of routes to follow. Nicatous Stream leads to "Kiasobeak," now called Nicatous Lake, from which you can easily reach the headwaters of four major river systems.

Nicatous Lake ➤ Pistol Green	7.75 mi
Description:	Flatwater, quickwater, marsh, Class I, II, III
Date checked:	2000
Navigable:	Medium water
Scenery:	Wild
Maps:	Nicatous Lake 15, Saponac 15; DL 34
Portage:	0.25 mi dam

There is a public landing at the small dam at the outlet. The river flows for 2.0 miles through boggy areas separated by short, boulder-strewn sections. Class I rapids commence after a long boggy stretch and increase without letup to Idiot Dog Falls, 50 yards of granite ledges, and Class III if there is enough water (3.0 mi). At the bottom, a crumbling log bridge has posed some hazards in the past. The bridge is a good picnic spot; just upstream on the left at bank level is a cold spring.

Below the bridge is another short, sharp pitch, then rapids diminish quickly. The final 3.0 miles flow through a swamp with gravel bars and pools; this is good moose country. There is a bridge and campsite a half-mile above the Passadumkeag.

Gassabias Stream

This stream is part of a major east-west Indian canoe route and also used to be the traditional approach to the Machias River in the days before roads. You can easily pole or paddle up and down Gassabias Stream with only a minimum of dragging in low water.

Gassabias Lake ➤ Nicatous Lake	3.0 mi
Description:	Flatwater, quickwater, rapids
Date checked:	2000
Navigable:	High, medium, and low water
Scenery:	Wild
Maps:	Nicatous Lake 15; DL 34 and 35
Campsites:	Red pine grove by the portage
	Outlet of Gassabias Lake
	North side of "Snakka"

The low bridge at the outlet of Gassabias Lake may have to be carried if the water is high. After a mile of deep-water swamp comes a mile of mossy boulders, but no rapids, where you must be alert for the problems in the low water. This ends at the CCC road bridge, where marsh begins again and continues to Great Falls. At Great Falls, the stream narrows and plunges 5 feet vertically in the next 200 yards. Soon you reach Nicatous Lake, just south of the "Snakka," a long, undulating stone ridge that almost cuts the lake in two.

The 2-mile portage to Fourth Machias Lake starts on the east shore of Gassabias Lake just to the left of a large stand of red pine. The portage trail begins as a groove cut into the peat bog from heavy use. The trail is passable, but difficult.

Kenduskeag Stream

Garland ➤ French Stream	7.5 mi
Description:	Quickwater, Class I, II

Date checked:	2000
Navigable:	High water (spring runoff or pond drawdown)
Scenery:	Forested
Maps:	Dover-Foxcroft 15, Stetson 15; DL 32
Portages:	2.75 mi L dam at Twin Brook lift over
	2.75+ mi L ledge lift over

Just below the dam at Garland, ME 94 crosses the stream. Put in here at relatively high water levels only. The first mile is mostly quickwater, with sharp turns and minor alder tangles. After the first mile, a rock-strewn channel requires quick maneuvering in spots, generally with stretches of quickwater below each rapid. This continues for about 0.5 mile to a road crossing and another 0.5 mile to the backup of a small, washed-out mill dam at Twin Brook. Burnham Brook enters on the left in this area but may be missed in the meanders.

Another 0.8 mile brings you to the old dam at Twin Brook. It may be lifted over on the left or might be run after scouting if water level is advantageous. Within 0.1 mile of the dam is another road crossing. Beneath this bridge is a ledge drop of 2 to 3 feet over which the current takes a sharp S-turn. After scouting from above the bridge, and with careful execution, the stream may be run to the left bank above the ledge, and the boat lifted over. It is slightly over 1 mile below the ledge to the next road crossing. Between the ledge and the crossing are more rapids interspersed with quickwater, much like the section above the pond. The remainder of the run to the ME 11/43 bridge is comprised of occasional rapids with numerous beaver dams, blowdowns, and tangles. The crossing of ME 11/43 is just (30 yards) upstream of the confluence with French Stream, which at this point is approximately the same size as the Kenduskeag. Take out here on the right under the bridge.

French Stream ➤ Kenduskeag   13.5 mi

Description:	Flatwater, quickwater, Class I, II
Date checked:	2000
Navigable:	Medium to high water (April, May)
Scenery:	Forested, rural

Maps:	Stetson 15, Bangor 15; DL 32
Portages:	11.5 mi ledge lift over
	13.5 mi ledge lift over

Below the ME 11/43 bridge, the river is doubled in size by French Stream entering right. The bridge at McGregor Mill is 1.25 miles, and it is another 1.25 miles to the second bridge. The current is fast, with some rapids up to Class II; then the river pools up for a couple of miles. There is little current and the water becomes deeper on its way to a rapid above a covered bridge at Robyville (7.0 mi). The bridge cannot be seen from the beginning of the rapid, but the change in terrain is obvious, as the river makes an S-turn over a ledgy drop, Class III.

The rapids for the next 0.75 mile are slightly harder. Just above the fourth bridge is a 3.5-foot drop over a ledge, which you may need to line or carry. The next ledge before the bridge in Kenduskeag is even more difficult.

Kenduskeag ➤ Flour Mill Falls   15.0 mi

Description:	Quickwater, Class I, II, III
Date checked:	2000
Navigable:	High water (March, April)
Scenery:	Forested
Maps:	Bangor 15; DL 32, 22 and 23

The bridge in Kenduskeag is the start of the Kenduskeag-to-Bangor race. The first 10.0 miles are meandering quickwater with a few riffles to Six Mile Falls, the only Class III rapid in this section. Six Mile Falls is a 200-yard Class III rapid at most water levels and is easily scouted and run on the left. The next 3.0 miles to Bull's Eye Bridge are mostly quickwater.

A put-in may be made at Bull's Eye Bridge. The 2.0 miles to the park and parking area above Flour Mill Falls are Class I–II rapids. Most paddlers take out on river left above Flour Mill Falls.

Flour Mill Falls ➤ Second Valley Avenue Bridge   0.5 mi

Description:	Class IV
Date checked:	2000
Navigable:	High water (March, April)
Scenery:	Forested
Maps:	Bangor 15; DL 23

This is a favorite after-work run for local paddlers. Put in at Valley Avenue above Flour Mill Falls. Be sure to scout the drop from the observation platform. The farther upstream you put in, the longer the warm-up. Flour Mill Falls has two distinct drops. The cleanest route at high water involves running the top drop on the right and grabbing a micro-eddy on the right. Then peel out and run the second drop right down the middle. Lower water necessitates approaching the second drop from the left, as the upper drop becomes dry on the right.

A ledge halfway to the Valley Avenue Bridge provides fine surfing. Eddy out right above the bridge. The drop below the bridge is the most dangerous on the river. A pour-over on river right creates a nasty hole, which might recirculate a boat or boater for an extended time. The best route is just right of the central bridge abutment. Aim for the second guardrail support from the right, and avoid the curler farther right and the smaller hole on the left. A short pool, offering excellent squirting, follows.

You can easily run the ledge at the old Maxfield Mill site on the left. The river then passes through Class II rapids to a Class III ledge, Shopping Cart. This area is the site of an annual slalom race. You will find good surfing and enders in the waves here.

Take out at a park on river right. The river then flows under the second Valley Avenue bridge and through downtown Bangor. The Penobscot is 0.75 mile downstream. The lower portion of the river is tidal.

Souadabscook Stream

Souadabscook Stream (alternate spelling: Sawadapskook) rises in Etna Pond and flows east to join the Penobscot River south of Bangor. It was one of the major Indian waterways, connecting the Penobscot and Kennebec watersheds; a portage connected to the Sebasticook River.

Black Stream ➤ Vatiades Landing	3.5 mi
Description:	Lake, quickwater, Class I
Date checked:	2000
Navigable:	High and medium water (mid-April to

early June)

Scenery: Rural, towns
Maps: Bangor 15; DL 22 and 23

Put in from US 2 at a culvert 3.75 miles west of Hermon. This culvert connects Black Stream, a tributary of the Kenduskeag River, to Souadabscook Stream in high water. There is little parking.

The 1.75 miles to Newburgh Road and the Maine Central Railroad crossings are all flatwater, except for a Class II chute over what appears to be a sunken stone wall. Newburgh Road offers good parking, and this section can be paddled upstream.

The pond is another 0.25 mile, and the outlet of the pond is 1.5 miles to the southeast. Vatiades Landing on Bogg Road is an additional 0.5 mile.

Black Stream, while a tributary of the Kenduskeag, is more likely to be paddled as an extension of this trip. It can be ascended from the culvert at the start of this trip 0.5 mile to a washed-out culvert or descended 1.0 mile to Black Stream Road (an alternate start).

Vatiades Landing ➤ Hampden 9.0 mi

Description:	Lake, flatwater, quickwater, Class II, III, IV
Date checked:	1990
Navigable:	High water (March, April)
Scenery:	Forested, rural, settled
Maps:	Bangor 15, Bucksport 15; DL 22 and 23
Portage:	7.0 mi L Grand Falls and Dam 0.5 mi

The flatwater section begins at Vatiades Landing on a side road just north of I-95. The stream is smooth at the start, as it goes south under I-95, and then flows into Hammond Pond, which often is still frozen when the stream is at its best. The outlet is 0.5 mile east across the pond on the northeastern corner.

The current gradually quickens, flowing through a deepwater swamp, and passes under I-95 twice more. Some warm-up around scattered rocks prepares you for the ledge just above Manning Mill Road, a drop of 2 or 3 feet, cleanest on the right. Manning Mill Road is the usual put-in for whitewater paddlers. The property on both sides of the river is private.

A pool below the bridge leads to a good surfing hole, followed by a sharper drop that is best run right center. A harder ledge lies just above Emerson Mill Road. The exciting route is down the middle, although there is a viable route on the left.

Good surfing waves are found below the bridge. Scout from the right side. Crawford's Drop is often considered Class IV. The best route is on the far left, although there is an interesting route on the right. The drop below Papermill Road often has high waves.

This bridge offers a possible take-out and is the beginning of the portage around Grand Falls, a dangerous Class V drop. Put in below the dam that follows the drop. A series of ledges leads to flatwater above the dam in Hampden. Take out on the right at the waterworks. The Penobscot is 0.25 mile below.

Marsh Stream

Marsh Stream flows eastward from Monroe to tidewater on the Penobscot.

Monroe Center ➤ West Winterport	9.5 mi
Description:	Flatwater, quickwater, Class I, II
Date checked:	2000
Navigable:	High water (spring)
Scenery:	Forested
Maps:	Brooks 15, Bucksport 15; DL 22
Portage:	9.25 mi e dam in West Winterport

There is a good trail on the left to the put-in at the base of the falls. A mile of Class I rips slows down through bottom farmland. The ME 141 bridge is passed at 3.0 miles. Just before the Marsh Stream Road bridge (5.75 mi) is Crooked Rip, a right-left-right ledge drop, Class II in low to moderate water. The junction with the North branch is another 0.25 mile.

The deadwater starts above the dam in West Winterport.

West Winterport ➤ Frankfort	6.5 mi
Description:	Quickwater, Class I, II, III

Date checked:	2000
Navigable:	High water (spring, after heavy rains)
Scenery:	Forested
Maps:	Bucksport 15; DL 22 and 23
Portages:	5.0 mi L Flatrock Falls 100 yd
	(6.5 mi e dam)

This is a nice day trip with a variety of whitewater. Put in from Loggin Road in West Winterport just off ME 139. It starts with a couple of miles of quickwater, which is followed by three Class I rapids.

Just above a snowmobile bridge (3.25 mi) is a double ledge, running at 45 degrees to flow (Class II). In another 0.75 mile is rock garden (Class I–II).

Beyond the railroad bridge (possible access) are Railroad Rip, which has complicated currents, and Pine Island Rip (Class II). Run left of the island; to the right is disastrous. Portage or line from the island if necessary. Scout before running.

Around another corner is Flatrock Falls (5.0 mi), Class IV–V. The run-out is poor, as the river immediately becomes wider, shallow, and full of boulders and logs. One Class II drop comes before the final 1.5 miles mostly on flowage above the dam at Frankfort.

The last mile on the North Branch of the Marsh River is tidal on the Penobscot River.

Chapter 5
Allagash Wilderness Waterway

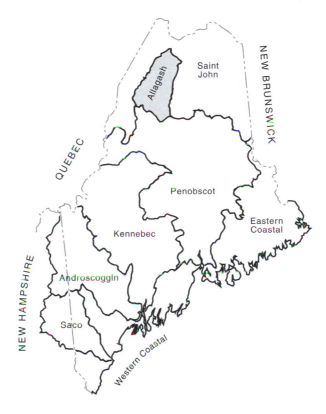

**ALLAGASH
WILDERNESS
WATERWAY**

N

Scale in miles

0   10   20

St John River

● Allagash

Allagash River

Musquacook Stream

First Musquacook Lake

Long Lake

Third Musquacook Lake

Clayton Lake ●

Umsaskis Lake

Fifth Musquacook Lake

Chemquasabamticook Stream

Clear Lake

Allagash River

Churchill Lake

Chemquasabamticook Lake

Eagle Lake

Allagash Lake

Chamberlain Lake

Allagash River

Maine's best-known canoe route has attracted paddlers to the Allagash and its headwater lakes for more than a century. Since Thoreau ventured into the Allagash waters across Mud Pond Carry, the name Allagash has conjured up images of wildness and adventure by canoe. Today, the Allagash is one of few eastern U.S. rivers that can provide a remote paddling-trip experience of a week or more throughout the summer season. The legendary Allagash is Maine's only designated Wild and Scenic river, and since 1967 most of its shoreline has been owned by the state and managed as the Allagash Wilderness Waterway.

For some who do the Allagash trip, it symbolizes an achievement, the culmination of a series of trips, with the Allagash providing the finishing touch. For others, it is the beginning (maybe the first experience in a canoe or kayak), with other rivers to follow depending upon the individual's affinity for backwoods and black flies, rain and rapids, winds and waves, and all the features of an extended paddling trip. People from all over the world come to Maine just to do the Allagash trip, and even for some Maine residents paddling the Allagash is the fulfillment of a lifelong dream.

Between ice-out and mid-June, fishing is the primary use of the Allagash waters. As the season progresses, paddlers are drawn to the wilderness setting for its traditional canoe- and kayak-camping experience. Heaviest paddle-tripping use occurs between mid-July and mid-August. In the middle of the summer, solitude may be hard to find, especially if you schedule your trip to run from weekend to weekend as most parties do. If you wish to encounter fewer people on the waterway, visit in mid- to late June, late August, or September.

There is no need to purchase USGS maps unless you are paddling into the Allagash Wilderness Waterway instead of using a vehicle access point. A map of the waterway is available free of charge from the Maine Department of Conservation, Northern Region, 106 Hogan Road, Bangor, ME (207-941-4014). Waterway rangers can also supply you with this map, and it is available at the North Maine Woods checkpoint as you drive in to the waterway. This official map shows the location of the eighty-plus campsites, but does not show topography or all existing roads.

DeLorme Mapping Company publishes a *Map & Guide of the Allagash/St. John Rivers*, which shows campsites, roads, trails, and topographic features. It is for sale in many stores throughout the state and can be ordered from DeLorme at P.O. Box 298, Yarmouth, ME 04096 (800-561-5105).

If you plan to drive to the put in, a current copy of the DeLorme *Maine Atlas and Gazetteer* is a must. The atlas shows every road and trail, and newer editions have topographic features. The maze of logging roads you will have to negotiate can be confusing to those unfamiliar with the area, and road signs are rare. This atlas can be purchased directly from DeLorme (see above) and is available throughout Maine in most convenience stores.

Waterway camping fees are collected at North Maine Woods gates on the private roads leading to the waterway. In 2001, Allagash Wilderness Waterway camping fees are $4 per person per night for Maine residents and $5 for non-residents, with no fee for children under age 10. Campsites along the waterway are available on a first-come/first-served basis and cannot be reserved.

In addition, there are private road use fees to drive in to the river. For current rates contact North Maine Woods at P.O. Box 425, Ashland, ME 04732 (207-435-6213). In 2001, North Maine Woods user fees are $4 per person per day for Maine residents and $7 for non-residents, with no charge for those under age 15 or over age 70.

North Maine Woods also can supply you with a list of outfitters, guides, and shuttle services that operate in the Allagash region.

For those who fly by float plane into the Allagash, registration and camping fees will be collected by the first waterway ranger encountered. Float planes are allowed to land only at certain designated locations within the waterway, so be sure to consult with your flying service while planning your trip itinerary. Flying services that provide flights to the Allagash are located in Greenville, Shin Pond, Millinocket, and Bangor.

From Chamberlain Bridge, the southernmost vehicle access point, the distance is 87.5 miles to the end of the Allagash Wilderness Waterway at West Twin Brook. Most parties continue on to Allagash Village, another 6.0 miles, before taking out. The trip from Chamberlain to Allagash will take six to nine days (five to eight nights) depending on wind and water level and your paddling pace and daily mileage.

There are waterway Ranger Stations at Chamberlain Thoroughfare Bridge, on Allagash Lake, at Churchill Dam, on Umsaskis Lake Thoroughfare, and at Michaud Farm. A ranger is also usually present on Eagle Lake and at Round Pond.

Establishment of the Allagash Wilderness Waterway

A hydroelectric dam on the Saint John River was first proposed in the 1920s. The site chosen was Rankin Rapids, 9.0 miles downstream from Allagash Village. A dam at that location would have wiped out the lower portions of both the Allagash and the upper Saint John Rivers. In the late 1950s, there was renewed interest in damming the Saint John, but public pressure ultimately prevented the construction of a high dam downstream from the mouth of the Allagash River.

In August 1962, the Natural Resources Council of Maine recommended land acquisition and management of the Allagash by the state or federal government. The following year, the Bureau of Outdoor Recreation in Washington recommended federal protection for the river. Pressure from the federal government for protection of the river through land acquisition led to the state's establishment of the Allagash Wilderness Waterway on December 28, 1966. The act setting up the waterway authorized a bond issue of $1,500,000 ". . . to develop the maximum wilderness character of the Allagash Waterway," which was passed by Maine voters and matched by federal funds. The state acquired a corridor averaging 500 feet wide along the shore of the river and all the lakes it flows through from Telos Dam north to West Twin Brook, including Allagash Lake and Allagash Stream. The act also placed some restrictions on land use within 1.0 mile of the shorelines of the waterway.

One of the first projects undertaken by the state was the reconstruction of Churchill Dam to ensure that the flow through Chase Rapids could be regulated and maintained throughout the paddling season.

In 1970 the governor of Maine applied for and received federal

Wild and Scenic river designation for the Allagash, and existing dams were grandfathered as historic structures. The Allagash was the first state-administered "wild" component of the Wild and Scenic River System.

The protection afforded the Allagash River applies to development, dam construction, and timber harvesting. Guidelines were established with the federal "wild" designation calling for strictly limited access points, temporary bridge crossings, relocating or discontinuing roads, and restricting public use of private roads passing through the waterway. In 1999 a ten-year management plan for the waterway was developed that brought the Allagash under public scrutiny. The plan, adopted in 2000, authorized a number of new road access points. The increase raised concerns about possible negative effects on the wilderness experience of waterway users. One new access point in particular, John's Bridge, spurred much public debate over management of the Allagash, and remains controversial in 2001.

Camping use since 1973 has numbered approximately 45,000 to 50,000 visitor nights between ice-out and the end of September. While overall camping visitor numbers have remained flat in recent years, by 2001 the trend shows an increase in shorter visits and day use.

Early Logging along the Allagash

The Allagash is a river rich in human history, and the remnants of that history add to its appeal as a paddling trip. In 1835, logging began to have an impact on the Allagash region. As was the case all over the state, the early loggers built dams at the outlets of the lakes to store and release water into the rivers to drive logs downstream to a mill. Today, only a trace of old driving dams can be found at the outlet of Allagash Lake and Mud Pond. The remnants of Long Lake Dam still form a substantial obstruction that is mostly underwater.

Dams are of particular interest on the Allagash because of the diversion of much of its headwaters into the East Branch of the Penobscot. A dam at the site of Lock Dam raised the level of Chamberlain and Telos lakes so that the water would flow east, rather than north. Telos Dam was built to control the flow into the East Branch. A dam at the site of the present Churchill Dam raised the level of the water in Eagle, Churchill, and Heron lakes. This allowed booming of logs on these lakes to another dam at the southern end of Eagle Lake that functioned as a lock. There, the logs were raised up to Chamberlain Lake, from which they were boomed down to Telos Dam and into the Penobscot watershed.

Unique to the Allagash were the Eagle Lake Tramway, used for 6 years from 1903, and the Eagle Lake and West Branch Railroad, that operated over a 13-mile roadbed between Eagle and Chesuncook lakes from 1927 to 1933. The remains of the tramway are still visible close to the old locomotives near Eagle Lake. You can still paddle through remnants of the railroad trestle crossing the north end of Chamberlain Lake.

Parties traveling the river stop to view the remains of two lombard log haulers at Cunliffe Depot, the site of a long-gone logging settlement. Other evidence of lumbering history can be seen at campsite locations such as Long Lake Dam and Allagash Falls.

The history of the river is told in *The Allagash* by Lew Dietz (Holt, Rhinehart and Winston, 1968 and reprinted in 2000 by Down East Books). This book adds meaning to many of the places of interest along the river and gives you a picture of life in the Maine woods during the past two centuries. Another book, *Allagash* by Maine guide and author Gil Gilpatrick, gives a sense of evolving human use of the area first as a hunting territory of Penobscot Indians, followed by the river's logging history and the recreational paddling tradition.

The Allagash Wilderness Waterway Trip

The most popular vehicle access points at the southern end of the waterway are Chamberlain Thoroughfare Bridge and Indian Stream. Both are reached from Greenville or Millinocket by private logging roads that are open to the public. Be prepared to pay user fees to pass through gates on all these roads. From Ashland, you can use the American Realty Road to reach Long and Umsaskis Lakes, and Churchill Dam. Churchill Dam and Umsaskis can also be reached by continuing north from Chamberlain Bridge.

Chamberlain Thoroughfare Bridge ➤ Lock Dam   9.5 mi

Description:	Lake
Date checked:	2000
Navigable:	Spring, summer, fall
Scenery:	Wild
Maps:	Churchill Lake 15, Umsaskis Lake 15, DL 55 and 56
Portage:	9.5 mi Lock Dam 20 yd
Campsites:	See Allagash Wilderness Waterway map

The boat landing is to the east of the bridge. After unloading, vehicles must be left in the large parking lot across the road and to the southwest. Check at the waterway Ranger Station for updates on weather and parties ahead of you.

Chamberlain is a very large lake with a northwest/southeast orientation, and the prevailing NW wind can make travel difficult and dangerous for small craft. Exercise caution and good judgment when crossing bays in Chamberlain and keep an eye to the sky.

Lock Dam ➤ Churchill Dam   18.75 mi

Description:	Lakes
Date checked:	2000
Navigable:	Spring, summer, fall
Scenery:	Wild; tramway and trains—southwestern end of Eagle Lake; moose in early morning and evening, especially in Heron Lake
Maps:	Churchill 15, Umsaskis 15, DL 55,56
Portage:	18.75 mi L Churchill Dam 50 YD
Campsites:	See Allagash Wilderness Waterway map

At the right end of Lock Dam, there is a short lift-over into the stream below. In 0.5 mile, you reach Martin Cove at the southern end of Eagle Lake. Beaver may have dammed the stream in one or two places but canoes and kayaks can usually be pushed over the top.

No trip down the Allagash is complete without a visit to the tramway and the locomotives. The trail begins at the end of a narrow inlet on the shore of Eagle Lake located due south of Farm Island (6.0 mi from Lock Dam). Look out for metal spikes in logs underwater as you paddle into the inlet. The trail leads past the locomotives to Chamberlain Lake, parallel to the old tramway, which can be seen in the woods to the right. At the Chamberlain end of the trail are the remains of the engines that powered the tramway.

Johns Bridge (12.25 mi) crosses the thoroughfare between Eagle and Churchill Lake, and 6.5 miles beyond is Churchill Dam (18.75 mi), where you take out on the left.

Indian Stream Access

For those wishing to skip Chamberlain Lake and a day of paddling, Indian Stream provides access to Eagle Lake in a cove southwest of Lock Dam and about the same distance from the northerly destinations. The Indian Pond road turns right off the Telos road 9.3 miles north of Chamberlain Bridge. Follow the Indian Pond road to the bridge over Indian Stream. You will pass the Indian Pond campsite on the left. When you reach the stream, there is a small parking area to the right and a closed gate just beyond the bridge. Walk your boats for about 0.5 mile down Indian Stream to Eagle Lake.

Indian Stream ➤ Churchill Dam	18.75 mi
Description:	Small stream, lakes
Date checked:	2000
Navigable:	Spring, summer, fall; Low water—may have to drag or lift in a few places in stream
Scenery:	Wild
Maps:	Churchill Lake 15, Umsaskis Lake 15, DL 55 and 56
Campsites:	See Allagash Wilderness Waterway map

Indian Stream enters Eagle in a shallow cove at the south end of the lake. In high water the stream may be paddled. There are some rocks to avoid and low-hanging branches make poling difficult. In most conditions boats will have to be walked down the stream.

Once in Eagle Lake, continue north to Churchill Dam as if paddling from Lock Dam.

Churchill Dam ➤ Long Lake Dam	18.75 mi
Description:	Quickwater, Class I, II, lakes
Date checked:	2000
Navigable:	Spring, summer, fall (chase rapids—controlled release)
Scenery:	Wild, moose along river, in delta before Umsaskis
Maps:	Churchill Lake 15, Umsaskis Lake 15; DL 55, 56, and 61
Portage:	0 mi Churchill Dam—50 yd from Churchill Lake take-out
Campsites:	See Allagash Wilderness Waterway map

If paddling from the lakes, the take-out is on the left before the dam. If putting in at the dam, river access is on the left below the dam and the parking lot is behind old boarding house building on the west side of the river.

The deteriorating 1968 timber crib Churchill Dam was removed in 1997 and replaced with a concrete dam. During the paddling season, enough Churchill Dam gates are kept open in the morning to provide a medium water level for Chase Rapids. In high water the gates may be kept open longer. Be sure to check with the ranger at the dam to find out what time gates will be shut down. Waterway rangers provide a portage service for gear around the first six miles of the river. A minimal fee is charged for the service and most canoe-trippers use it.

The first 1.5 miles of Chase Rapids are Class II and the most difficult. Just after a big eddy there is another drop as the river turns sharply right. About 1 mile farther there is one more Class II section, and the rest of Chase Rapids is Class I and quickwater to the remains of a washed-out bridge. Gear that has been portaged by the ranger can be picked up by landing on the right shore just above or below the old bridge abutment. After the gear pick-up, minor rapids and quickwater continue for most of the remaining distance to Umsaskis Lake (8.5 mi).

The next 9.75 miles up Umsaskis and Long Lakes and beyond are flat. At the north end of Harvey Pond, there are some riffles at the outlet. About 0.5 mile downriver look for the horizon line formed by the remains of Long Lake Dam (18.75 mi). The portage trail and campsites are on the right. The dam can be run only in high water, and even then must be scouted to find the deepest channel, as metal spikes protrude throughout the underwater woodwork of the dam. **Caution!** Not only have boats been ripped open, but paddlers have also been injured. In medium water some paddlers line their boats along the left shore after checking for spikes underwater. The old logs and cribworks are "slick as a smelt" so watch your step.

Long Lake Dam ➤ St John River   44.25 mi

Description:	Lake, quickwater, Class I, II
Date checked:	2000
Navigable:	High and medium water (mid-May through July, generally)
	Low water (if you can't pole, you may have to wade and drag in places)
Scenery:	Wild
Maps:	Umsaskis Lake 15, Round Pond 15, Allagash Falls 15, Allagash 15; DL 61, 62, 66, and 70
Portage:	30.0 mi R Allagash Falls 0.25 mile
Campsites:	See Allagash Wilderness Waterway map

In a dry season, you should not have any illusions that the water level of the Lower Allagash will be similar to that in Chase Rapids. The flow from Churchill Dam, where all but the fish ladder may be closed at night, is not sufficient alone to provide good paddling farther downstream, where the riverbed is much wider. The depth of the water below Long Lake depends largely on the contributions of all the small streams along the way. If they are low, you will have to pick your channels carefully, and occasionally you may have to pole or walk your boat through shallow sections, particularly below Allagash Falls.

Below Long Lake Dam, intermittent riffles continue for 9.75 miles to Round Pond. After the outlet of Round Pond (11.25

mi) Class I Rapids and quickwater alternate for 18.75 miles to Allagash Falls (30.0 mi). The only long stretch of flatwater is Musquacook Deadwater, which begins about 2 miles before the mouth of Musquacook Stream (15.75 mi) and extends for about 2 miles north of it. There is a Waterway Ranger Station in the field at Michaud Farm (26.75 mi) beside a wide bend in the river to the right. Paddling parties are expected to stop and check with the ranger at Michaud Farm. After the farm the river splits into several channels with many islands before coming back together just above Allagash Falls.

Allagash Falls (30.0 mi) is 3.25 miles below Michaud Farm. **Caution!** You should stop at the portage on the right bank above the rapids that precede the falls. Below the falls, the river continues much as it does above for the remaining 14.0 miles to Allagash Village. The only Class II water begins 7.5 miles below the falls at Twin Brook Rapids (37.5 mi). Twin Brook is the end of the state-owned Allagash Wilderness Waterway but the river continues another 6.75 miles to its confluence with the St. John in the town of Allagash.

There is one last rapid as the river completes a long oxbow before the ME 161 bridge. You can take out on the left just above the bridge (44.0 mi), or a little way below on the right where the Allagash and St. John waters start to mingle (44.25 mi). Landowners at these sites usually charge a small per-boat fee to take out. Remember to ask for and obtain permission before crossing property lines.

Alternative Routes into the Waterway

By Canoe: To Allagash Lake

Upper Allagash Stream ➤ Allagash Lake   3.75 mi

Description:	Small stream, quickwater
Date checked:	2001
Navigable:	Spring and high water
Scenery:	Wild
Maps:	Allagash Lake 15, DL 55

Upper Allagash Stream can be reached by several different roads after passing through the NMW Caucomgomoc Checkpoint. Be aware that although roads may be on the map, they are not necessarily in passable condition.

The stream is flatwater with swift current. Be on the lookout for obstructions from blowdowns or beavers. When you see Johnson Stream entering on the right (2.0 mi), it is 1.75 meandering miles farther to Allagash Lake (3.75 mi). The outlet is due east 3.25 miles (7.0 mi).

Johnson Pond ➤ Allagash Lake   3.0 mi

Description:	Flatwater
Date checked:	1997
Navigable:	Spring, high water
Scenery:	Wild
Maps:	Allagash Lake 15; DL 55
Campsites:	On island in Johnson Pond

In high water, you can float a canoe most of the way down the stream from Johnson Pond to Allagash Stream. There may be obstructions as it is not used frequently anymore. In low water the stream is not passable. If you must portage, there is a grown-over tote road close to the right bank that may or may not be a passable carry trail.

If you fly into Johnson Pond you will land at a small island. It is 1.25 miles from the island in Johnson Pond to Allagash Stream, followed by a 1.75-mile paddle down the latter to Allagash Lake (3.0 mi). To the east 3.25 miles, is the outlet (6.25 mi).

Allagash Lake Outlet ➤ Lock Dam   9.5 mi

Description:	Lakes, quickwater, Class I, II
Date checked:	2000
Navigable:	Spring, early summer (fall or low water, wading)
Scenery:	Wild, Little Allagash Falls, remains of Trestle of the Eagle Lake and West Branch RR (1927–1933)
Maps:	Allagash Lake 15, Churchill Lake 15; DL 55

Portages:	3.25 mi L Little Allagash Falls 150 yd
	9.5 mi Lock Dam 20 yd
Campsites:	See Allagash Wilderness Waterway map.

Below the lake, Allagash Stream flows for 2.75 miles to Little Round Pond. There are continuous rapids, up to Class I, in the first part, but the last mile consists of quickwater. The portage around Little Allagash Falls (3.25 mi), at the outlet of Little Round Pond, is on the left through the campsite areas.

The stream below the falls, 2.25 miles long, has Class I rapids, except for three places. The first is a ledge about 0.25 mile below the falls that can be avoided by staying along the right shore and going to the right of a small island. A second ledge farther on must be lifted over on the left. Finally, be on the lookout for a logging bridge, because underneath there is a short rapid that you should scout.

The gradient gradually lessens as you approach Chamberlain Lake (5.5 mi). It is a 4-mile paddle down the lake, past the railroad trestle (6.5 mi), to Lock Dam (9.5 mi).

If you are en route from Allagash Lake to Churchill Dam, you can avoid 7.5 miles of paddling, an important consideration if there is a strong headwind, by portaging along the abandoned tramway from the northern tip of Chamberlain Lake to Eagle Lake. Included in the bargain is a 0.5-mile carry, as well as a visit to the trains.

By Canoe: The Long Trips to Allagash Lake and Chamberlain Lake

A trip on the Allagash Wilderness Waterway, with Allagash Lake on the itinerary, takes eight to ten days if you put in above Allagash Lake. If you wish to plan a longer trip, you can do this by beginning at Chesuncook Lake on the West Branch of the Penobscot. It takes an additional three or four days from Chesuncook Dam to the Allagash by Mud Pond or Caucomgomoc Lake.

Long before today's network of logging roads into the Allagash region, the earliest trips on the Allagash usually began at Greenville and followed a route that went up Moosehead Lake, across North East Carry to the West Branch of the Penobscot, down the latter to Chesuncook Lake, and then by either Mud Pond to Chamberlain or Caucomgomoc Lake to Allagash Lake. The two routes detailed below use Chesuncook Dam landing at the southern end of Chesuncook Lake as the starting point, but you can drive to the West Branch below Seboomook Lake, paddle downstream to Chesuncook Lake, and head north for either route. You can also drive to Caucomgomoc Lake or Umbazooksus Bridge, or for those with weeks of time, you can still start your trip at Moosehead Lake in Greenville and follow the route paddled and portaged by Thoreau into the Allagash, although that route is not outlined here.

Chesuncook Dam ➤ Allagash Lake by Caucomgomoc 35.25 mi

Description:	Class I, II (if traveled in reverse)
Date checked:	2000
Navigable:	Spring, summer, fall
Scenery:	Wild
Maps:	Harrington Lake 15, Ragged Lake 15, Chesuncook Lake 15, Allagash Lake 15; DL 49, 50, and 55
Portages:	26.0 mi L Caucomgomoc Stream 1.5 mi 32.25 mi Allagash Carry 3.0 mi
Campsites:	10 sites Chesuncook Lake BPL $ 19.75 mi L Black Pond (S end) permit 26.0 mi L Caucomgomoc Portage NMW $ 32.25 mi (N shore) NMW $ car 35.25 mi Allagash Portage (N end) AWW $

From the landing at Chesuncook "dam" there are 26.0 miles of paddling up Chesuncook Lake and the length of Black Pond to the 1.5-mile Caucomgomoc Portage. The trail begins a short distance up Caucomgomoc Stream on the left at the campsite and leads to a logging road, which you follow to the right. A second road comes in on the left not far from the Caucomgomoc Dam (27.5 mi).

The rapids in Caucomgomoc Stream are easy enough that you can pull up the stream if there is enough water. The only difficulty, going up- or downstream, is a ledge approximately two-thirds up the stream, about opposite where the trail joins the logging road. When you first see the ledge, take out on the left up a steep bank to the trail leading to the logging road. Go right on the road and follow it to Caucomgomoc Dam.

The next leg of the trip is a 4.75-mile paddle up Ciss Stream (deadwater) and across Round Pond to the campsite (32.25 mi). The 3-mile Allagash Carry begins at the campsite and Ts off the logging road that goes around the northern shore of Round Pond. The carry trail is a hardened road. About halfway along the carry, go left where the road forks, onto the less-traveled road. You will come to a closed gate that can be carried around. Always remember to ask for and obtain permission before crossing property lines. As you near the end of the portage, an old trail at a fork leads left to the ranger camp on Allagash Lake. The right fork, a smaller footpath, leads to a campsite on the lake.

The outlet of Allagash Lake (40.0 mi) lies 4.75 miles northeast of the end of the portage.

Chesuncook Dam ➤ Lock Dam by Mud Pond	31.25 mi

Description:	Lakes, Class I
Date checked:	2000
Navigable:	Spring, summer, fall
Scenery:	Wild, moose in Umbazooksus Lake
Maps:	Harrington Lake 15, Ragged Lake 15, Chesuncook 15; DL 49, 50, 55, and 56
Portages:	21.5 mi R Umbazooksus Dam 10 yd
	22.25 mi R Mud Pond Carry 1.75 mi
	31.25 mi Lock Dam 20 yd
Campsites:	10 sites on Chesuncook Lake BPL, 2 on Umbazooksus Stream
	22.5 mi Mud Pond Carry (S end) NMW $

It is a 20.25-mile paddle from the landing at Chesuncook "dam" to the head of the lake at Umbazooksus Stream, where in high water you must portage a low bridge. After the bridge, you paddle past dry-ki for 0.75 mile, after which you work your way up Umbazooksus Stream. Carry on the right around the remains of the dam on Umbazooksus Lake (21.5 mi). Be on the lookout for moose while crossing Umbazooksus.

The Mud Pond Carry begins on the northeastern shore of the lake, 0.75 mile from the dam. The trail crosses the old roadbed of the Eagle Lake and West Branch Railroad (1927–1933), passes through the campsite, crosses a logging road flanked on both sides with deep water-filled ditches, and then continues through attractive woods to Mud Pond (24.0 mi). While Mud Pond Carry is named after the pond, the name is an apt one and the carry is notorious for the character-building challenge of its knee-deep muck. Make sure your footwear is securely fastened, and have a careful and safe carry.

Across Mud Pond, 1.25 miles, is the outlet (25.25 mi). The brook below can be run in high water, but part of it must be waded, lined, or poled down in medium water. There is also a portage trail to the right of the brook that may be brushy. It is 0.25 mile from Mud Pond to Mud Cove on Chamberlain Lake. Lock Dam (31.25 mi) lies 5.75 miles to the north.

By Canoe: to Eagle and Churchill Lakes

Haymock Lake ➤ Eagle Lake   8.0 mi

Smith Brook is mostly a small, easy stream, with a waterfall to lift over not far above Eagle Lake. This route is rarely used and may need clearing of brush or blowdowns.

Cliff Lake ➤ Churchill Lake   4.0 mi

Cliff Lake lies southeast of Churchill Lake. It is rarely used as an access route to the Allagash. There is a campsite and water access at the southeast end of the lake, although road conditions may or may not be passable. It is 2.0 miles across the lake and through Twin Lake to the outlet at South Twin Brook. If the water is high enough to run, this brook provides 2.0 miles of easy rapids to Churchill Lake. If the water is too low, you may have to wade with the boat. It is then 4.5 miles across Churchill Lake and through Heron Lake to Churchill Dam.

Chemquasabamticook Stream

The stream flows north from the lake of the same name, known also as Ross Lake. The latter has a large surface area, a factor that contributes to a relatively steady flow in Chemquasabamticook Stream, particularly above Clayton Lake. Nonetheless, this river requires the high water of May and early June since above Clayton Lake there is a mile-plus-long section with a gradient of 40 feet per mile that requires a good flow. The drop in this section is steady, and there are no large rocks in the riverbed, so the rapids are Class II.

Seventeen miles of the river (over half of it) are rapids, all relatively easy, with the most difficult being below Clayton Lake. It is a very scenic, semiwilderness trip than can be done in little over half a day in high water.

Chemquasabamticook Stream joins the Allagash Wilderness Waterway at Long Lake 4.5 miles north of the American Realty Road, from which Ross Lake can be reached. For paddlers continuing down the Allagash, it is 47.25 miles to the Saint John River, in which case the most practical access to Ross Lake may be by floatplane.

Ross Lake ➤ Long Lake		27.0 mi
Description:	Lake, flatwater, Class I, II	
Date checked:	2000	
Navigable:	High water (mid-May to early June)	
Scenery:	Wild	
Maps:	Clayton Lake 15, Umsaskis Lake 15; DL 55 and 61	
Campsites:	Ross Lake (NE shore) NMW $ car	

The first 3.5 miles below Ross Lake are easy rapids, which begin to slacken at a bridge. Then, for 1.5 miles, there is a deadwater, in which there are two dry-ki dams; the first must be lifted over, but the second may be paddled around on the left. The flatwater ends (0.5 mi), the current picks up, and the river drops steadily for 4.0 miles to an old logging camp (9.0 mi), where the current slackens. After 4.0 miles of meandering, the stream opens into Clayton Lake (13.0 mi). It is about 1 mile across the lake to the outlet (14.0 mi).

Below Clayton Lake, the stream drops steadily for 9.5 miles, providing good Class II whitewater. The river gradually becomes shallower and wider until it reaches slackwater (23.5 mi). After 3.5 miles of flatwater, it ends at Long Lake (27.0 mi). To the north, 3.0 miles, is Long Lake Dam (30.0 mi).

Musquacook Stream

Musquacook Stream flows north from a series of lakes east of the Allagash River, joining the latter 4.5 miles below Round Pond. In the spring when the water is high, the stream offers many miles of enjoyable whitewater up to Class III. The trip from Fifth Musquacook Lake to Allagash Village, a total of 52.5 miles, can be done in three days.

The stream begins at Clear Lake, an appropriately named body for water that has no tributaries to bring in the organic matter that colors most of Maine's paddleable waters. Access is difficult since the logging roads to it are not generally open to the public. Thus, a floatplane is the only practical access. The mile from Clear Lake to Fifth Musquacook Lake is hard, requiring portaging (including bushwhacking) into and out of a deadwater between the two lakes.

The remainder of the stream from fifth Musquacook Lake makes an excellent trip of lakes and rapids for 25.25 miles to the Allagash River. Fifth is not accessible by road, but Second can be reached at the campground on the American Realty Road.

Fifth ➤ Second Musquacook Lake	7.0 mi
Description:	Lakes, quickwater, Class I, II
Date checked:	2000
Navigable:	High water (mid-May to early June)
Scenery:	Wild
Maps:	Musquacook Lakes 15; DL 62
Portages:	4.0 mi L Fourth Musquacook Lake outlet
	5.25 mi L Musquacook Dam 0.75 mi

Fifth Musquacook Lake is a horseshoe-shaped lake 2.25 miles long, whose only access is by floatplane. The 0.5-mile long stream from the outlet is wide and deep when the water is high, but narrow and difficult when low. There is a 0.5-mile paddle on Fourth Musquacook Lake to its outlet, which is clogged with dry-ki, requiring a short carry left. The 1-mile run to Third Lake (5.0 mi) is a fast run of easy Class II rapids.

It is 0.5 mile across Third Lake to the outlet, where the dam is washed out and easily run in high water. The 1.5 miles of stream to Second Musquacook Lake (7.0 mi) is Class I–II. Just before Second Lake, the American Realty Road crosses the stream.

Second Musquacook Lake ➤ Allagash River	18.25 mi
Description:	Lakes, flatwater, Class I, II, III
Date checked:	2000
Scenery:	Wild
Maps:	Musquacook Lakes 15, Allagash Falls 15; DL 62
Portage:	1 long portage
Campsites:	(0) mi R Squirrel Pocket NMW $ car
	5.25 mi L Musquacook Dam NMW $

The washed-out dam at the end of first Musquacook Lake (5.25 mi) is followed by Horse Race Rapids, which are extremely rough. A portage leads through the campsite left to an old tote road that follows the stream for 0.75 mile to where you can put in.

Below the portage the gradient lessens, and there follows about 2.5 miles of flatwater to lower Horse Race Rapids (9.25 mi), which are Class III and can be heard as you approach them. A loaded canoe may have to be lined in a few places. The remaining 8.5 miles to the Allagash River at Musquacook Deadwater are all rapid, Class I–II.

Chapter 6
Saint John Watershed

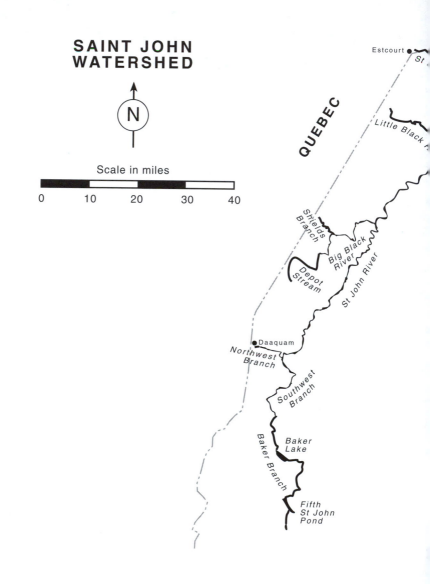

SAINT JOHN
WATERSHED

N

Scale in miles

0   10   20   30   40

Estcourt

QUEBEC

St

Little Black R

Shields
Branch

Big Black
River

Depot
Stream

St John River

Daaquam

Northwest
Branch

Southwest
Branch

Baker
Lake

Baker Branch

Fifth
St John
Pond

Madawaska

St John River

St Agatha
Long
Lake

Fort Kent

Mud
Lake

Van Buren

St Francis

Guerette

Cross
Lake

Eagle
Lake

Little Madawaska
River

lagash

Eagle Lake

Square
Lake

St Froid
Lake

Fish River

Caribou

Salmon
Brook

Fish River
Lake

Fish River

Beaver
Brook

Washburn

Portage
Lake

Portage

Aroostook River

Presque Isle

Little Machias River

Ashland

Squa
Pan
Lake

Prestile
Stream

Machias River

Mars Hill

Mooseleuk Stream

Aroostook River

Masardis

Bridgewater

Presque Isle Stream

eleuk
Lake

Whitney Brook

gan Stream

Oxbow

St Croix Stream

an
ke

B Stream

Millinocket
Stream

Houlton

linocket
Lake

Meduxnekeag River

New Limerick

South Branch

Cary

NEW BRUNSWICK

Saint John River

Perhaps Ogden Tanner says it best in his book *The Maine Woods* (New England Wilds/Time-Life Books): "Famous though the Allagash may be, not many people have even heard of the upper Saint John." The entire Saint John River is 450 miles long, which makes it 50 miles longer than the Connecticut and, next to the Saint Lawrence, the longest river in the Northeast. It starts in the remotest corner of Maine, loops north and east to form part of the border with Canada, then sweeps south and east through New Brunswick to the Bay of Fundy at Saint John. It was named by the Frenchman Samuel de Champlain, who was nosing along the coast in 1604 and happened to sail into its mouth on the feast day of Saint John the Baptist. For the upper Saint John, which Champlain never saw, the original Native American name Wollastook is far more descriptive: it means "beautiful river."

From 4th Saint John to Baker Lake, the upper Saint John starts shallow and narrow with drops and pitches that make it runnable only at spring's high water levels and after heavy downpours. Because there are no major lakes or dams to provide holding waters, the Saint John runs off quickly after spring snowmelt. Heavy cutting all along the Saint John also contributes to quick run-offs. Because of the vagaries of weather, the amount of snow at snowmelt, and rain (or lack of it), there is perhaps no guaranteed best time to run the Saint John River. The surest times are at spring run-off (which can happen in a week or can stretch into a month) and following a downpour, which can happen anytime. The best formula for a successful run on the Saint John is as follows: Realize that the river rises one vertical foot for each inch of rain; that it takes 24 hours to reach that one foot; that it will hold 24 hours; that it will go back to its pre-rainfall level after another 24 hours. There are two points on the river where the cubic footage of water is measured 24 hours a day and is recorded via satellite and available at the following two websites: http://me.water.usgs/gov and http://water.usgs.gov/me/nwis or at USGS in Augusta, ME (207-622-8201).

A final, very important ingredient of the Saint John pre-plan formula is the weather forecast. There are many choices. One which has proved reliable for years is North Winds Weather in Sandwich, NH (603-284-7718). If called a week before your trip, this service will put together a 5- to 10-day report for the Saint John River Valley from Baker Lake to Dickey. (Expect to pay a fee for this service; it may well be your most important expenditure!) This report will assist immeasurably in planning where to put in or whether to put in at all. Spelled out, this means if you have a given cfs of 1,500 feet at Nine Mile Bridge and 3,000 feet at Dickey, the water is spread from the upper to lower Saint John. If the weather report includes rainfall pre-trip and during trip, add up the inches, factor in the number of hours, and you can discern ahead of time a best-case scenario of river heights and run-off times. It is vital to remember that high cfs at Dickey and low cfs at Nine Mile interpolate into good water downriver, not upriver, suggesting a put-in north of Nine Mile. Conversely, if water is high at Nine Mile and some rain expected, you can assume you will get through, especially if you speed up your trip (miles per day) and/or put in downriver. Runnable pitches are from 1,000–1,500 and above at Nine Mile and 2,500–3,000 and above at Dickey. This formula obviously works best for those who can pick up at any given time and leave, rather than for those who must stick to an agenda. Even an agenda set in concrete, however, can be molded by the weatherman and the cfs reports as to where to put in and where to take out and/or whether to start at all.

Other important pre-planning factors have to do with where you decide to put in and take out, how you decide to travel (by road or by air), and how to set up your shuttle vehicles if they are to be used. North Maine Woods, Inc. (207-435-6213) is in charge of the road system, fee schedules, and permits for the Saint John area. NMW officials must be contacted for their map and outfitter packet. They need your itinerary to figure your day and night user fees and to give you permission to use fires at their official campsites. They will also provide information about road fees and gate schedules. There are as many methods of accessing and egressing the Saint John River as there are drive-in and drive-out sites, each dependent on your itinerary. For the most part, access will/can be at Fourth Saint John (fly in only), Fifth Saint John (fly and/or drive), and Baker Lake (fly and/or drive). Because a preponderance of river travelers start at Baker Lake, road access may be made through the province of Quebec, Canada, to Saint Aurelie, then east on the International Paper Company road to Baker or through Maine to Greenville, NNE to Kokad-jo, left onto the Golden Road, right onto the Ragmuff Stream Road to Caucomgomac NMW gate, and on past Saint Francis Lake to Baker Lake. One can also travel through Maine to Millinocket and then west on the Golden Road to Ragmuff, and then as above. As of June 2001, 5th Saint John is accessible by vehicle, albeit with difficulty. One can put in at the bridge site north of Saint John Pond depot or at the outlet of 5th Saint John.

If you use an outfitter, he/she will drive your vehicles around to your take-out point. If you have the time, inclination, and road knowledge, you can shuttle your own vehicles to the take-out point. If you choose to use friends or to hire help, they can take an extra vehicle and transport your vehicles from your put-in to your take-out point.

"Wallastook" (Beautiful River), the Saint John (from 4th to Ft. Kent) is a magnificent river to run, comparable in the East to a climb of Everest. Flowing 159 miles from start to finish, she rises embryonically at Fourth with riffles, alder, and fords. She expands from 20 ft of brook at Fourth to 300 to 600 ft of stream below the SW Branch, to 800 to 1,500 ft of river at Ft. Kent. She grows at each inlet, forming major rapids at Big Black and Big Rapids above Dickey. Four major rivers, each larger than the Baker Branch, swell her sides from the SW Branch to the NW Branch to the Big Black, to the Allagash. A myriad of brooks and streams from Turner to Brailey to Doucie to Knowles, Burntland to Nine Mile, Chimenticook, Pockwock, Ouellete, and Fox all add their waters to the expanding Saint John, each demanding a look-see, a thrown fly.

Because a majority of paddlers put in at Baker Lake, we will start the mileage from that point and end the mileage at Allagash Town. We will, however, show mileage from 4th to 5th Saint John Ponds; from 5th Saint John Pond to Baker Lake, and from Allagash Town to Fort Kent as separate trips. You can add them if you include them in your trip. As these waters flow geographically from one to the other, we will describe them as a continuum—4th Saint John to Ft. Kent.

Moody Bridge ➤ Allagash Town		72.25 mi
Description:	Quickwater, Class I, II, III (at high water)	
Date checked:	2001	
Navigable:	High water—after snowmelt and heavy rainfall medium water—following rainfall	
Scenery:	Wild	
Maps:	Beaver Pond 15, Clayton Lake 15, Rocky Mountain 15, Allagash 15; DL 54, 60, 61, 70 and 66	
Campsites:	34.69 mi R Red Pine Grove	
	36.40 mi L Burntland Brook	
	44.03 mi L Nine Mile Bridge	
	54.01 mi R Connor's Farm	
	55.11 mi L Seven Islands	
	58.22 mi L Priestly Campsite	
	63.93 mi L Simmonds Farm	
	68.90 mi L Basford Rips	
	73.73 mi L Big Black	
	75.35 mi L The Birches	
	79.06 mi L Seminary Brook	
	80.46 mi R Boom Chain	
	80.69 mi L Long Rapids	
	87.70 mi L Castonia Farm	
	88.67 mi L Quellette Farm	
	90.53 mi L Fox Brook	
	94.93 mi L Poplar Island	
	101.97 mi L Dickey	
	104.81 mi R Allagash Town	

For the next 25.0 miles, from Moody Bridge to Priestly Campsite, the river has good current with occasional easy rapids. In medium to low water, the river is shallow in many places, requiring that you choose your route carefully. As is so frequently the case of canoe and kayak travel at low water on many Maine rivers, the Saint John lends itself to the use of the setting pole. Setting pole notwithstanding, occasionally it will be necessary to handline or walk your boat. In high water travel is almost effortless. At mid to high water Rocky Rapids are instructive in the art of going slower than the current through high-standing waves; they lead to Red Pine Grove on the right and a real widening and slowing of the river for 2.0 miles to Burntland Brook. Between Burntland and Nine Mile Bridge there are numerous turns hosting fastwater that behoove the paddler to start each corner on the inside so as to have the option to go wide or not as the rip develops. Nine Mile, as storied by Hamlin, was a settlement through the thirties and still harbors many an historic cabin, an empty bridge abutment, and gauging stations.

Seven Islands, the major logging-resupply and horse-rehab depot of the early 1900s, lies 9.0 miles downriver and stretches, island by island, flat and grassy from Connor's Farm on the right past the Seven Islands campsite on the left. Priestly Campsite, site of the old Priestly Bridge, is a drive-in site off the Saint Pamphille Road. Priestly Rapids, below Priestly deadwater, are a true anomaly of this evasive river—hidden at high water, a runable rapid at mid to low water. Simmonds Farm is a grassy knoll on the west shore across from a large island.

Below Simmonds Farm there is a shallow section for several miles and there are two small rapids: Basford Rips, located at the two right-hand turns that precede Big Black Rapids. **Caution!** Big Black Rapids are 1.0-mile long and may reach Class III depending on the water level. They begin in a sharp left-hand bend of the river. Since you cannot see them as you approach the corner, it is advisable to stop on the left shore where there is a good path and look them over. They are the most difficult rapids between Baker Lake and Big Rapids farther on; because of their remoteness, they deserve respect. The rapids consist of two sharp drops with an easier section in between. There are boulders, ledges, and standing waves. At high water the safest route to follow is down the right-hand side. At mid to low water start left, eddy right at the midsection, ferry left, eddy back and finish on the right side; or start left, ferry right in the middle, leading with the stern, going slower than the current, and then run out the third pitch on the right side. Following 1.0 mile of mostly smoothwater, the Big Black River enters on the left.

The Saint John, swollen by the flow from the Big Black River, continues for the next 24.0 miles with a good steady current, broken several times by short drops that are Class I in high water and somewhat more difficult when the river is lower.

Then you reach the beginning of Big Rapids, located below a sweeping left turn in the river with a field and a large log house on the left. Downriver from the log house at river left, there is a road that you can use to portage wanigan around Big Rapids. Like Chase Rapids on the Allagash, it is best to run Big Rapids with empty boats. If you choose not to run Big Rapids, however, you may take out at this spot. **Caution!** Big Rapids is 2.0 miles long, Class III, and difficult in high water. It should be scouted from the left bank. Most of the rapids on the Saint John get easier as the water rises because they are flooded out. This one does not because it has many large boulders that produce heavy waves. The best route to run this rapid is to stay far left all the way through; the last part is the most difficult. Below Big Rapids, the river flattens, passes under the bridge in Dickey, and through Allagash Town where the Allagash River enters on the right. Campsites along this section from Moody Bridge to Allagash are numerous and spaced at convenient intervals. Most sites are on river-left; toward the lower sections, the sites are accessible by car.

Allagash ➤ Fort Kent	27.91 mi
Description:	Quickwater, Class I, II
Date checked:	2001
Navigable:	High (4000 cfs or above at Dickey)
	Medium (2,500–4,000 cfs or above at Dickey)
Scenery:	Rural
Maps:	Allagash 15, Saint Francis 15, Eagle Lake 15, Fort Kent 15; DL 66 and 67

Campsites:	5.0 mi R Cross Rock
	8.5 mile R Rankin Rapids (not easily recognized dirt road leads up from river)
	11.0 mi R Pelletier
	Numerous islands below Saint Francis

For the first 11.5 miles the northern bank of the Saint John is wild and the southern bank has a few houses and fields along the highway, which follows the river closely some of the way. Below Saint Francis it flows between Maine and New Brunswick in a rural setting all the way to Fort Kent. This section can be run easily in less than a day except when the water is low. The current is strong for 11.5 miles to the Saint Francis River which enters on the left. There are three short rapids, Cross Rock (4.25 mi), Golden (5.5 mi), and Rankin (8.75 mi). They rate up to Class II in medium water, but they are largely flooded out when the river is high. If you are going to be picked up by floatplane in Saint Francis, stop at least a mile above the town to avoid having to paddle back upstream to the plane. Below the Saint Francis River (11.5 mi), the Saint John is broader and flatter but with good current for the rest of the way to Fort Kent where the Fish River enters on the right (28.0 mi).

Saint John River (Northwest Branch)

The Northwest Branch rises in Beaver Pond near Lac Frontiere and flows south to Powers Gore, where it is joined by the Daaquam River—a stream running north, parallel to the Southwest Branch, until it turns east and crosses the boundary to join up with the Northwest Branch. The American Realty Road, which comes in from Daaquam, Quebec, follows the Daaquam River and the Northwest Branch, and then crosses the main Saint John River several miles below. The customs stations on this road are not open nights or Sundays. If the water is high enough, you can paddle down the Daaquam River and the Northwest Branch practically from the border.

Daaquam ➤ Southwest Branch   8.5 mi
Description: Quickwater, Class I
Date checked: 2000
Navigable: High water
Scenery   Wild
Map: Beaver Pond 15, DL 60 and 54

Put in on the Daaquam River at Daaquam Forest Service Headquarters. It is nearly 2.5 miles down the Daaquam River to the junction with the Northwest Branch, where it becomes a broader stream, and then 6.0 miles to the junction with the main stream. In this distance the river is mostly smooth. Below the confluence with the Southwest Branch, there is a larger boulder patch followed by riffles and good current for the remaining 4.5 miles to the American Realty Road.

Saint John River (Southwest Branch)

This is a common approach to the Saint John River early in the season, giving the longest continuous run.

Fourth Saint John Pond Outlet ➤
Fifth Saint John Pond Outlet   6.56 mi
Description: Ponds, flatwater, Class I, II (depending
                         on cfs)
Date checked: 2001
Navigable: High water only—following snowmelt
                         and after heavy rainfall
Scenery: Wild
Maps: Saint John Pond 15; DL 48 and 54
Campsites: 0 mi 4th Saint John outlet, E shore,
                         small
                         6.0 mi NW shore at canal 5th
                         Saint John Pond
                         6.56 mi NE shore at outlet 5th
                         Saint John Pond

From 4th to 5th Saint John Ponds, the Baker Branch is small enough to crowd the paddler with alder and block him/her with dry-ki dams. The old dam at 4th has long been washed out. Immediately below the outlet, the stream consists mostly of fast, shallow riffles, with no big rocks; then it deepens and slows until, about halfway down, there is a dry-ki dam in an alder swamp. The lower section speeds up, leading to a short, sharp pitch just above and at a bridge site near the inlet to 5th Saint John Pond. At this pitch (as at so many places on the Saint John at low- to mid-flow levels,) one should stand and pole, slowing the boat to a manageable speed. Shortly below this pitch, the stream enters 5th Saint John. Two campsites are at the north end, 3.5 miles down the pond.

5th Saint John Pond Outlet ➤ Baker Lake Outlet   19.32 mi

Description:	Lakes, flatwater, Class I, II
Date checked:	2001
Navigable:	High water only—following snowmelt and after heavy rainfall
Scenery:	Wild
Maps:	Saint John Pond 15, Baker Lake 15; DL 48 and 54
Campsites:	0 mi 5th Saint John outlet
	16.58 mi Baker Pond, SE shore
	19.32 mi Baker Pond, N outlet

Below 5th Saint John sluiceway, the first 4.0 miles are difficult. The river runs fast with sharp turns and drops that require quick maneuvers to avoid being swept against the outside banks. Stow poles inside and beneath thwarts. (If they trail behind the boat, they can be snapped off.) The rapids are not difficult, but they are continuous and demand constant attention. In this section there are two old logging bridges that may block the river (depending on the water level) and two dry-ki dams which require very short portages or drags without unloading gear: first on the left and then on the right. Other than the possibility of a log or fallen tree, there are no more obstacles. For the next eight miles, the current remains strong with rapids most of the way to a long dead-water. After 4.5 miles of flatwater, the river empties into Baker Lake. The first campsite is immediately to the right (16.58). The next site is at the outlet on the west shore (19.32). This is a long, arduous 16.58 miles from 5th outlet to Baker inlet—equal to many 30-mile days on larger rivers.

Wagner Forest Management, Ltd, Bangor, ME (207-990-0050) is responsible for managing lands (including 4th and 5th Saint John Pond areas) that were formerly owned by Gross National Product Company. Brian Rolfe, Wagner forester, is their man in the field for the 4th and 5th Saint John areas as of June 2001. His cell phone is 207-557-9624. Although difficult to reach, he relates that he seldom hears of a happy paddler from 4th to 5th but always hears paddlers extol the trip from 5th to Baker.

Baker Lake Outlet ➤ Moody Bridge		32.67 mi
Description:	Flatwater, Class I, II	
Date checked:	2001	
Navigable:	High water—after snowmelt and heavy rainfall	
	Medium water—following rainfall	
Scenery:	Wild	
Maps:	Baker Lake 15, Beaver Pond 15; DL 48 and 54	
Campsites:	0 mi Baker Outlet	
	4.69 mi R Turner Bogan	
	8.57 mi R Flaws Bogan	
	17.74 mi L Southwest Branch	
	18.20 mi L Sunset Island	
	21.67 mi L Doucie Brook	
	23.24 mi R Knowles Brook	
	28.88 mi R Northwest Branch	
	31.98 mi L Ledge Rapids	
	32.67 mi Moody Bridge	

In this section, the Saint John grows to become a large river. Below Baker Lake, the Baker Branch is still small enough so that the forest grows right to the water's edge. As you approach the confluence with the Southwest Branch, you can begin to see the effect of the tremendous force behind the ice as it breaks up in the spring. Where there are sharp bends and a strong current, the ice has scraped and sometimes broken off the trees on the outside of the turns. Continuing downstream, the size of the river increases, and the scouring of the riverbank is such a regular occurrence during ice-out that few trees grow near the water except alders, which are relatively unaffected as the ice rides over them.

There are numerous easy rapids for 4.69 miles to Turner Brook which enters on the right. There is a campsite just above at Turner Bogan on the right. For the next 8.0 miles the river is mostly flat. Flaws Bogan campsite (8.57 mi) is located on the high right bank a little south of the forest service camp. Approximately 14 miles north of Baker Lake, the current picks up. In the remaining 4.0 miles, the rapids increase to Class II as you approach the Southwest Branch.

At the Southwest Branch, there are several good campsites. The first is on the left across the confluence with the Southwest Branch, and it must be anticipated in order to reach it without being washed downstream. Simply eddy left into the SW Branch and ferry across stream to the site. The next site, also on the left, is more easily reached. It is a small site at the head of Sunset Island.

Below the confluence with the Southwest Branch (17.74 mi), there are 11.14 miles of smooth- and quickwater all the way to the Northwest Branch. About 4.0 miles below the Southwest Branch, there is a campsite on the left, across from Doucie Brook; shortly thereafter there is a site at Knowles Brook, river-right (23.24 mi). There are a few riffles as you approach the Northwest Branch. Just below, on the right, is a nice, small, high-bank campsite. After the confluence with the Northwest Branch (28.88 mi), there is a large boulder patch followed by riffles and a good current to the Realty Road (32.67 mi) where Moody Bridge crosses the Saint John River. Just below the boulder patch, which requires careful maneuvering, is a heavy pitch at high water. With laden canoes a good path is to start right, move to center at the first corner, skirt stacks, following right beyond the streamlet and cabin, and edge left at the runout. Shortly after this pitch is Ledge Rapids and a campsite on the left shore. Skirt Ledge Rapids right and Moody Bridge soon looms ahead. There are 5 sites here. They are good and well maintained. Remember that they are drive-in sites.

Big Black River

In many respects, the Big Black River resembles the Saint John. It is a large river with alternating sections of slow- and fast-moving current. The rapids are generally shallow, and they tend to get easier as the water gets higher, although a few may generate large waves at times of heavy runoff. The water level is responsive to rainfall, and the river is likely to show daily fluctuations that can be easily measured.

Below the mouth of Depot Stream and above the bridge near the top of Connors Sluice there are a few cabins, but the remainder of the river is wild. Many of the banks are heavily forested, but Ninemile Deadwater, which used to be flooded, is bordered by extensive and open low-lying areas. At the end of Connors Sluice, there is a large meadow that is similar to the one at Seven Islands on the Saint John River.

The Big Black River can be reached by road most easily from Quebec. At Saint Pamphile, a North Maine Woods road crosses the border and soon divides. The road to the left crosses Shields Branch, which provides a flatwater access to Ninemile Deadwater that is used by anglers in motorboats. Straight ahead is the bridge near the top of Connors Sluice. The one to the right crosses the river close to the border. The river from that point to Depot Stream is mostly flat.

An alternative means of access is to fly into Depot Lake.

Depot Stream ➤ Saint John River	22.5 mi
Description:	Flatwater, quickwater, Class I, II
Date checked:	2000
Navigable:	High water (mid-May to early June)
	Medium water (scratchy by mid-June)
Scenery:	Wild
Maps:	Seven Islands 15, Round Pond 15; DL 61
Campsites:	5.0 mi R Connors Sluice (meadow at end) NMW $
	10.25 mi L Ninemile Deadwater (First right turn in T14, R14) NMW $
	13.75 mi L Big Black Dam NMW $
	17.5 mi L Fivemile Brook NMW $
	20.5 mi L Twomile Brook NMW $

Below the mouth of Depot Stream, there are 2.5 miles of flatwater to the beginning of Connors Sluice, a fast and easy 2.5-mile Class II run that ends at the beginning of Ninemile Deadwater (5.0 mi). In 2.75 miles, Shields Branch enters on the left.

Ninemile Deadwater extends all the way to Big Black Dam (13.75 mi). The washed-out dam is runnable. The remaining 8.75 miles to the Saint John River are a mixture of intermittent Class I and II rapids and quickwater, with the most difficult sections being just above and below Fivemile Brook (17.5 mi).

Depot Stream

Depot Stream is a tributary of the Big Black River. Depot Lake, below which the stream is runnable, is located close to the Quebec border; it is a remote body of water. A trip from the lake to Allagash is 72.5 miles. There are no portages, and the hardest rapids, other than Big Rapids on the Saint John, are Class II.

Depot Lake cannot be reached by road, but you can drive from Quebec to at least three places along the upper half of the stream.

Depot Lake ➤ Big Black River	19.0 mi
Description:	Flatwater, quickwater, Class I, II
Date checked:	2000
Navigable:	High water (mid-May to early June)
Scenery:	Wild
Maps:	Depot Lake 15, Seven Islands 15; DL 60 and 61
Campsites:	8.0 mi L Old MFS camp (grassy bluff) NMW $

From the outlet at the northern end of Depot Lake, there are 3.0 miles of flatwater to a logging bridge, followed by 0.75 mile of easy Class II rapids that lead to another flatwater section 4.0 miles long. Much of this section is through alder swamps and extensive low-lying areas, where there are occasional views of Depot Mountain ahead.

As it passes around the northern side of the mountain, the stream enters a narrow and densely wooded valley and Class II rapids begin (7.75 mi). In 0.5 mile, there is a bridge where the road to the fire tower crosses. (To reach the tower follow the road to the south right. Keep left at the fork. Distance is 1.0 mile.)

Rapids and quickwater continue for the next 7.0 miles to the bridge on the logging road from Saint Pamphile to Allagash (15.25 mi). There is quickwater for most of the remaining distance to the Big Black River (19.0 mi).

Shields Branch

Shields Branch rises in Quebec and flows across the international boundary into Maine. Although the upper part can be paddled, it has no access. The road from Saint Pamphile, mentioned in the description of the Big Black River, crosses Shields Branch about 3 miles above the junction of that stream with the Big Black and provides an opportunity to reach the latter below Connors Sluice. The 3.0 miles of meandering river give an easy and pleasant paddle through wild country.

Little Black River

The Little Black River rises in Quebec and flows in a southeasterly direction to the Saint John River, which it reaches at Dickey. It is navigable from the international boundary all the way to the Saint John. The river is most easily reached by a private road of the Seven Islands Land Company, which runs south from Estcourt in Quebec. This road reaches the river about 2 miles from the international boundary. Always remember to ask for and obtain permission before crossing property lines. There is a public campground here, which makes a good starting point. The trip is fastwater most of the way, with two rapids, both usually runnable.

T19 R12 bridge ➤ Saint John River		27.0 mi
Description:	Quickwater	
Date checked:	2000	
Navigable:	High water (spring or after heavy rains)	
Scenery:	Wild	
Maps:	Rocky Brook 15, Rocky Mountain 15, Allagash 15; DL 66	

You can put in at the campground on the private road at the bridge over the river in T19 R12. From here, there is a good current to the forks where the West Branch comes in. There is a very fast rapid here, about 0.6 mile long. Below this rapid the river has a good current for the 9.0 miles to Boat Landing Camp at the end of a spur of the same private road from Estcourt. There is a public campground here on the northern bank of the river. Below Boat Landing Camp, the river meanders for 10.0 miles through a boggy section, although it does have well-defined banks. About 1 mile more below this section, Johnson Brook enters on the right; there is a public campground here near the road that comes upstream from the mouth. From Johnson Brook, there are 5.0 more miles of fastwater to the mouth, with a falls about halfway down. This is usually runnable but should be looked over first. In high water, a carry will be necessary; the carry trail is on the left. From here to the Saint John River, it is all easy but with a good current. Almost directly across the Saint John is the town of Dickey, where paddlers may take out on ME 161 if they do not wish to run down that stream.

Saint Francis River

The Saint Francis River rises near Whitworth, Quebec, and flows southeast into Pohenegamook Lake. Upon its exit from this lake, it becomes the international boundary for the rest of its course to its confluence with the Saint John River. It flows eastward on a very meandering course to Blue River, Quebec, where it turns almost due south for a number of miles. Finally, just above Glazier Lake, it flows southeast toward the Saint John. The water holds up well because of the many lakes, so that from Blue

River down, at least, it may be run at any time. The best approach is from the Maine side of the river.

Estcourt ➤ Blue River	24.0 mi
Description:	Quickwater, Class I
Date checked:	2000
Navigable:	Medium or high water (spring and early summer)
Scenery:	Wild
Maps:	Beau Lake 15; DL 67

This section is very winding. Although the water holds up well, it may become quite scratchy in a dry summer, so the best time for running is probably spring and early summer. There are no serious rapids and few obstructions; but some of the old dams, which have been largely washed out, may require a lift-over or lining down. At Blue River the Riviere Blue enters from the north, adding considerably to the volume.

Blue River ➤ Beau Lake	10.0 mi
Description:	Quickwater
Date checked:	2000
Navigable:	Spring, summer, fall
Scenery:	Wild, rural
Maps:	Allagash 15, Beau Lake 15; DL 66 and 67

This portion of the river carries somewhat more water and can usually be run at any time. It has many meanders but no rapids of any consequence. It provides a pleasant, easy paddle with forested banks on the Maine shore; most of the time, there are fields on the Canadian side.

Beau Lake ➤ Saint John River	22.0 mi
Description:	Lakes, quickwater, Class I, II
Date checked:	2000
Navigable:	Spring, summer, fall
Scenery:	Wild
Maps:	Saint Francis; DL 67

This is probably the most interesting stretch of the whole river, as it comprises lake, rapid, and fastwater paddling. Like the

Allagash, which it resembles, it can be run at any time. The road running south from Blue River ends at Beau Lake, but it gives paddlers a chance to select this section without necessarily running the 10.0 miles down from Blue River if they wish. You can put in at the upper end of Beau Lake and paddle down the 6.0 miles to the narrows at the southern end, after which there is 1.0 mile more of wide, lake-like stream. Halfway down you pass the Quebec–New Brunswick boundary on the left, before the river becomes narrow for another 1.0 mile, with a small pond partway down.

The river then enters Cross Lake, down which you paddle less than 0.25 mile to the outlet on the eastern shore, or all the way down the lake, 0.5 mile to the southern end. The 0.75 mile of river to the Upper MacPherson Pond includes the 0.33-mile-long Cross Lake Rapid (Class III), which must be scouted! The water is heavy and in high water can be dangerous or impossible for a loaded boat. The 0.5-mile carry from the southern end of Cross Lake to Upper MacPherson Pond would be the wise choice for less experienced paddlers.

Upper MacPherson Pond is 0.75 mile long. At its southeastern corner, the river turns southeastward and in 300 yards flows into Lower MacPherson Pond, down which you paddle 1.0 mile to the short stretch of river leading into Glazier Lake. This lake is 4.0 miles long to the Narrows; then it is 0.5 mile more to the outlet. From the outlet of Glazier Lake, there are 2.0 miles of fastwater to Falls Brook. Here, where the brook enters on the right at a sharp left turn, is the 0.33-mile-long Falls Brook Rapid. This can be a difficult spot and should be looked over, especially at high water.

In another mile, after the river has made a sharp right turn, you come to the Horseback Rapids. These are composed of two short, but sharp, drops. Scout before running. There are a number of twists and turns in the next 2.0 miles to the MacDonald Rock Rapid. This is about 0.33 mile long and has high waves in high water. In low water, there are many rocks and fast boat handling is necessary.

From here it is about 1 mile to the Saint John River, which you reach opposite the town of Saint Francis, Maine.

Fish River

The Fish River rises from the confluence of a number of brooks in Township 13 Range 8, 2.0 miles south of Fish River Lake. For all practical purposes, the lake may be considered as its source. From here it flows eastward to Portage Lake, on which the town of Portage is located. It then takes a northerly route to flow into the Saint John River at Fort Kent. The upper headwaters are in wild country and must be paddled early in the season when the water is fairly high. Except for wet seasons, summer travel may be impractical. From Portage Lake down, the stream is larger and much of it is composed of lakes, so that travel at most seasons is practical. Many paddlers combine it with the lakes of the East Branch, which joins it at Eagle Lake, to make a long trip.

Fish River Source ➤ Portage	24.0 mi
Description:	Lakes, flatwater, quickwater
Date checked:	2000
Navigable:	High water
Scenery:	Wild
Maps:	Fish River Lake 15, Winterville 15, Portage 15; DL 63 and 64
Portage:	8.5 mi Fish River Falls

An unmarked private road from Portage crosses the Fish River practically at its source above Fish River Lake. Always ask for and obtain permission before crossing property lines. A branch of this road, which swings north and down the Red River to Eagle Lake, has a side road, which reaches Fish River Lake at the outlet. You can also fly in to the lake, where there are two sporting camps. If you put in at the road crossing above the lake, there are 2.0 miles of easy travel with a good current north to the lake. There is a sporting camp 0.25 mile away from the inlet on the western shore and another halfway down the lake on the eastern shore. It is 3.0 miles down the lake to the game warden's camp at the outlet at the northeastern corner.

From the lake, there is 0.5 mile of river to Round Pond, where there is a public landing and campsite; then it is 0.5 mile across the pond. Just below the pond, the Fish River Falls are located, and a short portage is necessary. Fish River Falls may be run, but it is a heavy Class III+ section. The next 2.5 miles are quickwater, with minor rips. The river then becomes smoothwater through marshland fringed by forest, good moose country, for most of the 10.0 miles to Portage Lake. It is then 3.0 miles down the lake to the village of Portage at its southeastern corner.

Portage Lake ➤ Eagle Lake		24.0 mi
Description:	Lakes, flatwater	
Date checked:	2000	
Navigable:	Spring, summer, fall	
Scenery:	Forested	
Maps:	Portage 15, Eagle Lake 15; DL 63 and 67	

This section is all smoothwater or lakes. It is often run in the reverse direction starting at the head of the East Branch chain of lakes. From Portage, it is 4.0 miles down the lake to the outlet at the northern end. For the next 10.0 miles to Saint Froid Lake, the Fish River offers smooth paddling through boggy woodlands. There is an excellent beach as you enter Saint Froid Lake.

Saint Froid Lake is 7.0 miles long and less than 1.0 mile wide. About 4.0 miles down, the Red River enters on the left. In another 3.0 miles, you reach the foot of the lake, and here the 3.0-mile-long Nadeau Thoroughfare leads to Eagle Lake, where this route meets that coming down the East Branch. There is a good campsite across Eagle Lake from the inlet, at Cozy Point on the northeastern shore just east of Oak Point.

Eagle Lake ➤ Saint John River		20.5 mi
Description:	Lakes, flatwater, quickwater, Class I, II	
Date checked:	2000	
Navigable:	Medium water	
Scenery:	Forested, rural	
Maps:	Eagle Lake 15, Fort Kent 15; DL 67	
Portage:	16.0 mi R Fish River Falls 20 yd	

From the inlet of Eagle Lake to Eagle Lake village is less than 2 miles. Eagle Lake is a very beautiful, narrow lake. It is about 5 miles from Eagle Lake village to the Outlet near Wallagrass. Below, there are 4.0 miles of smooth river to Soldier Pond, where there is a bridge (10.0 mi). Here the quickwater begins.

A mile below Soldier Pond there is a 4-foot drop, which may be run on the right (Class II) or lifted over on the left. There is quickwater for the next 5.0 miles to the second Fish River Falls, a Class V drop. **Caution!** Stop well above the falls on the right and line the boat down to the carry trail, starting from an eddy at the lip of the falls on the right. If the falls is run, it must be run on the right over the drop, because the easy-looking left chute has many very sharp rocks and cross-currents.

Below the falls, it is 2.5 miles to a railroad bridge; then comes Martins Rapid, a Class II drop 200-feet long, which must be run on the right. In another 0.5 mile, below the road bridge, the river splits. To the right is easy Class I, but to the left is a Class II+ drop, which may be re-run because of the nice pool at the bottom. The remainder of the way is Class I to the Fort Kent Blockhouse, an excellent take-out just above the confluence with the Saint John River.

Fish River (East Branch)

The East Branch of the Fish River is little more than a chain of lakes, which are lined with many cottages and year-round homes. The trip comprises the major part of what is commonly called The Fish River Lake Trip. The northern end of Long Lake, the highest in the chain, is in the towns of Saint Agatha and Madawaska, only a few miles from Saint John River. Most of the lakes run in a northwest-southeast direction, with the short bits of connecting river cutting at right angles to this trend, so that you travel in a zigzag route, which finally brings you to Eagle Lake considerably to the south. Here, you meet the main stream of the Fish River and can either go up that stream to its headwaters or down it to the Saint John River at Fort Kent, only a few miles from where you started. This trip is one of the best-known in northern Maine and can be done by careful novice paddlers.

Saint Agatha ➤ Eagle Lake   28.0 mi

Description:	Lakes
Date checked:	2000
Navigable:	Spring, summer, fall
Scenery:	Forested
Maps:	Frenchville 15, Square Lake 15, Stockholm 15, Eagle Lake 15; DL 68

The usual starting point is Saint Agatha at the northwestern end of Long Lake. Although this lake is 10.0 miles long, the paddler wishing to make a fast trip will turn into the eastern arm in 6.0 miles and follow this 3.0 miles to the town of Sinclair at the western end. There are three state campsites on the lake: one at Berube Point on the eastern shore opposite the western arm, one on the southeastern shore at the mouth of Mud Brook, and one on the southern shore of the western arm 2.5 miles from Sinclair. At Sinclair there is a short 0.5-mile passage through the thoroughfare to Mud Lake, sometimes called Salmon Lake. There is a 2-mile paddle the length of this lake. A lunch site is located on the southern shore about 1.5 miles down. At the southwestern corner the outlet leaves. It is 1.5 miles down this thoroughfare to Cross Lake, which is reached on the eastern shore about halfway down. The northern end of the lake has a number of cottages on both shores. The only campsite on this lake is 1.0 mile diagonally northwest across the lake from the inlet, at Matrimony Point. From this campground or from the inlet it is 3.0 miles to the outlet at the southwestern corner, where a short thoroughfare 1.0 mile in length leads into Square Lake. This is a large lake some 7.0 miles long and 2.0 miles wide with an extensive shoal in the middle. Because of this shoal and the fact that the wind is funneled between mountains, this lake can be dangerous in the wind, which may come up suddenly; therefore, stay close to the shore.

It is about 3 miles northwesterly across the lake to the outlet far up on the northwestern shore. This is a wilder lake than Cross Lake, and many paddlers will want to spend some time on it using some of the four campsites available: one at Salmon Point on the southeastern shore, one at Goddard Cove on the southern shore at the mouth of Little Goddard Brook, another on the western shore at the big hill 3.5 miles south of the outlet, and another on the western shore 1.5 miles south of the outlet at Limestone Point. The thoroughfare from Square Lake to Eagle Lake is 3.0 miles long, with a good campsite halfway down on the northern bank at the mouth of Halfway Brook. Eagle Lake is formed in the shape of an L. The thoroughfare from Square Lake reaches the lake at the halfway point of the east-west leg on the northern shore. From here, it is 4.0 miles west to the inlet of the main stream of the Fish River 1.0 mile east of Eagle Lake village on the southern shore. From this point, you can ascend the main stream or descend to the Saint John River. There is a nice campsite on the northern shore just east of Oak Point, on Cozy Point. Many paddlers may wish to spend some time on the eastern bay of the lake east of the inlet. There are three campsites here: one on the southern shore in Three Brooks Cove at the mouth of Middle Brook, one on the southeastern shore 3.0 miles east of the thoroughfare, and another one 4.0 miles from the thoroughfare. You can take out at Eagle Lake village or continue the trip as desired.

Aroostook River

The Aroostook River is formed by the union of Munsungan Stream and Millinocket Stream in the unincorporated townships north of Baxter State Park and follows a winding course northeast to the Saint John River in New Brunswick. The first part of the river is forested and wild; the lower portion is through farmland; and the last few miles are difficult whitewater.

Pending settlement of the boundary between the United States and England, the Aroostook valley became the prey of lawless trespassers who removed large amounts of timber. The Maine legislature authorized a company of volunteers to suppress this illegal traffic. On February 8, 1839, 200 men under Captain Rines reached Masardis Stream and fell unexpectedly upon the trespassers, who offered only slight resistance. Flushed with success, the company advanced to the Little Madawaska River, where they met a reverse. Captain Rines was captured and carried off to Fredericton. These events precipitated the Aroostook War, a general call to arms in which there was no loss of life, and which was finally settled by the Webster-Asburton Treaty of 1842.

Around 1900, the Aroostook River was used to gain access to the Upper East Branch of the Penobscot River from Moose Brook, which flows into Millinocket Lake. The Aroostook was also used, as it is still by a few, to gain access to the Seboeis River and Grand Lake Seboeis, with a 0.75-mile carry from the West Branch of Carry Brook. This brook flows into La Pomkeag Stream and then into the Aroostook River about 10 miles west of Oxbow.

Libby Camp ➤ Oxbow Landing		17.0 mi
Description:	Quickwater, Class I	
Date checked:	2000	
Navigable:	High water (spring)	
Scenery:	Wild	
Maps:	Millinocket Lake 15, Grand Lake Seboeis 15; DL 57	

Put in where Pinkham Road crosses Munsungan Stream, or farther down at Oxbow Road. This latter road also crosses Millinocket Stream. Libby Camp is at the confluence of Millinocket Stream and Munsungan Stream and can be reached by either. The first 7.0 miles to Mooseleuk Stream have a fast current with occasional riffles, followed by 1.0 mile of deadwater to La Pomkeag Stream. After 7.5 miles of current to Baste Rips (Class II), it is 1.5 miles to Oxbow Landing, where motorboats can be launched.

Oxbow Landing ➤ Washburn		44.0 mi
Description:	Flatwater, quickwater, Class I	
Date checked:	2000	

Navigable:	Spring, summer, fall (some shallow spots)
Scenery:	Forested, towns
Maps:	Grand Lake Seboeis 15, Oxbow 15, Ashland 15, Presque Isle 15, Caribou 15; DL 57, 58, and 64

After 3.0 miles of deadwater, the river swings north, and the barely noticeable entrance to the Oxbow is on the right. You can make a side trip of 1.0 mile to this overgrown marsh. The deadwater continues 3.0 miles to Shepard Rips (Class I), where there is a camp on a bluff on the left. The river runs slowly east/north, where there is an excellent campsite at the turn, and then east again for 8.0 miles to the mouth of the Saint Croix Stream (and a good take-out just up Saint Croix Stream at ME 11 bridge) in Masardis (14.0 mi). Several small ledges are found here. The 5.0 miles of slow water to Squa Pan Brook is largely through farmland, which cannot be seen from the river. In 5.0 more miles, you pass the site of an old logging bridge, and shortly after that the Machias River (24.0 mi). The next mile contains some Class I rapids to the ME 11 bridge in Ashland (access here). It is another mile to the Little Machias, and 1.0 mile more to Sheridan, with a railroad bridge and the remains of an old logging dam. This can be run, lined, or carried on the right. Six miles below is Pudding Rock, a large rock face on right with some ledges on the left; there is a good access to the river here.

At the island before Beaver Brook, 3.0 miles farther, the left channel leads to a campsite on a high bank on the left. The river winds through islands for 2.0 miles to Gardner Brook Rapids (easy Class I).

This is the end of the wilderness run, as many camps are along the shore for the 6.0 miles of quickwater to Washburn. At the railroad trestle are the remains of an old logging dam, and then a landing and a good parking place just above the Washburn Bridge (44.0 mi).

Washburn ➤ Fort Fairfield   37.0 mi

Description:	Flatwater, quickwater
Date checked:	2000
Navigable:	Spring, summer, fall
Scenery:	Rural, towns
Maps:	Caribou 15, Presque Isle 15, Mars Hill 15, Fort Fairfield 15; DL 64 and 65
Portage:	14.0 mi e Caribou Dam 0.5 mi

Much of this run is through potato fields, although the banks are often wooded. The river is swift, with many small rips through islands to Crossville, where there is a white church steeple on the left. The river passes under a railroad bridge a mile below Crossville and enters Rum Rapids, Class II in low water, but tending to wash out in higher water. The next 7.0 miles to the US 1 bridge in Presque Isle (11.0 mi), where Presque Isle Stream enters, have good current and pass many islands. The 14.0 miles to the dam at Caribou are smooth. The carry on the right is shorter but difficult; the left is 0.5 mile on a good road behind the power plant. It is 5.0 miles to the Little Madawaska River at Grimes Mill, and 7.0 miles to the ME 165 bridge at Fort Fairfield (37.0 mi).

Fort Fairfield ➤ Saint John River   11.0 mi

Description:	Flatwater, Class II, III, IV, V
Date checked:	2000
Navigable:	Above 15,000 cfs—dangerous; 2,800–5,000 cfs—best level for all boats
Scenery:	Wild
Maps:	Fort Fairfield 15; DL 65
Portages:	4.0 mi R Dam
	5.0 mi Dam

If you continue across the international boundary you must report to customs, located 3.0 miles east of town of ME 167, and also check the dam release for the day.

Flatwater continues to the dam, 4.0 miles from Fort Fairfield, and 1.0 mile beyond the Canadian border. Portage right.

The next mile is through a canyon, Class IV–V, where the

river drops 75 feet. The canyon should be run only after complete scouting because it contains very few eddies and a 180-degree turn in the middle of the gorge. The last drop is the most difficult, where the river makes a right-angle turn against a rock wall.

Below the second dam, you enter immediately into Class II rapids for 1.5 miles, to a Class III ledge with the chute on the left, and then into more Class II rapids to the Limestone River on the left. The last major rapid starts under the Trans-Canada Bridge; the size of this rapid is deceiving because of the height of the bridge, and it can easily swamp an open boat. The last 2.0 miles to the Saint John are flatwater.

Munsungan Stream

Both the upper end of Chase Lake and the outlet of Munsungan Lake can be reached by good gravel roads.

Chase Lake ➤ Libby Camp		16.0 mi
Description:	Lakes, flatwater, Class I, II	
Date checked:	2000	
Navigable:	High water (spring)	
Scenery:	Wild	
Maps:	Spider Lake 15, Millinocket Lake 15; DL 56 and 57	

Chase Lake is 1.5 miles long. The outlet is a 0.5-mile long shallow stream with Class I rapids. It is then 5.0 miles down Munsungan Lake to a broken logging dam, which can be run. There are 1.5 miles of Class I rapids and ledge drops to Munsungan Falls, a heavy Class III rapid, which should be scouted from the right bank. The worst drop is around a corner and cannot be seen from the start. Just below is a steel logging bridge.

Six miles of quickwater follow to a collapsed bridge. This section may have to be carried; then there are 3.0 miles of Class I rapids to Libby Camp, where Millinocket Stream joins to form the Aroostook River.

Machias Stream

The Machias Stream flows south and then west from Machias Lake in T12 R8 to the Aroostook River near Ashland. The river is about 39 miles long and drops 420 feet, making it an excellent whitewater trip for a weekend. In the early spring, the river can be run in a day with water up to Class IV. The Machias runs through mountainous and heavily forested country, with many signs of the old logging days. Because of heavy logging in the recent years, the river must be run early because there is a very fast runoff. It also can be run after heavy rains.

Pratt Lake ➤ Big Machias Lake Outlet	8.0 mi
Description:	Lake, quickwater
Date checked:	2000
Navigable:	High water (spring)
Scenery:	Wild
Maps:	Mooseleuk Lake 15; DL 63
Campsites:	7.0 mi on northern shore at Twentymile Brook
	8.0 mi Big Machias Lake outlet car

The outlet of Pratt Lake is at the northernmost point, where you enter a small but swift stream. This flows through some ponds for about 2 miles. After 3.0 miles, you enter Big Machias Lake. The outlet is 3.0 miles down the lake at the eastern end.

Big Machias Lake ➤ Aroostook River	32.0 mi
Description:	Flatwater, quickwater, Class I, II, III
Date checked:	2000
Navigable:	High water (very fast-Class III)
	Medium water (scratchy)
Scenery:	Wild
Maps:	Mooseleuk Lake 15, Greenlaw 15, Ashland 15; DL 63, 57, and 64
Portage:	15.0 mi L Rand Crossing car; many other undeveloped campsites

Scout the old dam at the outlet, which can be run but contains many rocks. Below the dam is good current for a mile and then 2.0 miles of Class II rapids to Russell Crossing, where there was once a bridge on the American Realty Road. The heavy rapids continue about a mile, followed by 3.0 miles of Class II rapids to McKeen's Crossing and Rowe Brook (6.0 mi). After 9.0 miles of good current, you go under the Rand Crossing Bridge from Ashland, where there is a large public campsite on the left side.

Below here, the river has good current 8.0 miles to the deadwater behind a dam. In the middle of the swamp just before the South Branch enters is a set of Class I rapids where a clay deposit was once mined from the river. Six miles below Rand Crossing is a deadwater 3.0 miles long formed by an old dam now almost gone, which can easily be run in the log chute on the right side.

Below are Class II+ rapids for 4.0 miles; then good current follows for 4.0 miles. Suddenly, Ashland is around a bend. Just below the town is a Class III+ set of ledges, which should be run left to right in medium and low water, but on the far right in high water. Then go under a bridge, and in 0.5 mile enter the Aroostook River.

Little Machias River

The Little Machias River rises to the southwest of Portage, flowing southeast to Little Machias Lake. From there, it flows southeasterly through wild but swampy land to the Aroostook River below Ashland.

Little Machias Lake ➤ Aroostook River	6.0 mi
Description:	Flatwater, quickwater, Class I
Date checked:	2000
Navigable:	High water
Scenery:	Wild
Maps:	Greenlaw 15, Ashland 15; DL 63 and 64

The first 3.0 miles are wild, swampy country; the lower 3.0 miles are swift current with occasional rips. The confluence with the Aroostook is halfway between Ashland and Sheridan.

Beaver Brook

Beaver Brook drains an extensive forest area to the east of Portage Lake. The brook is smooth with good current and about ten good permit campsites along the way. The country is wild and untouched by camps, roads, or signs of logging; it is a good place to see moose and waterfowl. The campsite at the mouth of Beaver Brook is the nicest on the Aroostook River.

West Branch Beaver Brook ➤ East Branch   5.0 mi

Description:	Quickwater
Date checked:	2000
Navigable:	High water
Scenery:	Wild
Maps:	Ashland 15, Portage 15; DL 64

This section can be run down from the ME 11 bridge in Winterville in high water only and is rapid, with many blowdowns.

Confluence ➤ Aroostook River   8.0 mi

Description:	Quickwater, Class I
Date checked:	2000
Navigable:	High or medium water
Scenery:	Wild
Maps:	Ashland 15, Portage 15; DL 64

From the bridge on a dirt road just below the confluence, the brook is mostly smooth, with a few rips and chutes for the first 3.0 miles to enliven the trip. It then winds through the alder in a swamp, but in the last 3.0 miles to the Aroostook there are again rips and quickwater. When the brook takes a sharp bend to the left, the Aroostook River is beyond the high bank directly ahead.

Salmon Brook

Salmon Brook is a rapid stream, which rises in Salmon Brook Lake and flows southeast to the Aroostook River at Washburn.

New Dunn Town Road ➤ Aroostook River   4.0 mi

Description:	Class II

Date checked:	2000
Navigable:	High water (spring only)
Scenery:	Wild
Maps:	Caribou 15; DL 64

Put in from the Story Brook Fire Tower road. The stream drops 40 feet to the Aroostook River, all in an even gradient, providing easy Class II rapids for the entire distance. It makes a good stream to warm up on in the spring. Take out at the town landing in Washburn.

Little Madawaska River

The Little Madawaska River rises in Bog Pond about 6 miles west of Perham in T14 R5, and flows northeast to Stockholm, and then southeast to the Aroostook River at Grimes Mill. The beginning and end of the river are very swift, but the middle section is swampy and slow going. Above Blackstone, access is poor and there are many blowdowns.

Blackstone Siding ➤ Stockholm		13.0 mi
Description:	Quickwater	
Date checked:	2000	
Navigable:	High or medium water	
Scenery:	Forested, town	
Maps:	Portage 15, Caribou 15, Stockholm 15; DL 64 and 68	
Portage:	13.0 mi L dam in Stockholm 400 yd	

The first 5.0 miles to Madawaska Lake Outlet are quickwater and easy rapids through softwood swamps. An alternate starting point is Madawaska Lake, running the 1.0 mile down the outlet, which increases the size of the river considerably. The next 4.0 miles to the ME 161 bridge and the following 2.0 miles are swift, and then 2.0 miles of deadwater and swamp bring you to the dam in Stockholm.

Stockholm ➤ Aroostook River		22.0 mi
Description:	Flatwater, quickwater	
Date checked:	2000	

Navigable:	High water (dangerous below ME 89)
	Medium water (recommended)
Scenery:	Forested, rural, towns
Maps:	Stockholm 15, Caribou 15, Fort
	Fairfield 15; DL 68 and 65

There is 1.0 mile of quickwater below the dam, then 7.0 miles of meandering swampland to the US 1 bridge at Acadia. Three miles of quickwater follows; after another 5.0 miles there is a dam, then 2.0 miles of meanders through open farmland to another bridge on the Loring Access Highway. There, the river quickens for the next mile to the ME 89 bridge, which should be approached on the extreme left.

The last 3.0 miles to the Aroostook are very swift and meandering. Almost every bend has overhanging or fallen trees. Stay near the inside of the bends and be prepared to land should the river be blocked.

Presque Isle Stream

Presque Isle Stream rises in the unorganized townships southeast of Ashland and flows northerly to the Aroostook River at Presque Isle. Starting at Presque Isle Lake, the stream is steep and blowdowns are frequent, so the recommended starting point is Grindstone.

Grindstone ➤ Aroostook River		15.0 mi
Description:	Flatwater, quickwater	
Date checked:	2000	
Navigable:	High water (spring)	
Scenery:	Wild, town	
Maps:	Presque Isle 15; DL 64 and 65	

The first 8.0 miles are swift, with the Presque Isle Rapids (Class I) at the foot of Hobart Hill. The next 5.0 miles are the backwater from the rock dam at Presque Isle, located directly below a bridge. This can be run on the right center (Class III+) in high water or lined on the right at low water. The last 2.0 miles to the Aroostook River are quickwater with a few rips.

Prestile Stream

Prestile Stream is formed by the junction of a number of brooks in Fort Fairfield. It flows south through Easton, Mars Hill, and Blaine to Bridgewater. There, it turns east, crosses the international boundary, and flows into the Saint John River a few miles south of Florenceville, New Brunswick.

Westfield ➤ Canadian Border	14.5 mi
Description:	Flatwater, quickwater, Class I
Date checked:	2000
Navigable:	High water (upper sections)
	Medium or low water (lower section)
Scenery:	Wild
Maps:	Mars Hill 15, Bridgewater 15;
	DL 59
Portage:	6.0 mi R Robinson Dam

From Westfield to Mars Hill, the river runs southeasterly with fine views of the long ridge of Mars Hill. The going is hard, with many low trees and blowdowns, to the backwater of the washed-out Mars Hill Dam (4.5 mi).

Below the old dam there are easy rapids for about a mile, then 3.5 miles of good current to the backwater of the Robinson Dam (10.5 mi), which is carried on the right.

Below Robinson Dam the stream is much larger and passable at most seasons. About 1 mile below the dam at Robinsons, the river crosses the town line into Bridgewater and turns east. About 3.5 miles down, Whitney Brook enters on the right and in less than 0.5 mile the international boundary is reached. The customs station is on the road on the left bank. For paddlers not wishing to continue into Canada, take-out here or at the bridge just above the entrance of Whitney Brook.

Whitney Brook

Whitney Brook is formed in Bridgewater by the junction of the northern and southern branches. About 1 mile below this junction, the brook is crossed by Rumford Road and US 1. Below here it is navigable, although it is best done with relatively high water. The brook flows on a northeasterly course to meet the Prestile Stream less than 0.5 mile west of the Canadian border.

Bridgewater ➤ Prestile Stream		4.0 mi
Description:	Quickwater, Class I	
Date checked:	2000	
Navigable:	High water	
Scenery:	Forested	
Maps:	Bridgewater 15; DL 59	

From the pond at Bridgewater, there are 4.0 miles of easy rapids and fast current to the junction with Prestile Stream, passing a very low bridge 2.0 miles down. Take out in the large field in front of customs.

Meduxnekeag River

The Meduxnekeag River rises in Ludlow, flows southeast to New Limerick, then east to Houlton, where it turns north and slightly east to the Canadian border. Here, it turns east to join the Saint John River near Woodstock, New Brunswick.

New Limerick ➤ Houlton		11.0 mi
Description:	Flatwater, quickwater	
Date checked:	2000	
Navigable:	High or medium water (spring, early summer)	
Scenery:	Forested	
Maps:	Myrna Mills 15, Amity 15; DL 53	
Portage:	(11.0 mi dam in Houlton)	

Below the dam at New Limerick, the river has a good current partly through swamps for the 2.0 miles to Green Pond, where the outlet is only 200 yards away along the southern shore to the east. From here the river is larger, and in 3.0 miles of a somewhat meandering course, you reach the outlet of Nickerson Lake on the right. This lake, a favorite spot for summer cottages, is only 1.0 mile up the outlet. In 3.0 miles more, you reach Carys Mills and the entrance of the South Branch just below on the right. With the added water the stream is now quite large for the 3.0 miles to the dam at Houlton.

Houlton ➤ Canadian Border	9.0 mi
Description:	Flatwater, quickwater
Date checked:	2000
Navigable:	Spring, summer, fall
Scenery:	Forested, rural
Maps:	Houlton 15, Amity 15; DL 53 and 59

The stream is now large and flows northward for some 8.0 miles with no obstructions; then it turns east and in 1.0 mile more crosses the border between Monuments 27A and 27. The nearest customs station is 1.0 mile south at the road crossing, so most paddlers would probably take out at the road bridge about 2.5 miles upstream from the international boundary.

Meduxnekeag River (South Branch)

The South Branch of the Meduxnekeag River is formed by the junction of a number of brooks in Cary. From there, it flows north through Hodgdon to Houlton, where it joins the main river at Carys Mills.

Cary ➤ Meduxnekeag River	9.0 mi
Description:	Flatwater, quickwater, Class I
Date checked:	2000
Navigable:	High and medium water
Scenery:	Forested, rural, towns
Maps:	Houlton 15; DL 53
Portages:	5.0 mi L dam at Hodgdon 10 yd
	(9.0 mi L waterfall at Carys Mills)

Just above the Oliver Road Bridge at Cary, the South Branch is joined by Davis Brook and becomes quite large. There are 4.0 miles of meandering stream to the big pond at Hodgdon, followed by 1.0 mile down the pond to the town. There is a dam just above the bridge; portage 10 yards on the left by a small public landing. There are Class I–II rips for 100 yards below the dam, followed by 1.0 mile of good current to a broken log dam. This dam may be runnable but is apt to be blocked by debris. Two more miles of quickwater and riffles bring the paddler to a bridge on the dirt back road from Hodgdon to Carys Mills. Within 0.5 mile you come to an area of meanders and alder that continues for 0.75 mile. Once out of the bushes, the current quickens again and occasional Class I rapids appear. These become more frequent and interesting after a nearly right-angle turn to the right. A slight turn to the left signals the beginning of a series of low ledges above the first of two bridges at Carys Mills. There is a falls dropping in several sections just below the bridge. Below the falls there are 100 yards of Class I water to the main river.

B Stream

B Stream rises in Hammond and flows southeast to the Meduxnekeag River in Houlton. It is fed by a number of brooks with swampy areas on their courses, so it should hold water well later in the paddling season. From B School in southeastern Hammond, the river drops 120 feet in 8.0 miles to Houlton.

Hammond (Sixth Bridge) ➤ Houlton	4.25 mi
Description:	Quickwater, Class I, II
Date checked:	2000
Navigable:	Medium water
Scenery:	Forested
Maps:	Houlton; DL 59 and 53

Starting at the sixth bridge above the confluence with the Meduxnekeag, this stream can be paddled in mid-June if it has not been too dry. There is quickwater and Class I riffles, occasionally obstructed by trees, to the high bridge near BM 373 (1.5 mi). Below this bridge, the stream is somewhat larger and deeper and paddlers are not so hampered by trees. The third bridge marks the beginning of a mile-long section where ledges cross the stream at varying angles, creating intermittent Class II rapids, one or two of which may be tricky at high water. This section ends at a bridge on the back road to Ludlow, which is the last convenient take-out; beyond, access from I-95 is impractical and the area around the US 2 bridge is urbanized, with a low dam just above it.

Chapter 7
Western Coastal Watersheds

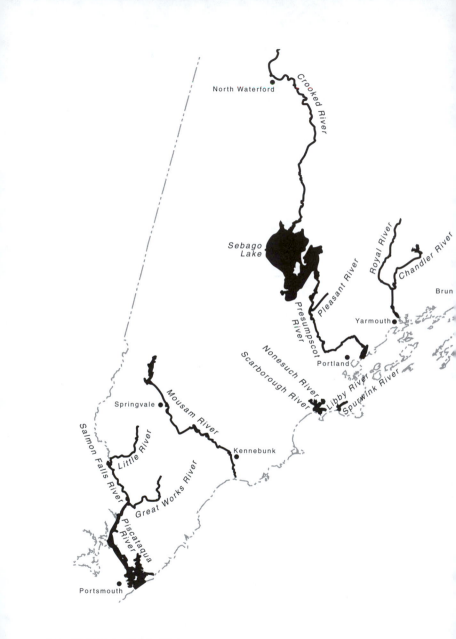

North Waterford

Crooked River

Sebago
Lake

Royal River

Chandler River

Pleasant River

Brun

Presumpscot
River

Yarmouth

Nonesuch River

Portland

Scarborough River

Libby River

Spurwink River

Springvale

Mousam River

Kennebunk

Salmon Falls River

Little River

Great Works River

Piscataqua
River

Portsmouth

Augusta ●

Weeks
Mills

*Sheepscot
Pond*

West Branch

Sheepscot River

Gardiner ●

Kennebec River

● Searsmont

Appleton ●

Medomak River

● Whitefield

St George River

ance River

Sheepscot

Damariscotta River

Pemaquid River

Oyster River

Wiscasset

● Waldoboro

ath ●

South
Warren

● Thomaston

WESTERN COASTAL
WATERSHEDS

Scale in miles

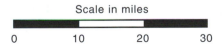

0   10   20   30

Little River

The season is short but exciting on the Little River. Go early in the morning or on an overcast day, because the river heads into the afternoon sun for most of its length.

Lebanon ➤ Salmon Falls River	11.25 mi
Description:	Flatwater, quickwater, Class I, II
Date checked:	2000
Navigable:	High water (late March to early May)
Scenery:	Forested
Maps:	Berwick 15; DL 2

The usual put-in is below the broken dam beside an old mill in Lebanon. In high water, the river can be run above the mill, either from Fall Road (1.0 mi upriver) or from ME 11/US 202 (3.0 mi above the mill). Determined explorers occasionally start even higher up. The river above the mill is quite narrow with Class I–II rapids and numerous obstructions.

From the mill there are two rapids, one at a broken dam in the first mile. In the next mile, from the Lord Road bridge to the bridge on Little River Road, the river is smooth and winding. The next 4.25 miles to Stackpole Bridge pass through an area known as "the Marshes," where the river maintains a good current around numerous tight twists and turns. Occasional breakthroughs create some confusion, but careful observation of the current will guide you through easily.

Whitewater enthusiasts frequently begin at Stackpole Bridge (6.25 mi); under the bridge is a small drop over a ledge. The next 2.0 miles are smooth and slow until the river reaches a small Class I rapid, followed soon after by 0.25 mile of Class I rapids up to Messenger Bridge, where Pine Hill Road and Little River Road meet.

Below Messenger Bridge (8.25 mi) there is another Class I rapid, an easy Class II rapid, and finally a 0.75-mile-long, hard Class II rapid. The river is narrow enough that you must pick either the left or right side—there is no room for a middle route—and the only clear passage involves switching occasionally from a course down one side to a course down the other. Stop and scout frequently unless you like piling up onto ledges and into impassable rock gardens. One particularly interesting spot has a car-sized boulder perched on top of a ledge left of center; the usually runnable channels lead you within an arm's length of it.

The long rapid ends with a small ledge in a sharp right turn. The last 0.5 mile of this rapid, down to a back-road bridge (9.5 mi), is very scratchy when the rapids above are marginally runnable; flatwater follows. One half-mile above the Hubbard Road bridge (11.25 mi), there is a broken dam at the end of a sharp S-turn that can be run with extreme caution or lined from the right bank.

The Little River empties in to the Salmon Falls River (11.25 mi) just below the Hubbard Road bridge. Somersworth is 5.0 miles downstream (16.25 mi).

Great Works River

This unassuming little river claims the distinction of having turned the first water-powered mill in the United States, in the section of South Berwick called Great Works. Mills continued there without a break for over three hundred years, until the 1940s, when the remaining few fell into disuse.

North Berwick ➤ South Berwick	11.5 mi
Description:	Flatwater, quickwater, Class I, II
Date checked:	2000
Navigable:	High water (late March to mid-May, passable at most water levels for last 3.5 mi)
Scenery:	Forested
Maps:	Kennebunk 15, York 15, Dover 15; DL 2 and 1
Portage:	11.5 mi Rock Gorge 1.0 mi

The best place to put in is at the bridge on Madison Street. Use the Maine Atlas to find Madison Street, across from where ME 4 and ME 9 merge from the south in the town of North Berwick.

The first 5.0 miles to Emerys Bridge on Hooper Sands Road are narrow and winding, and the river shallows out early in the season. The next 3.0 miles to Junction Bridge, at the western end of Emerys Bridge Road, hold water a little longer. Both sections are prone to blowdowns.

The final 3.5-mile section from Junction Bridge to the village of Great Works is runnable except in very dry summers, and it is entirely flatwater. Take out at the Brattle Street bridge (11.5 mi) 0.25 mile below the ME 236 bridge.

Caution! Below the Brattle Street bridge there is a dam and falls called Rocky Gorge. Stay well above it. Continuing to the Salmon Falls River, into which the Great Works River flows, is difficult because this obstruction requires a mile-long portage. There is another dam 1.0 mile downstream at the confluence with the Salmon Falls River. The deep impoundment above this hydroelectric dam is Leigh's Mill Pond, a local swimming/fishing hole. If you want to explore this section of the river up to Rocky Gorge, the river crossing at Leigh's Mill Pond on Vine Street would be the best access.

Mousam River

The Mousam River flows into the sea at Kennebunk. There is usually not enough water in the upper section for a good run except in the spring and just after Labor Day, when Mousam Lake is drawn down.

Mousam Lake ➤ Estes Lake		14.0 mi
Description:	Lakes, flatwater, quickwater, Class I, II, III	
Date checked:	2000	
Navigable:	High water (early spring and early September, annual drawdown of Mousam Lake)	
Scenery:	Forested, rural, towns	
Maps:	Berwick 15, Kennebunk 15; DL 2	
Portages:	3.5 mi L 1st and 2nd dams in Springvale	
	4.0 mi R small dam in Springvale	
	4.5 mi e 1st dam in Sanford	

6.0 mi L 2nd dam in Sanford (cross over
 first bridge)
(14.0 mi R Estes Lake Dam)

The river below the dam on Mousam Lake can be reached by turning off ME 11/109 at the Emery Mills Market. If there is a boiling flow at the base of the dam, there is sufficient water for this trip.

In the 3.0 miles to the first millpond in Springvale, there are three sharp drops to watch out for. The first is under a power line. The second is a short distance below the ME 11/109 bridge (1.25 mi). This drop could be Class III and should be scouted. If the water is too low for this rapid it is too low for the trip. Scout this rapid from a bridge about 50 yards downstream from the ME 11/109 bridge. The third drop is about 1.0 mile farther.

At Holdsworth Park on ME 11/109 in Springvale, there is good access to the pond above the first dam. If continuing downstream, take out left of the dam (3.5 mi), portage along Water Street about 1,000 feet, and put in below the second dam. There is a third dam (4.0 mi) just upstream of an abandoned stone railroad bridge.

The first dam in Sanford (4.5 mi) is followed by quickwater to the millpond above the second dam (6.0 mi). Take out on the left, cross the river via Washington Street, follow Pioneer Avenue downstream, and put in by the Emery Street bridge. Then there is quickwater with some debris for 3.0 miles to the ME 4 bridge.

Below ME 4 (9.0 mi) is 0.5 mile to the ruins of Jagger Mill Dam, which can be run. Quickwater continues for most of the way to Mousam Lake (13.0 mi), which is near the head of Estes Lake. When the lake opens up, turn right to reach the dam (14.0 mi).

Estes Lake ➤ Kennebunk		12.0 mi
Description:	Quickwater, flatwater, rapids	
Date checked:	2000	
Scenery:	Rural	
Maps:	Kennebunk 15; DL 2, 3	

Below the powerhouse there is a short rapid, followed in 0.5 mile by a gauging station on the right, the Whichers Mills Road bridge, and a dam. This dam should be carried on the right and the put-in made below a sharp fall and rapid, at the head of Old Falls Pond. Then 1.5 miles of paddling brings you down the pond to the high-power dam at the end. This should be portaged on the left, down a steep hill 150 yards. Below the start about 200 yards, just around the bend, is a sharp rapid, which should be scouted before running if the river is in flood. Once through the rapid, the river becomes quiet with a fair current and good hemlock woods on the right bank. The valley soon widens out, and in 4.5 miles you come to the bridge at West Kennebunk. The old dam just below the bridge has a short rapid just below it.

In 0.5 mile more, the railroad culvert is reached; in another 200 yards is a dam at a mill, where there is a short, steep carry on the right bank to the rapids. These 0.25-mile-long rapids are easily run to the slackwater, which continues for 1.0 mile to the Maine Turnpike bridge. The next 2.0 miles of meandering river to the US 1 bridge in Kennebunk pass through farmlands on both sides. In Kennebunk, it is best to take out above the bridge. The rapids below drop to tidewater.

Tidal Rivers South of Portland

Paddling in tidal marshes does not involve either the risks or the specialized equipment required for paddling along exposed shorelines. Both open canoes and flatwater kayaks, along with basic quickwater paddling skills are generally sufficient. Birders and amateur naturalists will find salt marsh exploration particularly enjoyable.

Scarborough, Nonesuch, Libby, and Spurwink River

Description:	Tidal
Date checked:	2000
Navigable:	Anytime; check tide chart
Scenery:	Rural, settled, salt marsh
Maps:	Portland 15; DL 3

Scarborough River

The Scarborough River is formed by the joining of Cascade Brook and Dunstan River near West Scarborough, which is also called Dunstan Corner. It is the largest of several streams emptying into the estuary that separates Pine Point from Prouts Neck. For a 4.75-mile trip, put in at the Scarborough Marsh Nature Center (which provides boat rentals and guided trips) near the time of high tide. The Nature Center, a Maine Audubon Society location, is south of US 1 on ME 9 (Pine Point Road).

For the first 0.5 mile or so, you will actually be on the Dunstan River. Cascade Brook enters through a culvert on the right. About 3 miles farther on, the river passes under a railroad trestle. The current at the strength of the ebb can be quite strong, and it passes through the trestle at a 45-degree angle. Paddlers without whitewater experience, or who are not alert, can get into difficulty here. Another mile through the widening estuary brings you to the Pine Point town landing.

Nonesuch River

The Nonesuch River has a long course through the upland parts of Scarborough, but it is so frequently obstructed by alder and fallen trees that it can be recommended only to dedicated bushwhackers.

For the recommended trip, put in at ME 207 just west of Black Point village. The river can be ascended at least 1.5 miles from here or paddled 4.0 miles down with the tide.

Downstream of this point you encounter a railroad trestle. Alternatively, you can put in at the state boat ramp on Clay Pits Road and skip it. Other than that, there are no impediments to the take-outs at either Pine Point or Ferry Beach on Prouts Neck.

Libby River

The Libby River is substantially smaller than either the Scarborough or the Nonesuch. Put in from ME 207 just west of ME 77. Respect the no trespassing signs along the river, and remember to ask for and obtain permission before crossing property lines. The Libby becomes a little scratchy at low tides. This river is excellent for viewing wildlife. You can paddle through the culvert under ME 207. Take out at Ferry Beach, which has a parking fee in the summer.

Spurwink River

The Spurwink River is not connected to the others and is of a somewhat different character. Those wishing to tour the narrow passages of the marsh can put in from Spurwink Avenue for the East Branch or from Fickett Road for the West Branch. From either point, it is 0.5 mile to ME 77, where a side road on the right comes right down to the river. This is a better start for the lower Spurwink.

The side road ends at what appears to have been an old ford, and its remnants form a Class I riffle and eddies on the ebb. There is also a lot of current under the ME 77 bridge. From ME 77 to Higgins Beach is about a mile past scenery that is more varied than the typical marsh. No good take-out or any free parking is available at Higgins Beach, which is a popular bathing beach. Often, there is an impressive surf that closes out the mouth of the river at half tide or lower. Plan to return to ME 77 (about a 5-mile round trip). If you start at high water and set a leisurely pace down and back, you may end up dragging your canoe or kayak over sandbars the last 0.25 mile up to ME 77.

Presumpscot River

The Native Americans named the river the Presumpscot, meaning the "river of many falls." Indeed, it was once an appropriate name: Wescott's Falls, Great Falls, Whitney's Falls, Island Falls, Dundee Falls, Leavitt's Falls, Gambo Falls, Little Falls, Mallison Falls, Saccarappa Falls, Ammonscongin Falls, and Presumpscot Falls all claimed the river as their home in the 1600s.

The river has changed dramatically since Europeans arrived and began developing industries along the Presumpscot's banks. Perhaps the Native Americans would have renamed the river

"river of much sludge, pollution and foam" as detritus from saw mills, paper mill effluent, town sewage, and the like poured into the waters that once teemed with salmon and other fish.

At its worst, the Presumpscot became so polluted that there was no measurable oxygen in the river at all. The water resembled a "root beer float" and was considered dead. Abandoned by all who lived nearby, its only value was its use as a cheap and convenient place to dump waste. Today the river is cleaner, but still remains one of the more-polluted rivers in Maine.

Five of the ten dams on the Presumpscot are up for relicensing by the Federal Energy Regulatory Commission. The Friends of the Presumpscot River has opposed the relicensing of three: Little Falls, Mallison Falls, Saccarappa, and supports the relicensing of two (Dundee, Gambo) provided certain conditions are met. Contact FoPR for more information: www.presumpscotriver.org.

The Presumpscot River is the largest freshwater input to Casco Bay. At times the river is a boulder-strewn rapid, at other times a calm ripple in forested ravines, and at others, placid pond water. It discharges 39,000 cubic feet per minute and falls 270 feet during its journey. Ten dams account for most of the elevation drop. The Presumpscot flows 25 miles, from Sebago Lake to Casco Bay, passing through Windham, Gorham, Westbrook, Falmouth, and Portland.

Sebago Lake Basin ➤ Smelt Hill Dam	23.5 mi
Description:	Lakes, flatwater, quickwater
Date checked:	2000
Navigable:	Spring, summer, fall (dam controlled)
Scenery:	Forested, rural, settled
Maps:	Portland 15, Gray 15; DL 5
Portages:	1.25 mi R Sebago Lake Basin Dam 80 yd
	2.1 mi R Eel Weir Canal Dam 140 yd
	3.25 mi R Great Falls Dam 140 yd
	5.0 mi R Dundee Dam 340 yd
	8.1 mi R Gambo Dam 150 yd
	9.75 mi L South Windham Dam
	10.33 mi R Mallison Dam 1.0 mi
	15.5 mi L Saccarrappa Dam 0.33 mi

Portages *(cont.)*:   16.5 mi R Cumberland Mills Dam
                                      2.75 mi
                            23.5 mi R Smelt Hill Dam 230 yd to
                                      continue or 610 yd to take-out

Access at White's Bridge Road is gone. Everything is fenced and parking is nonexistent. You can paddle down Jordan Bay from the Raymond Beach and Boat Launch on US 302 but that adds about 4 miles of big-lake paddling to the trip. Because of the orientation of Sebago, in any wind, trouble waves are guaranteed. From White's Bridge Road it is 1.2 miles across the basin to the Sebago Lake Basin Dam which maintains the lake level.

Portage on the right of all dam works. It is recommended that Eel Weir canal not be used for boating—use the river itself. Subject to water levels (releases from the Basin dam), the river needs at least April level to be runnable. Put in at the base of the ME 35 bridge. There is public parking on the east side of ME 35. This section of the river is small, mixed Class I and easy Class II, until Eel Weir Dam, and thus the end of the canal, come into view. There is a river-wide ledge here which is not runnable due to problems at the base of the vertical portion. Line or portage river left (about 200 ft).

The unrunnable ledge is in deadwater where you will see the Eel Weir dam to your right. Portage Eel Weir Canal Dam river right, and put directly into the head of North Gorham Pond. There is a stand of large pine trees at the portage site.

It is 1.2 miles to the take-out at the Great Falls Dam. Portage along North Gorham Road to the head of Dundee Pond. There is access at Pettingill Park in 0.33 mile on the left. Then it is a 1.5-mile paddle to Dundee Dam, where you should start a portage at left of center on right wing dam. Proceed to the dam access road, which is 0.5 mile of private road off Hurricane Road, go left, then right along the old canal path and put in at the end of the tailrace. Watch carefully to follow the trail as it leaves the gravel roads—signs are not always in place.

Finally the trip is on the river and not ponds. It is 1.25 miles to Babb's Bridge, a replica of an 1864 covered bridge which burned in 1973. The mouth of the Pleasant River is passed on the left in 0.6 mile. It is 0.5 mile up the river to the River Road access in Windham. In 1.8 miles, the Gambo Dam is reached on the Gambo Road. Portage to the right of an island before the bridge, and continue along the old gunpowder mill foundations to put in across from the powerhouse.

The riverbanks continue to be mostly forested in the next 1.6 miles to the South Windham Dam. A rather long portage of 0.9 mile is mandatory at this point due to private property, and no easy access or egress exists before the Mallison Dam and its power canal in 0.6 mile. Take out before the US 202/ME 4 bridge on the left and cross the bridge going 0.4 mile south to ME 237. Go left for 0.2 mile to Mallison Street on the left. In 0.1 mile, turn right onto Canal Street and go 0.2 mile to the gate to the powerhouse. Go through the parking lot to the put-in down a steep bank, always being aware that you are on private property and obtain permission before crossing (postings everywhere).

The next stretch of 5.0 miles is the longest section of continuous paddling on the river. It extends to the Saccarrappa Dam in Westbrook passing the Little River on the right in 0.75 mile. A private take-out on the left 0.2 mile above the falls is recommended, but remember to ask for and obtain permission before taking out. Portage to Bridge Street, and put in on river right downstream of the bridge. A short paddle of 1.2 miles through the wooded backyards of Westbrook ends at the River Road bridge just before the Cumberland Mills Dam. You can take out on the right in the Sappi Fine Paper parking lot. Remember to ask for and get permission before taking out.

From the Cumberland Mills dam the river is steady, deep, and murky down to the US 302 bridge. There is no marked public parking under this bridge. Below this bridge are the remains of Riverton Park on the right, now a patch of woodland. It is 2.0 miles to the Maine Turnpike bridge. Continuing with good current and wooded banks, you pass the Piscataqua

River, which might offer a mile or so of flatwater paddling. Smelt Hill Dam comes in 1.25 miles with a well-marked portage trail. A take-out here is possible with a 0.33-mile uphill portage on the dam access road through pretty woods to the Falls Road near Pleasant Hill Road. This road is private property, so under no circumstances block or park on it. To continue, put in at tidewater and in 0.25 mile pass under the high bridge. Continuing 0.5 mile farther is the ME 9 bridge and last take-out before the large estuary. This 0.75-mile section should be timed with a high tide due to mud flats at low tide.

Crooked River

The Crooked River flows from Songo Pond near Bethel south to the Songo River and Sebago Lake. Mostly it is clean and attractive, and for 53.0 miles it has scenery that includes forests typical of northern Maine (alder swamps, and stands of red maple). Many sections have a remoteness that road and topographical maps do not suggest. From the river, North Waterford is not very pretty, but the settlements of Bolsters Mills and Scribners Mill farther downstream are slices from New England's past.

In the spring, the river offers a pleasant combination of rapids and smoothwater. Below the ME 118 bridge in East Waterford, there are ten sets of rapids, which are mostly Class II with a few Class III drops. In high water, there are several sections with heavy waves. Because of the river's relatively small drainage area, the water level changes from hazardously high to undesirably low in a matter of weeks.

Albany ➤ North Waterford		9.0 mi
Description:	Flatwater, Class I, II	
Date checked:	2000	
Navigable:	High water (April)	
Scenery:	Forested	
Maps:	East Stoneham, North Waterford; DL 10	

The Crooked River here is small. In a few places, fallen trees block the stream, and in the middle section alder crowds the channel. The current is fastest at the beginning where it flows through forest, portions of which have been selectively cut.

Where the gradient lessens, the river meanders through alder thickets.

A convenient starting point within sight of the highway is from a bridge on a logging road that leaves ME 5/35 just over 5 miles north of Lynchville. For 0.75 mile, there is a mixture of rapids and flatwater. Stop above an old bridge by an abandoned farm (1.5 mi) to scout the rapids below. One half-mile below the second highway bridge, the stream enters an alder swamp through which it meanders for 2.5 miles to the ME 35 bridge in Lynchville (7.5 mi). For the next 1.5 miles to the ME 35 bridge in North Waterford (9.0 mi), the river is flat and wider.

North Waterford ➤ East Waterford	12.0 mi
Description:	Flatwater, quickwater, Class II, III
Date checked:	2000
Navigable:	High water (April)
	Medium water (May, shallow rapids)
Scenery:	Forested, towns
Maps:	North Waterford, Norway 15; DL 10

The banks of the river in North Waterford are not very attractive. Beginning at the broken dam below town, though, there are a couple of miles of good rapids mixed with quickwater. The last 6.0 miles are very crooked, with leaning swamp maple crowding the stream.

Below the ME 35 bridge less than 0.5 mile, there is a broken dam that you should scout. Then there are easy rapids as the river flows past a lumberyard. About 100 yards beyond the point where the stream approaches the highway again, stop just above a cabin on the right (1.0 mi) to scout the steep Class III rapids beside the roadside rest area. Near the top, large boulders produce heavy waves in high water with no obvious channel. The lower section is 0.75-mile long, and it contains two easier Class II drops, which can be scouted from ME 118.

Below the last drop (2.0 mi), the river leaves the highway and runs deep and slow. A distance of 2.5 miles below the rapids, the outlet from Papoose Pond enters on the right, and in another 0.25 mile there is a bridge (4.75 mi). After 1.0 mile, the river passes below the cliffs of Pulpit Rock (5.75 mi). The second bridge below the rock is ME 118 in East Waterford (12.0 mi), and it is reached after 6.25 very crooked miles.

East Waterford ➤ Scribners Mill		17.0 mi
Description:	Flatwater, Class I, II	
Date checked:	2000	
Navigable:	Spring, summer, fall	
Scenery:	Forested, rural	
Maps:	Norway 15, Sebago Lake 15; DL 10, 4, and 5	
Portage:	(17.0 mi L dam at Scribners Mill 20 yd)	
Campsite:	4.75 mi L bottom of first rapids	

This stretch makes a pleasant one-day trip with a mixture of rapids and smoothwater. There are some cabins along the river below East Waterford and Twin Bridges, and also beside McDaniel's Rips near Sodom Road. Other than that, the river is secluded all the way to Bolsters Mills. The section between Sodom Road (a name that originated in the enmities aroused by a nineteenth-century land feud) and Twin bridges is especially scenic.

The rapids between East Waterford and Sodom Road provide nice whitewater runs for paddlers with skill and good judgment. Not all who try to run these rapids possess these qualities, and many boats have been wrecked in McDaniel's Rips.

Below the ME 118 bridge are 4.5 miles of winding river that lead to a 0.25-mile-long set of rapids that begin innocently enough. Soon, though, these lead to a very sharp Class III drop followed by easier rapids that have heavy waves in high water. The river should be scouted from the left bank. Below it are two pools separated by some riffles. Then you reach McDaniel's Rips (5.0 mi). Stop on the right bank and scout them, because they begin with a drop over a ledge at the site of an old paper mill.

After the ledges associated with the mill site, there is a narrow and surprisingly steep pitch ending with a boulder midstream. Because this rock is often covered by water and hard to spot, many paddlers have been too slow to choose a path around it and have broached on it.

Beyond (about 100 yards), the drops continue as Class II or III rapids (depending on the water level), which are 0.5-mile long and taper to smoothwater at the Sodom Road bridge.

Below Sodom Road (5.5 mi) there is slackwater for 3.0 miles to a power line (8.5 mi). Shortly after that is a nice, 100-yard Class II rapid with clear channels and large waves in high water, followed almost immediately by another shorter pitch, also with heavy waves in high water. In about 0.5 mile, there are more Class II rapids at Twin Bridges.

For 0.25 mile below ME 117 at Twin Bridges (9.5 mi), the rapids continue; then, there is smoothwater for 4.25 miles to Bolsters Mills (14.0 mi). A human-made rapid replaces the dam; the rapids lead to the 0.5-mile of natural Class II rapids that are below where the dam once was. These rapids are followed by 2.5 miles of slackwater broken by one short, easy pitch about halfway to Scribners Mill (17.0 mi). If you are continuing downstream, portage on the left; or you can run the dam at the right water level.

Scribners Mill ➤ US 302	15.0 mi
Description:	Flatwater, Class I, II
Date checked:	2000
Navigable:	Spring, summer, fall
Scenery:	Forested, rural
Maps:	Norway 15, Sebago Lake 15; DL 10, 4, and 5
Portage:	10.0 mi L Edes Falls 10 yd

This section is passable all summer, although there are a few short rapids that may have to be walked down. Between Scribners Mill and Edes Falls, the river meanders for many miles through a high-banked flood plain where some sandy beaches are exposed in low water.

The portion of the river from US 302 to the Songo River is not recommended. The banks are lined with many small cabins, and there are other encroachments of civilization (such as powerboats) that the sections upstream generally lack.

To reach Scribners Mill, head south on Maple Ridge Road, about 2 miles north of Harrison on ME 117. In about 2 miles turn left on an unnamed side road—it's less than a mile to the river. If you go too far, Maple Ridge Road meets Edes Falls Road in 1.5 miles. Put in below the dam on the left. After 0.5 mile of rapids, the river is flat and winding for 9.25 miles. Near the end of the flatwater, there are a few camps on the left, some Class I rapids, and, finally, a portage on the left around the old dam at Edes Falls. Sometimes you can pass the breached dam by running over a sloping ledge on the far right (Class III).

Below Edes Falls (10.0 mi) is 0.25 mile of Class I rapids, ending just below the bridge. The last 5.0 miles are mostly flatwater. There is a good access on the left bank at the ME 11 bridge (12.75 mi) and fair access at the US 302 bridge (15.0 mi).

The last 4.25 miles to the Songo River (19.25 mi) are flat, crooked, and unattractive. From the mouth of the river, continue straight ahead through the locks to the Bay of Naples (Brandy Pond) (20.0 mi), or turn left to Sebago Lake (21.75 mi).

Pleasant River

This Pleasant River is a tributary of the Presumpscot River, which drains Sebago Lake. The Pleasant River rises east of Little Sebago Lake and flows southwest to its confluence with the Presumpscot.

US 302 ➤ River Road	4.0 mi
Description:	Flatwater, quickwater, Class I, II, III
Date checked:	2000
Navigable:	High or medium water (April or May after heavy rains)
Scenery:	Forested, rural
Maps:	Yarmouth; DL 5

Put in on the right side of US 302 going north toward North Windham. The rapids are easy for the first half of the distance to a 6-foot drop in two stages (Class III). Scout or portage on the right. Quickwater continues below for another 0.25 mile

to another double-ledge combination (Class II+), a good surfing spot. The remainder of the distance is mostly quickwater.
Take out on River Road at Lovet Bridge. Watch for trees partially blocking the river.

Royal River

The Royal River rises in Sabbathday Pond in New Gloucester
and flows east, north, and then south in that town. It continues
southward through North Yarmouth to reach the Atlantic at
Yarmouth. Except for one or two short bits, it is mostly smooth;
the parts that can be most easily paddled are wholly smooth. As a
consequence, the river can be run almost any time of year. The
upper river can probably be run in high water, but the steep drop
at Upper Gloucester must be carried.

Mill Road ➤ ME 231	1.75 mi
Description:	Quickwater, Class I
Date checked:	2000
Navigable:	High water (April, early May, passable most summers)
Scenery:	Forested, rural
Maps:	Freeport 15; DL 5

Put in where Mill Road spans the Royal River (between ME
115 and ME 231). After a Class I chute below the bridge, it is
quickwater to the next bridge. This part of the Royal is often
interrupted by fallen trees and the thick undergrowth may
make portage difficult.

ME 231 ➤ Yarmouth Waterworks	7.5 mi
Description:	Flatwater, quickwater (in spring)
Date checked:	2000
Navigable:	High water (April, early May, passable most summers)
Scenery:	Forested, rural
Maps:	Freeport 15; DL 5

You can put in at the ME 231 bridge about 0.75 mile north of
BM 167 on the Freeport topographical map, but parking
space is limited. There is a Class I rip directly under the

bridge. In the spring, this part of the Royal has a strong but smooth current, occasionally interrupted by fallen trees and beaver dams, which may effectively block the small river. Thick undergrowth may make portaging difficult; you can always lift over the dam(s).

In 1.5 miles, the Chandler River enters from the left. At the confluence the Chandler is wider, but the current is slower. You can easily ascend the Chandler 0.25 mile to North Road, where there is a short, rocky rapid (Class II in medium water) under the road bridge. A short carry on either bank gives access to flatwater, which continues upstream for about 1 mile before the increasing frequency of fallen trees becomes a nuisance.

ME 9 is a little more than 0.25 mile below the confluence of the two streams, at Dunns Crossing, which offers a good off-road put-in. In summer, unless there have been heavy rains, there is no perceptible current below Dunns, and above it the current is not enough to impede upstream travel. The next 5.75 miles are smooth and meandering with no obstructions. You will see only a few houses and one lovely farm. The second of two railroad bridges signals the end of this section, with Yarmouth Waterworks on the right. The Waterworks is on East Elm Street, which joins North Road and leads back to Dunns, making for an easy car shuttle.

The Royal River now loses its placid demeanor as it plunges over the dam below East Elm Street and continues to fall until it reaches tidewater at ME 88.

Yarmouth Waterworks ➤ Town Landing   1.0 mi

Description:	Quickwater, Class II, III, IV
Date checked:	2000
Navigable:	High water (April, early May)
Scenery:	Settled, urban
Maps:	Yarmouth; DL 5
Portages:	R Below East Elm Street 100 yd
	R First old mill site 150 yd
	L Second old mill site 100 yd

The first half of this section runs through Royal River Park, in Yarmouth. Because of the four portages (total 0.33 mile), it is hard work for the amount of paddling actually done. Water levels are critical for safe and enjoyable run on those rapids that can be run.

Just below the East Elm Street bridge is a dam built on either side of a sloping outcropping of ledge. At an ideal water level, an expert kayaker might be able to slide down this ledge (Class IV) and run the short rocky Class III rapid just below it. There is also an old 10-foot-wide mill canal that exits the pond above this dam very near the Waterworks' parking lot and runs under the street. It looks runnable, but is not, as it contains two 90-degree turns, a 4-foot drop, and a lot of debris. Carry around the dam on either side of the canal.

Less than 50 yards below the confluence of the canal and the main river, the banks become vertical and the river turns into a Class II rapid that is the lead-in to a 12-foot drop over a nearly vertical ledge. This was once the site of a mill complex, the ruins of which make up the right bank. This fall could be run at some levels in a decked boat, but would be at least Class IV, as the run would require maneuvering both above and below the steep part. Carry by the paved path on the right; by the time you come to a suitable launching spot, the stream has subsided to Class I. In 200 yards, the river passes under US 1 and into the 100-yard-long pond formed by the dam above the Sparhawk Mill.

In high water, you can put in just below the fishway and run a strong Class II–III rapid down past the mill parking lot. Most of this rapid is too rocky to run at medium or lower levels, so you must take out on the right, carry across the bridge down into the mill parking lot, and put in from the left bank. Below the Sparhawk Mill rapid are 200 yards of quickwater and easy Class I rips. Now the river swings right and then slides into a series of broken and offset ledges at another old mill site. The lower half of this rapid is under the ME 88 bridge and is flooded out by high tide. With medium water and high tide, you have a choice of highly technical routes through the ledges down to flatwater just above the bridge. At low tide and high run-off, you still have several options on the upper part, but all routes lead to two successive heavy drops under the bridge. This rapid can vary from bony Class III to thundering Class IV, depending on the interaction of runoff and the tides.

There is a gauging station on the right that can serve as a take-out or a little farther downstream there is a take-out on the left at a public parking and picnic area. This spot is marked on the river by a bare ledge. Below the rapid is a pool and the high I-95 bridge. The town landing is 200 yards downstream on the left. It is reached by Bayview Street. There are 2.0 miles of pleasant tidal paddling to the Cousins River and Casco Bay, for those wishing an opportunity to relax.

Chandler River

The Chandler River rises in Pownal and flows southwest to the Royal River.

Runaround Pond ➤ Royal River	10.0 mi
Description:	Flatwater, quickwater, Class II
Date checked:	2000
Navigable:	High or medium water (April or May, some sections passable after heavy rains)
Scenery:	Forested, rural, settled
Maps:	Freeport 15; DL 5
Portages:	2.75 mi R dam 50 yd
	7.5 mi ledge lift-over

The dam at the foot of Runaround Pond is on Frickett Road halfway between North Pownal and ME 9, which are 3.0 miles apart. A paddle up the pond is possible for a warm-up.

Put in on Runaround Pond Road. To reach the put-in, it is necessary to carry your boat approximately 100 yards down the left side of the millpond below the old mill dam before reaching the stream. Getting into the millpond immediately at the road could be dangerous at high water as there is a possibility of being swept over the dam.

The first mile is choked with alder, but the struggle is rewarded by a subsequent mile of lovely woodland paddling in fair current to Poland Rang Road. Just below this bridge is 0.25 mile of millpond. Portage on the right along Lawrence Road to where the stream is again large enough for a canoe or kayak. A few yards of riffles bring you to the Lawrence Road bridge. In 0.5 mile there is a small broken weir that requires a lift-around unless the water is high. In 0.5 mile you pass Sweetser Road, and 0.25 mile below is 0.25 mile of rapids that are Class II when runnable. The one possible channel has lots of turns. Beyond the rapids is 1.0 mile of quickwater to Elmwood Road. To Hadsey Road is 0.75 mile of quickwater; the hardwood gives way to alder, but there is still room to paddle. The last mile is uneventful except for two ledges halfway along. The first is a sloping drop of 1.5 feet, the second is a 1-foot vertical drop. These might be up to Class II in high water and must be lifted around in low water. You can take out at Milliken Road, but the climb up is steep on either side.

Just below Milliken Road is a jagged ledge drop, which probably can never be run clean. The ledge drop is surrounded by barbed-wire fences. The river meanders 3.0 miles with some current to North Road and is occasionally obstructed by fallen trees.

Under the North Road bridge is a short rip. It is 0.25 mile to the Royal River and another 0.25 mile down it to ME 9 at Dunns Corner, where there is good off-road parking.

Paddling upstream from the lower end is also possible for a mile or more.

Cathance River

The Cathance River rises north of Bradley Pond and flows south to Topsham; there, it turns abruptly and flows northeast to tidewater at Bowdoinham. The river is very small, alternating smooth stretches with short rapids and ledges. These may be run, lined, or carried, depending on water height, type of boat, and skill of party. This is a fun river for paddlers with good skill in whitewater and a realistic estimate of their abilities.

US 201 ➤ Bowdoinham 6.5 mi

Description:	Flatwater, quickwater, Class I, II, III, IV, V, tidal
Date checked:	2000
Navigable:	Medium water or after heavy rains
Scenery:	Forested, settled
Maps:	Bath 15; DL 6
Portage:	2.5 mi R 15-foot waterfall 50 yd

Put in at the boat launch from US 201 just north of Topsham/Brunswick. From this put-in the river is 20 feet wide, deep, and there is almost no current. For 0.5 mile, it follows under and along I-95. As it curves away, the current becomes noticeable. A mile from the start the first rapid is reached, runnable but scratchy, a taste of things to come. There are many short, steep pitches, each with a quiet pool below, and easy to scout. Several are narrow, sharp curves with a width of 4 to 6 feet. Each drop after the first one should be scouted. The channels often have snags or boulders obstructing them. **Caution!** The 15-foot waterfall (2.5 mi) starts with several small, easy, waves but **do not be fooled**; take out on the right as soon as you see the horizon line and before entering the rapid. Once in the rapid there is only one tiny eddy on the right to save you from being swept over the falls.

Below Cathance Road bridge is a 15-foot waterfall, which can be carried on the right. Access is very poor at the bridge. From this point, the river is a tidal marsh. The scenery is good, with only a few scattered cottages and many birds. The tide is a couple of hours later than Portland. Take out at a boat launching ramp at Bowdoinham.

Sasanoa River

The Sasanoa is an entirely tidal passage that runs northwest-southeast connecting the tidal parts of the Kennebec and Sheepscot Rivers. Midway through its course, at Hockomock Bay, it meets and mixes with the Back River. The Back River also connects the Kennebec to the Sheepscot, but goes northeast-southwest.

You can do the trip in either direction, but timing the tide is critical if you want to go with the current at the two tidal rapids known as Upper and Lower Hell Gate. High water at Bath is 1 hour later than at Portland; at Upper Hell Gate, 1 hour and 11 minutes later than Portland; Mill Point, 35 minutes later; and Robinhood, 14 minutes later.

Knubble Bay ➤ Bath	7.0 mi
Description:	Tidal, tide race
Date checked:	2000
Navigable:	Anytime (check tide tables)
Scenery:	Rural, settled, urban
Maps:	NOS chart 13293 preferred to Bath 15 and Boothbay 15; DL 6 and 7

You can reach the AMC Knubble Bay Camp by following Webber Road that turns left off the paved road to Robinhood. From the camp it is about 0.5 mile to Beal Island (camping by previous registration only, www.outdoors.org). Lower Hell Gate is between Beal and Westport islands. The current swirls through the crooked passageway, creating many low waves, irregular eddies, and, occasionally, small whirlpools. It might be considered Class II at maximum strength on the ebb 3 or 4 hours after high water; near slack, it is more like Class I. The correct exit from Hockomock Bay is hard to find without a chart or knowledge of buoy markings. The white dome of the Maine Yankee nuclear power plant on the northeastern arm of the Back River is the only real landmark.

Upper Hell Gate is 1.0 mile west of where the Sasanoa leaves Hockomock Bay; it is nothing more than the constriction of the already-narrow channel and will appear trivial to whitewater paddlers. A Class I chute with waves at most times, it can be tricky if powerboats are trying to pass at the same time.

In another 0.5 mile the Sasanoa opens into Hanson Bay, which is shallow and can be choppy in a blow. Follow the current between Preble and Sasanoa points and out into the Kennebec. Take out at the municipal floats just upstream of the US 1 bridge on the west or at the boat ramp near the sewage treatment plant 1.0 mile farther up the Kennebec.

Kennebec River

Bath to Lines Island and Return   6.0 mi

As a continuation of the Sasanoa River trip, or separately, it is not too difficult to continue up the Kennebec River to round Lines Island and return.

If the tide is ebbing, hug the western bank and use the eddies to get upstream. Then ferry across and go up Burnt Jacket Channel east of Lines Island and come back down the western channel with the main current.

Sheepscot River

The Sheepscot River rises in Montville and flows southwest through Palermo and Somerville to Whitefield, where it is joined by the West Branch. From there, it flows southward past Wiscasset to the sea between Georgetown and Southport.

Sheepscot Pond ➤ Coopers Mills   12.5 mi
Description:	Quickwater, Class I, II
Date checked:	2000
Navigable:	Medium and high water
Scenery:	Forested
Maps:	Vassalboro 15, North Whitefield; DL 13

North of ME 3 in Palermo, the Sheepscot is mostly impassable. From ME 3, it is 0.75-mile of flatwater to Sheepscot Pond. A dam and a state fish hatchery are at the outlet 3.0 miles down below the pond. Below the bridge at the hatchery, the river is only a canoe-length wide with steep rapids underneath overhanging branches, runnable only in high water. The river can be reached another 0.75 mile downstream. From this road to just north of ME 105 is flatwater with frequent beaver dams.

A short section of quickwater begins at an old dam site just north of ME 105 and extends south approximately 1,000 feet to the gravel road south of ME 105, followed by more flatwater to Long Pond. Three miles down Long Pond the pond narrows into a river again. Approximately 1 mile more brings you to a 7-foot dam above the old bridge at Coopers Mills.

Coopers Mills ➤ Whitefield   9.5 mi

Description:	Flatwater, quickwater, Class II, III
Date checked:	2000
Navigable:	High and medium water
Scenery:	Forested, rural
Maps:	DL 13

There is 1.0 mile of rapids below the dam, the first 0.5 mile of which is Class III in high water and too rocky at other levels. It is narrow with one sharp drop and overhanging obstacles, which make it dangerous. The next mile to the junction with the West Branch (2.0 mi) is mostly smoothwater.

If you wish to put in at the junction of the West Branch, it is probably better to use the side road (Howe Road) that crosses the West Branch just above the junction rather than attempt to take the boats down the steep bank from ME 218 on the eastern shore. The next 2.0 miles to the ME 126 bridge at North Whitefield (4.0 mi) are smooth going. There is a USGS gauging station at this bridge. The next 5.5 miles of winding river to Whitefield are smooth, past many fields and some wooded banks to a dam.

Whitefield ➤ Head Tide   6.0 mi

Description:	Quickwater, Class II
Date checked:	2000
Navigable:	High water (early to mid-April)
	Medium water (late April to early May, or after heavy rains)
Scenery:	Forested, rural
Maps:	Wiscasset 15; DL 13
Portage:	(6.0 mi dam)

This is a very popular open-canoe run in early to mid-April, as it is not too difficult and it usually ices-out before most other streams. However, it is dry and bony after the spring runoff.

Below the washed-out dam is a 2-foot ledge that makes an interesting sousehole at high water. The put-in is easier from the right, but take care not to block access to the private home just downstream, and always remember to ask for permission before crossing property lines. The pool below the ledge has a fast jet down its middle, which divides around a low island. Most of the river goes left, and beginners often have difficulty crossing the jet to get to a deep channel; the right channel is usually too shallow to run.

Fast current with some waves and occasional rocks continues for about 0.5 mile, and then winds down to mostly smoothwater that continues to a pair of old bridge abutments. There, the Wiscasset, Waterville, and Farmington Narrow Gauge Railway once crossed the river. There is a short Class II pitch here, then 1.0 mile of flatwater to the beginning of a 2-mile stretch of continuous Class II rapids through wooded banks. These rapids ultimately diminish to Class I riffles; then the river kinks left and right by a large rock outcrop on the left, 100 yards above the muddy take-out on the right bank above the dam at Head Tide. If water is going over the crest of this dam, the rapids above will be mostly low waves with few visible rocks. If more than 6 inches of the upstream face of the dam are dry, the rapids will be rocky and technical.

Head Tide ➤ Wiscasset		11.5 mi
Description:	Tidal	
Date checked:	2000	
Navigable:	Anytime	
Scenery:	Forested, rural	
Maps:	DL 13 and 7	

For the next 1.5 miles to Alna, the river winds, nearly meeting itself, flowing over a gravel bottom, which causes riffles in high water but is dry going in low water. Although the tidal effect is felt above Alna, the river is still moderate in size and provides a pleasant paddle for the next 5.5 miles to the bridge at Sheepscot. This is the second bridge to replace the original bridge, a toll bridge from 1794 to 1894 that provided the earliest crossing of the river. You may wish to take out here. Below the bridge is the reversing falls. You may wish to go down the widening estuary 5.0 miles to Wiscasset, which is well worth visiting with its charming old houses and interesting museum.

Sheepscot Reversing Falls

The waves and holes are formed by the outgoing tide dropping over a ledge. The flow begins 2 1/2–3 hours after high tide in Portland. (Tide charts are available on the Internet, in the local newspapers, and elsewhere.) The greater the difference in high and low tide heights, the better the wave.

Typically boaters squirt the eddy line while waiting for the wave to form. As the flow changes the wave gets steeper and more hole-like. There is a second wave/hole behind the first one and several other spots along the ledge to play in. There is plenty of room for novices to play while the wave is busy and also lots of room for swimming and multiple roll attempts/practice.

How to get there:

Head north out of Wiscasset on ME 218. Turn right on Sheepscot Cross Road (street sign is on the left). You will cross the river and can see if the falls have "reversed" by looking right. Take the next right.

You will pass a church and some houses. Turn down the next right (unpaved) road 0.5 mile and take the next right down a smaller dirt road. Parking is limited. This looks as if you are entering private property and you are! Remember to ask for and obtain permission before crossing property lines.

Follow the footpath on the right of the parking area down to the put-in on the upstream side of the falls and float around the point. Take-out is on the downstream side of the peninsula.

Sheepscot River (West Branch)

The West Branch rises in Palermo and flows south through China to join the main river in Whitefield. In the first few miles below Branch Pond, the river is small as it wanders through a swamp, is obstructed with debris, and has a few rocky, scarcely runnable rapids. The remainder of the river is a mixture of quickwater and rapids, with the blockage by trees becoming less frequent as the river becomes larger.

Weeks Mills ➤ Sheepscot River		11.25 mi
Description:	Quickwater, Class I, II	
Date checked:	2000	
Navigable:	Medium or high water	
Scenery:	Forested	
Maps:	Vassalboro 15, North Whitefield 15; DL 13	
Portage:	11.0 mi L ledge 25 ft or 100 yd, depending on water level	

This section of river is primarily gentle current flowing between evergreen-lined banks, interspersed by occasional rocky rapids.

The section of river immediately below Weeks Mills may be blocked by fallen trees. Check locally before starting. If the river is blocked, put in at the next bridge.

An abutment 1.5 miles above the ME 105 bridge has a chute through it. Starting shortly above the bridge is a rocky Class II rapid with a small ledge continuing down to the bridge. More smoothwater is followed by 0.5 mile of scratchy rapids. There are more easy rapids and some interesting rocks by a pool above the ME 11 bridge (9.0 mi). Anyone who has had difficulty with the rapids above should take out here.

Rapids start 0.5 mile above the next bridge, gradually increasing in difficulty, and culminating in an unrunnable drop over a ledge. When you see the bridge you still have enough time and distance to get to shore before the ledge.

Rapids continue below the bridge to the confluence with the Sheepscot River 0.25 mile below. The next take-out is 2.0 miles down the main river.

Damariscotta River

The Damariscotta River is a long freshwater lake separated by a high dam from a tidal inlet. There is a reversing falls above Damariscotta, below Salt Bay.

Damariscotta ➤ South Bristol	13.0 mi
Description:	Tidal
Date checked:	2000
Navigable:	Anytime
Scenery:	Rural, settled, towns
Maps:	Wiscasset 15, Boothbay 15 or NOS chart 13293; DL 7
Campsite:	10.5 mi Fort Island

Put in from the public boat ramp in Damariscotta at or shortly after high water, which occurs 16 minutes later than at Portland. The river is wide, and the well-marked channel is deep enough for sizable yachts. In about 5 miles, the channel makes a sharp kink to the right around a hidden ledge off the end of Fitch Point. The ledge, which uncovers at half tide, creates a minor tide rip when covered and large eddies when bare. In another 2.5 miles on the left you will see the University of Maine's Darling Center Marine Lab on Wentworth Point. You pass between Miller and Carlisle islands 1.0 mile farther; they make good lunch stops.

Two miles beyond Carlisle Island is Fort Island, which boasts a campsite and the remains of a very small redoubt. Between Fort Point, the eastern end of the island, and the left bank is a powerful tidal race. At strength, it sometimes tows the navigational buoy completely under. Give it the same respect as a Class II rapid. Even though wide open, the eddy lines are irregular and abrupt.

East Boothbay is 1.5 miles beyond Fort Island on the west. You could take out here, but parking near the water is limited and the shuttle route is circuitous. A better idea would be to cross 1.5 miles to South Bristol on the eastern bank and take out near the town float on the southern side of the gut near a small store.

Pemaquid River

The Pemaquid River starts at Pemaquid Pond and flows through Biscay Pond and then southward past Bristol until it reaches tidewater at Pemaquid.

The dam at Bristol has raised the level of the connecting streams above, but the dams farther downstream are out, leaving shallow rapids.

Pemaquid Pond ➤ Bristol Dam		6.5 mi
Description:	Lake, flatwater	
Date checked:	2000	
Navigable:	Anytime	
Scenery:	Forested	
Maps:	Waldoboro West, Louds Island, Bristol; DL 7	
Portage:	(6.5 mi R Dam at Bristol)	

This trip is highly suitable for beginning paddlers as it is all flatwater, but pleasant; it is best suited as a lake paddle rather than a through trip.

Start at a launching ramp at the northern end of Pemaquid Pond. Paddle 6.25 miles south to the outlet. You could take a side trip up the outlet stream 1.75 miles to Duckpuddle Pond.

Continuing south, it is 2.5 miles down Biscay Pond to its outlet, a short, marshy paddle to the ponded Pemaquid River and another 2.25 miles to the dam above Bristol.

Bristol ➤ Pemaquid		5.0 mi
Description:	Pond, flatwater, quickwater, Class I, II	
Date checked:	2000	
Navigable:	Medium to medium-low water	
Scenery:	Forested, rural	
Maps:	Bristol; DL 7	
Portage:	5.0 mi gorge 200 yd	

The middle section of this river is a delightful paddle but lacks a good access. It is guarded by awkward rapids at the beginning and end. If runnable, the rapids may be Class III. This section should be enjoyed on a warm day with fairly low water and the boat waded down the rapids. Portaging is not feasible at either end.

Because of the rapids below the dam and the gabions in the river, it is best to put in below the last bridge in Bristol, 0.75 mile below the dam. A short stretch of rapids leads to an open marsh with occasional beaver dams. In another mile, you reach the old dam above Bristol Mills Road. The steep drop there should be waded down.

From this bridge (do not trespass on private property) another 0.5 mile of river with some beaver dams leads into Boyd Pond. Going down the pond, keep right into outlet, where it is 1.75 miles of marsh and riffles to the final ledges, 0.1 mile above the ME 30 bridge at Pemaquid. Below the bridge, the river drops steeply for 200 yards through an old mill site and another 200 yards to tidewater.

Medomak River

The Medomak River rises in Liberty and flows south to the ocean at Waldoboro. The river is small and meandering above Medomak Pond. Below the pond, much of the distance is flat and probably passable at most water levels. But this stretch is interspersed with several rapids, which are impressive at high water and impassable at low water. All these drops were once dammed, but all traces of the dams are now gone except for the one below Flanders Corner.

Carroll Road ➤ Medomak Pond	6.5 mi
Description:	Flatwater, quickwater, Class I, II
Date checked:	2000
Navigable:	Flatwater (most water levels)
	rapids (medium to medium-high water)
Scenery:	Forested
Maps:	Jefferson, Waldoboro West; DL 13

The first mile below the ME 220 bridge is smooth. Just above the next bridge, the river drops through the rocky site of an old dam. This section should give a fair representation of water conditions for the rest of the river.

Shortly below the bridge, the Medomak fans out through a boulder field, which necessitates some lifting over for passage at any safe water level. At 0.25 mile below the bridge, a breach in the old dam can probably be run. After dispersing briefly through another boulder pile below the dam, the river flattens out into the beginning of a long, quiet section. Most of the remaining distance to Winslow Mills is flat, with occasional quickwater and riffles. Three ledges break this placid run. The first and easiest is around a left turn and ends in a pool. The second is slightly more difficult. The third is at least Class III and may be unrunnable at some water levels. In any case, it should be scouted.

The current picks up as the next bridge (8.0 mi) is reached. Around the corner below, it is a scratchy drop and then easier going to the next bridge (10.5 mi) at Winslow Mills, with a drop through the old dam site. The rapid below soon smoothes out to slow current to the US 1 bridge at Waldoboro. Take out at the picnic area downstream on the right on ME 32.

Rapids start around the corner, leading to a dangerous waterfall at an old dam site behind the Legion hall. In another 0.25 mile (immediately below the next bridge) is a dam. Following a short, rocky section, the river opens up into a wide, flat expanse above town. At the Main Street bridge (another 0.25 mile), the river falls over another rocky drop to tidewater.

Saint George River

A number of lakes near Liberty form the headwaters of the Saint George River. West of Searsmont, it becomes large enough to run in high water, and lower down it is passable at all seasons. It is an easy river, but nonetheless, there are a half-dozen places where you must use caution.

The Saint George is an outstanding choice for someone who wishes to travel through rural Maine. Although many miles of its banks are forested, the river flows through several small towns and past numerous farms. There are three large ponds where the typical view includes hillside fields and barns, although there are some cottages along the shores. An occasional pair of stone bridge abutments confine the river momentarily, and two washed-out dams suggest that the river is better left unharnessed.

The upper section of the river offers the most interesting paddling. Flatwater alternates with rapids and ponds. In high water, you can probably put in below the dam on Trues Pond in Montville, but a start above Woodmans Mills is not recommended in medium water. You may also begin on Quantabacook Pond off ME 3 and paddle south to the river at Searsmont.

The lower Saint George River can be run at all water levels. It is all lake or flatwater except for a total of 0.75 mile of rapids, where you will need to wade or drag in low water.

The 5.5 miles from Warren to Thomaston are tidal. The river here, somewhat wider and lined with salt marshes, is attractive.

A road map and the text that follows will supply all the information needed to run this river. Of the USGS maps, the Union quadrangle is the most helpful.

Woodmans Mills ➤ Seven Tree Pond		21.5 mi
Description:	Flatwater, quickwater, Class I, II, III	
Date checked:	2000	
Navigable:	High water (early May)	
	Medium water (some wading, early June)	
Scenery:	Forested, rural, towns	
Maps:	Washington, Searsmont Union; DL 14	
Portages:	5.5 mi L ledge drops in Searsmont	
	7.75 mi R dam 100 yd	
	17.75 mi e dam 50 yd/0.25 mi	
Campsite:	18.0 mi L in pine-hemlock grove	

Woodmans Mills is located on ME 173 about 3 miles west of Searsmont where West Appleton Road branches south and almost immediately crosses the river. There is a small ledge drop and some minor rips just below the bridge. Then, for 0.5 mile, the river is small and occasionally crowded with alder, but the current is strong.

For the next 4.0 miles, the river is mostly smooth. The flatwater is occasionally broken by short rips, which in high water are barely noticeable. After the first 1.5 miles, there is a 0.25-mile Class II rapid with a ledge near the beginning that must be lined in medium water and should be scouted in high water.

More rapids (4.5 mi) begin as you approach ME 173 west of Searsmont. **Caution!** They begin as Class II, but just above the ME 173 bridge (4.75 mi) there is an old washed-out mill dam that must be scouted. Class II rapids continue to a short flat-water section above the bridge in Searsmont.

Caution! In high water, stop above the ME 131/173 bridge in Searsmont (5.5 mi). There are two difficult ledge drops directly below this bridge. In medium water you can lift over the left side of each ledge, but you are likely to get wet doing it. Below, easy rapids taper to flatwater by the time you reach the outlet from Quantabacook Lake (5.75 mi). There is an alternative put-in in Searsmont on ME 173/131 at the Quantabacook outlet. This is the most popular put-in and the starting point for the Saint George canoe race. In approximately 2.0 miles there is a Class III rapid at the former site of a wooden dam.

Below the bridge at Ghent (7.75 mi), there is about 1 mile of Class II rapids. After 0.5 mile of quickwater, there is a short rapid called Magog Chute. It can be run at any level but should be scouted because, depending on the water level and paddler skills, it can be run left, center, or right. The next 4.0 miles to Appleton are mostly flat, but there is a 0.25-mile Class II rapid that begins at the ME 105 bridge (10.25 mi). Another one begins 0.25 mile above Appleton, where the banks of the river become steep (13.0 mi). These last rapids continue past Appleton, but under the bridge there is another ledge drop that can be lined in medium water and should be scouted in high water.

Below Appleton (13.25 mi), wide, shallow rapids continue for 0.5 mile, followed by 1.75 miles of flatwater to Sennebec Pond (15.5 mi). There is a boat landing at the southern end where ME 105/131 skirts the pond (17.5 mi). There is a dam 0.25 mile below Sennebec Pond. If you carry on the right and put in below it, there is 0.25 mile of Class II rapids with a sharp Class III ledge drop halfway down in the middle of an S-turn. There is a steep portage on the left. You may also portage the dam and rapids by following a dirt road between the river and the canal on the left-hand side. Near the end of the canal, continue straight to a stand of conifers where there is a campsite (18.0 mi).

A 1-mile section of quickwater begins a short distance below the pool by the campsite. In the first 0.5 mile, there are several large trees, which partially block the channel. The fastwater continues under the ME 17/131 bridge (19.0 mi) to a sharp, Class II rapid (19.25 mi) just above the bridge in Union. After 1.5 miles of quickwater and flatwater, the Saint George River opens into Round Pond (20.75 mi).

The outlet of Round Pond is directly to the east, with flatwater the remaining 0.5 mile to the ME 235 bridge (21.5 mi). This brings you to the edge of Seven Tree Pond where there is a public access ramp.

Seven Tree Pond ➤ Warren   8.75 mi

Description:	Lake, flatwater, Class I, II
Date checked:	2000
Navigable:	High water (early May)
	Medium water (early June)
	Low water (passable, some lining required)
Scenery:	Forested, rural, towns
Maps:	Union, West Rockport, Thomaston; DL 243

This section begins with a 2-mile paddle to the southern end of Seven Tree Pond, followed by flatwater most of the way to Warren. One half-mile past an old railroad trestle is Middle Road bridge (4.25 mi). Two miles beyond, the edge of a field on the right marks the beginning of 0.5 mile of Class I rapids. You pass under a power line 0.25 mile before reaching the rapids (8.25 mi) just above Warren.

The rapids at Warren begin with a sharp, turbulent drop between a pair of old bridge abutments. There is a steep portage on the left. Beyond, there is 0.25 mile of Class II rapids that end at a power line. There is a good take-out point on the right above the ME 90 bridge (8.75 mi).

Except at high tide, there is a short rip under the bridge in the town of Warren (9.0 mi), with more easy rapids continuing beyond when the tide is out. In the spring, passage down these rapids is blocked by a fish weir.

At low tide, there is a Class I rapid 0.75 mile below Warren. The river passes under US 1 (12.25 mi), widens, then passes through a narrow, wooded valley before reaching the Wadsworth Street bridge in Thomaston, where there is a boat landing on the right (14.5 mi).

Oyster River

The Oyster River rises in Rockport and crashes its way to tidewater on the Saint George River.

West Rockport ➤ Warren		11.5 mi
Description:	Flatwater, quickwater, swamp, Class I, II, III, IV	
Date checked:	2000	
Navigable:	High water	
Scenery:	Wild, forested	
Maps:	Thomaston, West Rockport; DL 14	
Portages:	Many	
	5.0 mi R Falls	
	8.0 mi R Falls	

From the start at Mill Street in West Rockport, the Oyster River is a tiny stream with more blowdowns than water. Two miles below an old dam site and ford (3.0 mi) is "Dan's Demise," a narrow gorge. Portage on the right. Just past East Warren Road (7.25 mi), there is a complicated set of ledges followed by a series of sharp drops ending at Great Falls, where there is good access. Below the falls, the river mellows and is wider to the Saint George.

Although short it is an intense run, frustrating in low water and hair-raising in high. Unlike most remote streams, it is conveniently located not more than a 30-minute drive from nice, warm eateries in Camden.

Down East Coastal Canoe Trail

Various people have been working to establish a relatively safe tidewater-paddling route with supporting campsites to make a weeklong trip from Portland to Pemaquid feasible. This is a brief excerpt from their material.

The recommended route starts from Spring Point, in South Portland. It goes between Peaks and Diamond islands and west of Long Island. The first campsite is Little Chebeague Island (6.0 mi).

The route then passes south and east of Great Chebeague Island and west of Hope, Bangs, and Stockman Islands. Turning east, it passes south of Basin and Potts Points to a campsite in Harpswell Sound (12.0 mi).

Continue north up Harpswell Sound; proceed through Erwin Narrows, Long Reach, and the Gurnet Strait, turning southeast into the New Meadows River. The portage to the Kennebec is made from Winnegance Bay to Winnegance Creek (Winnegance is a Native American word meaning "small portage"). Meadowbrook, a commercial campground, is near the portage trail (12.0 mi).

The portage starts at a boat-launching ramp at the eastern end of Brighams Cove. Continue over the ridge and along the trees beyond to the trail down to the water. A short portage must be made at the ME 209 bridge. Go up the Kennebec to Bath and turn east into the Sasanoa River to Beal Island, where advance reservations are required for camping (10.0 mi). Access at the AMC Knubble Bay Camp 0.75 mile to the southwest.

From Beal Island, continue south down the Sasanoa River, cross the Sheepscot River to Townsend Gut, continue across Boothbay Harbor, and round south of Spruce Point and north to East Boothbay. Portage from the boat ramp across the road into a pool and then through a culvert (when tide conditions permit). Go north up the Damariscotta River to Fort Island (12.0 mi).

Return to South Bristol, and go through the Gut to the finish at the boat ramp just north of Fort William Henry (5.0 mi).

Wind, weather, and fog conditions make it highly likely that the trip will be dealyed at some point. Allow for rest days or an alternate take-out when making plans.

The entire route is on National Ocean Survey Chart #13288 (Monhegan Island to Cape Elizabeth). Greater detail is found on #13293 (Damariscotta, Sheepscot, and Kennebec Rivers) and #13290 (Casco Bay).

For further information, contact the Maine Island Trail Association, 60 Ocean Street, Rockland ME 04841 (207-594-9209).

Chapter 8
Eastern Coastal Watersheds

EASTERN COASTAL
WATERSHEDS

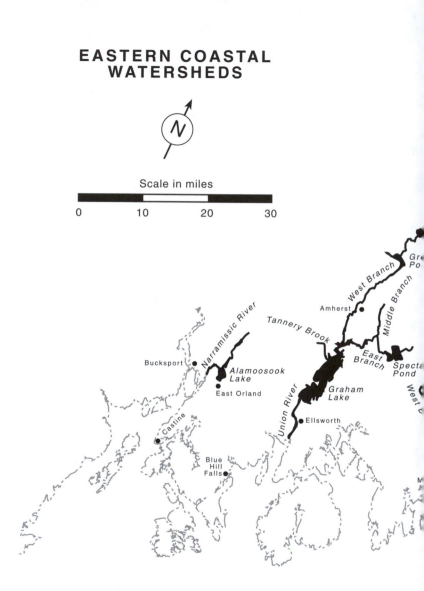

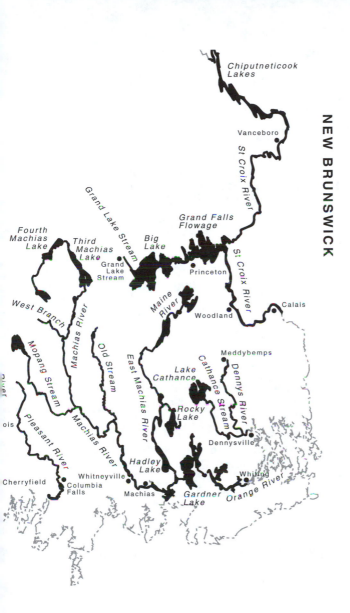

Blue Hill Falls

Blue Hill Falls is a tidal rip that is a good place for practice in handling rough water. You frequently see canoes and kayaks playing in these rapids.

There are approximately 100 yards of rugged whitewater that can be traversed repeatedly using the large eddy on the right. The trip can be run anytime the tide is right.

The falls is located by ME 175 where the bridge crosses the entrance to Salt Pond 3.0 miles southeast of Blue Hill.

Best runs start 3 hours after low tide. The falls start slowly and within 3 hours build up to Class IV.

Narramissic River

The Narramissic River is the outlet of Alamoosook Lake and is the last freshwater section of a collection of lakes and ponds that flow into the Penobscot River at its mouth. The tidal section below Orland is called the Orland River for the last few miles to the Penobscot.

The largest lake that drains into Alamoosook Pond is Toddy Pond, which is pretty and somewhat wild at the southern end; but its outlet is not runnable. The farthest upstream starting point is on Mill Dam Brook near Dedham. This flows into Long Pond, the outlet of which is Moosehorn Stream, which flows through Dead River to Alamoosook Lake.

Dedham ➤ Alamoosook Lake	10.25 mi
Description:	Lake, flatwater, quickwater, swamp, Class I, II
Date checked:	2000
Navigable:	Medium water, lakes anytime
Scenery:	Forested
Maps:	Orland 15, Bucksport 15; DL 23
Portage:	(10.25 mi dam at outlet)

The put-in is on ME 46 where several brooks join just below Dedham. The going is heavy through a swamp and over deadfalls and beaver dams to Long Pond (2.75 mi).

Continuing on Moosehorn Stream from Long Pond (4.75 mi), the river flows over a short rapid. There is quickwater and Class I rapids down to the ME 46 bridge, which is too low to pass under in high water. The stream slows for a while and then drops over the most difficult rapids on the trip. There, the stream is small and full of sharp turns under a small bridge on a dirt track. Soon it slows down and widens out, passing through a marshy area into the Dead River (7.5 mi), which is really a northern arm of the lake now, due to the backwater from the dam. It is 2.0 miles down Dead River to the narrows and another mile down the lake and around the corner to the dam.

Alamoosuk Lake ➤ Orland		3.0 mi
Description:	Flatwater, quickwater	
Date checked:	2000	
Navigable:	Spring, summer, fall	
Scenery:	Forested, rural	
Maps:	Orland 15; DL 23	
Portage:	(3.0 mi dam at Orland)	

This is a pleasant run through fields and woods that can be done as a return trip.

Union River

The confluence of the East and West branches of the Union River is now flooded out at the northern end of Graham Lake.

Graham Lake	14.75 mi

From the last bridge on the West Branch on ME 181, it is 2.75 miles to the confluence with the East Branch, and another mile to a boat ramp on the western bank. Beyond a large island the lake opens up, narrowing again toward the southern end and the dam.

Graham Lake ➤ Ellsworth	4.5 mi

Below the dam, the river is mostly smooth for the next 4.0 miles to Ellsworth, except for a bit of quickwater at Ellsworth Falls halfway down. Below the high dam at Ellsworth, the river is tidal.

Union River (West Branch)

The West Branch of the Union River is formed by a collection of brooks south of Passadumkeag Mountain and flows south to meet the sea south of Ellsworth. There, it feeds into the complex of bays around Mount Desert on the eastern side of Penobscot Bay. When the water is high, it offers relatively easy paddling with easy rapids. It should generally be run before the black-fly season.

The "Union River canoe trip" starts at Brandy Pond, follows Brandy Stream to Main River and from there to Great Pond. The West Branch of the Union is the outlet of Great Pond.

Brandy Pond ➤ Great Pond		8.5 mi
Description:	Flatwater, quickwater	
Date checked:	2000	
Navigable:	High water	
Scenery:	Forested	
Maps:	Saponic 15; DL 25 and 34	
Portage:	6.5 mi short carry	

Brandy Pond can be reached from the private road, open to the public, which runs north from the ranger's cabin on ME 9 at Beddington. The outlet, Brandy Stream, carries the drainage from Passadumkeag Mountain. These two streams join to form Main Stream, which for the next 3.0 miles meanders westward until it turns south. About 1.5 miles below this turn it passes under the bridge of the logging road, and 0.5 mile below this bridge fastwater begins and continues for 1.0 mile to Great Pond. At 0.5 mile below the junction with Alligator Stream there is a short, but difficult, carry over a 6-foot pitch. Main Stream enters Great Pond near the middle of the northern shore. From here, it is 2.0 miles across the pond to the outlet at the southeastern end.

Many paddlers may want to avoid this section because of the long shuttle and the difficult carry around the 6-foot pitch, which can only be run by expert paddlers.

Great Pond (Dow Pines) ➤ Amherst		11.0 mi
Description:	Quickwater, Class III, IV	
Date checked:	2000	

Navigable:	High water (April and May)
Scenery:	Forested, blueberry barrens
Maps:	Saponac 15, Great Pond 15; DL 34 and 24
Portages:	Optional, see text.

Great Pond can be reached by a good road that leaves ME 9 about 1 mile past Aurora. There is a landing at Dow Pines; ask for and obtain permission to park there at the main office.

From Dow Pines to the outlet is 1.0 mile of lake paddling. The dam that used to mark the beginning of the Union River is now gone. The river starts with 2.0 miles of flatwater that lead to a gentle Class II ledge drop under a defunct logging bridge. More flatwater leads to a Class II, 2-foot ledge drop that is best run on the right center. Next are 200 yards of easy Class II water that lead to a pool above Hell's Gate (3.25 mi). Stop and scout; a portage can be done on either side. Hell's Gate is a three-step, Class III drop that can approach Class IV at high water. To run this drop, start left, go center, and end left.

The next 6.0 miles are mostly smooth, but there are three significant ledge drops that should be scouted. The first of these drops is Class III–IV. There is a clean chute on the left side of the 5-foot drop while the easiest portage is on the right. The next rapid is a 3- to 4-foot drop that is rated Class III, IV. It is best run or portaged right. The Gauging Station is a popular take-out on Tannery Road (10.25 mi). The final drop (Class IV) is found in a right turn just past the Gauging Station and just above the Tannery Road bridge. Scout and run on the right. A tricky left turn leaves little margin for error. After the rapid, there is a take-out under the bridge on the right; or you can continue another 0.75 mile to ME 99 and take out there.

Amherst ➤ Graham Lake		6.0 mi
Description:	Quickwater, Class II	
Date checked:	2000	
Navigable:	Spring, summer, fall	
Scenery:	Forested	
Maps:	Great Pond 15, Ellsworth 15; DL 24	
Portage:	3.0 mi R waterfall	

The next 3.0 miles are meandering quickwater to a 10-foot waterfall, followed by 100 yards of Class II. Following this, you reach the backwaters of Graham Lake. Take out at Goodwin Bridge on ME 181 (6.0 mi).

Union River (East Branch)

The East Branch of the Union River drains a number of ponds east of Beddington, and flows west and then south into the upper end of Graham Lake north of Ellsworth to join the main river.

Steep Landing ➤ ME 179	14.25 mi
Description:	Lake, flatwater, quickwater, marsh, Class I, II
Date checked:	2000
Navigable:	Spring, after heavy rains
Scenery:	Wild, forested
Maps:	Great Pond, Lead Mountain 15; DL 24
Portages:	7.5 mi R Ledge Falls (optional)
	10.5 mi R Island Rips (optional)
Campsite:	3.0 mi Spectacle Pond

Steep Landing is where the esker crosses the river 2.0 miles below Rocky Pond. Do not try to drive down the hill the last 100 yards to the put-in; it is very steep.

The East Branch is half the size of the West Branch. The crossing of Spectacle Pond and the 2.5-mile flat paddle at the end tend to discourage the whitewater enthusiast, but the paddler with an appreciation for diversity will be delighted by the East Branch.

From Steep Landing to Spectacle Pond the river is small and flows through alternating forests and bogs. There is a short Class I rip just before the entrance to the pond (2.75 mi). Spectacle Pond has few camps and little boat traffic in spring, as well as good sand beaches and campsites.

A 3-mile paddle across the lake through the Narrows brings you to "Poison Ivy Pitch" (5.75 mi), a short, sharp drop, Class II in high water. In 1.0 mile, the Bog River (alternate start) comes in on the left, bringing a substantial volume of water.

The bog section ends at Ledge Falls (7.5 mi). Look for granite ledge on left. Portage right if desired. Ledge Falls is the site of an old timber dam; logs from the old dam sometimes tear free and complicate the lower end of this Class II–III drop.

Shortly after, the "Ramp," a delightful 2-mile section of narrow, snaky river loaded with blind bends and boulders, begins. **Caution!** Although no drop here is greater than Class II in high water, you can come upon downed trees very suddenly. The ramp ends at the junction with the Middle Branch, where you can take out (9.5 mi).

More rips are just below. A quarter-mile beyond a bridge you will find Island Rip (10.25 mi). A small channel of the river cuts right (not passable) to form a small island and a large island just beyond. The optional portage is on the right at the head of the large island; it is very easy to miss. Island Rip is 100 yards long, Class II–III, with many boulders and holes. The worst part is at the start. Below are two small Class I rips. The "Stanmoddar" (11.75 mi) is a huge, erratic boulder. Local Saxon legend has it that "Stanmoddar" gave birth to a myriad of boulders in this area.

The next 2.5 miles are smooth with little current. Take out at the large sawdust pile on the left, or below the ME 179 bridge on the right in the pool.

ME 179 ➤ West Branch   5.0 mi

Description:	Flatwater, quickwater, Class I, II
Date checked:	2000
Navigable:	High and medium water (until mid-June), after heavy rains
Scenery:	Wild
Maps:	Great Pond, Ellsworth 15; DL 24
Portage:	2.25 mi R waterfall 50-300 yd

This section is seldom paddled. About 0.5 mile below ME 179 is a ledge drop that you should look at. Pleasant paddling takes you in 1.0 mile to a bouldery bend, Class I–II (1.5 mi). Use caution on sharp bends here as they blend together.

Get out before two stone bridge abutments (the jaws of death), and scout the rapids below. Class II–III rips begin and continue right to the brink of Siltstone Falls (2.25 mi), a definite portage. Watch carefully for the portage! As there are no good eddies or rescue spots before the falls, this is one place where "going for it" may result in "getting it." Portage right. Below the falls is another short drop that changes in difficulty as the level of Graham Lake rises and falls.

There is no take-out at the confluence. Paddlers going upstream on the West Branch could drag over a peninsula (4.5 mi) to the right to the West Branch, and paddle 2.0 miles up to ME 181. From the confluence it is 12.0 miles south to Graham Lake dam. Take-out may be possible at a boat ramp on the western shore (6.25 mi).

Union River (Middle Branch)

This smaller branch of the Union River is the least used. The heaviest use is by people fishing; they usually put in at ME 9 and paddle upstream into the large bog paralleling the Whaleback.

ME 9 ➤ East Branch	6.5 mi
Description:	Flatwater, quickwater, swamp, Class I
Date checked:	2000
Navigable:	High or medium water (spring)
Scenery:	Wild
Maps:	Great Pond 15; DL 24

Below ME 9 the Middle Branch flows through a swamp with occasional beaver dams. Swamp gives way to forest, and soon the first of two Class I spots occurs. This is followed in 1.5 miles by the other Class I spot. Access is available at an old bridge crossing just before the East Branch.

Tannery Brook

Tannery Brook begins in Burnt Pond on the border of Dedham and Otis. It flows eastward through Otis and Mariaville to Graham Lake. The river drops 195 feet in 5.0 miles, but much of it is in the first 0.25 mile.

ME 180 ➤ Graham Lake   4.5 mi
Description: Class I, II, III
Date checked: 2000
Navigable: High water
Scenery: Wild
Maps: Orland 15, Ellsworth 15; DL 24

Put in at the ME 180 bridge. The river is small, and most of
the way is Class I, interspersed with ledge drops, Class II and
III. Shortly below the ME 181 bridge, it flows into Graham
Lake.

Narraguagus River

The Narraguagus flows from Deer Lake to tidewater at
Cherryfield. In the 40.0 miles described here, it drops 391 feet,
more than any coastal stream east of the Penobscot, except for
the Saint Croix, which is appreciably longer. It also has more
access points than the rivers to the east, because a road of some
kind parallels it the entire distance. Fortunately, the attractive-
ness of the river is scarcely affected, and it appears as wild as any
in Maine.

Deer Lake ➤ Deblois   25.0 mi
Description: Lakes, quickwater, Class I, II
Date checked: 2000
Navigable: High water (May)
Scenery: Forested
Maps: Tunk Lake 15, Lead Mountain 15; DL
                         34, 24, and 25
Campsites: 0 mi Deer Lake MFS $ car
                         1.25 mi L Twenty-eight Pond, permit
                         19.5 mi L Beddington Lake Outlet,
                         permit

The drop in this section is 230 feet, virtually all of which is
runnable in season. The rapids are Class I and II, except near
the end at Rock Dam Rips, a Class III pitch.

The first 4.0 miles are flat and should be avoided by paddlers
pressed for time or unwilling to cope with windfalls and

beaver dams. It is worth doing, but it will take 2 to 3 hours to paddle from Deer Lake through the Oxbow to the outlet of Haycock Pond, where the river approaches the road for the first time. Below the Oxbow, where the river flows slowly through a large meadow, there is a good current with many interesting rapids.

Lead Mountain, located north of the Airline (ME 9) and just west of the river, is a 1,475-foot landmark that is visible from various points along the Narraguagus as far upstream as the Oxbow.

It is 0.75 mile from the MFS campsite on Deer Lake to the outlet. Enroute you pass the road from Beddington, and if you can just squeeze a loaded canoe or kayak through the culvert, there will be plenty of water downstream. Below the dam for 1.25 miles the stream is flat, small, and occasionally blocked by deadfalls and choked with alder. After a log bridge (2.0 mi), the widened river meanders for 2.0 miles through the Oxbow, where there are beaver dams and a few trees across the water.

Below the Oxbow, the river approaches the road (4.0 mi), and the current picks up. As it passes Bracey Pond (out of sight to the west), there is a log bridge (6.0 mi), which is a good access point. In 0.75 mile, there is another bridge (6.75 mi); after this, there is 1.0 mile of easy rapids that end just above a large dry-ki dam. The latter may be passable on the left if the water is high enough. There is quickwater to Third Pond, and below that more good current to Twenty-eight Pond (11.0 mi).

After Twenty-eight Pond, there is good current for 3.0 miles, followed by 1.5 miles of intermittent Class I and II rapids to the Airline bridge (16.25 mi) and continuing for another 0.5 mile beyond. The paddle down Beddington Lake, beginning 1.0 mile past the Airline, may seem confusing if you follow the topographical map too closely, because the water level has dropped since it was made.

Below the old dam (19.5 mi), there is good current for 1.75 miles to Bog Brook, where it picks up. Then, 1.75 miles later, below a huge boulder on the right and out of sight around a bend to the left, is Rock Dam Rips (23.0 mi), a nice Class III rapid less than 100 yards long that should be scouted from the left bank. Beyond the rapids a short distance, there is an abrupt 3-foot ledge drop, which is easily lined down on the left. Soon the current slackens to quickwater. There is a short, easy rapid a little way above Deblois (25.0 mi). Land just above the ME 193 bridge because there is some very rough water below called Great Falls. There is a good 0.33-mile-long portage trail on the railroad tracks.

Deblois ➤ Cherryfield	17.25 mi
Description:	Flatwater, quickwater, Class I, II, III
Date checked:	2000
Navigable:	High or medium water (May through June)
	Low water (passable)
Scenery:	Wild, towns
Maps:	Tunk Lake 15, Cherryfield 15; DL 25
Portages:	0 mi R Ledges at Deblois 200 yd
	0.25 mi R Ledges 150 yd
	15.75 mi L Stillwater Dam 50 yd

The lower part of the Narraguagus is most easily characterized as a flatwater river that winds in a shallow, wooded valley. In a few locations, the blueberry barrens are visible on the hills above. From the power-line crossing to Little Falls, the banks are more open, with a thick growth of bushes and small plants overlooked by numerous dead elm trees.

At the beginning are two sections that must be portaged. Just north of the bridge in Deblois, there is a path along the river that leads in 0.33 mile past a cabin to the flatwater below the second impassable drop. In high or medium water, the part between the drops can be run. Descend to the river when you have reached the lower corner of the field (about 200 yards), and run easy Class II rapids to a pool. Take out a short distance below the pool on the right before a cabin, and portage again about 150 yards around the falls.

In the first 0.75 mile below the second portage, there are a few short Class I–II rips. Then, for approximately 9.0 miles, the river is quickwater, with a good current that lessens as you continue downstream. The only landmarks are a power line (4.25 mi) and Schoodic Brook (9.25 mi), which enters on the left as the Narraguagus turns right.

A short distance below Schoodic Brook you reach the first of two easy Class II rapids that precede Little Falls. The falls are, in fact, a Class II rapid, about 100 yards long with heavy waves in high water. The house on the left bank is owned by the Maine Atlantic Salmon Commission (www.state.me.us/asa/), and public access to the river is available here.

Below Little Falls, there are three Class II rapids, the first of which is almost flooded out in high water. Then flatwater continues past the confluence of the West Branch (15.25 mi) to Stillwater Dam.

Below Stillwater Dam (15.75 mi), there are nearly continuous rapids for 1.5 miles until you reach tidewater. The rapids are Class III, with three difficult pitches: just above and 50 yards below the railroad bridge, and just before the first road bridge. The other section are easier, but here the Narraguagus is a big river. The rapids reach tidewater about 100 yards above the US 1 bridge (17.25 mi).

Narraguagus River (West Branch)

The West Branch of the Narraguagus River rises just west of Beddington in T22 MD, and flows southeast more or less parallel to the main river until it joins it a few miles above Cherryfield. The upper part of the river is too small for paddling until it nearly reaches Deblois. You can reach it here, and run down to the main steam with easy rapids and good fishing along the way.

Denbow Heath ➤ Sprague Falls		14.0 mi
Description:	Flatwater, quickwater, swamp, Class I, II, III, IV	
Date checked:	2000	
Navigable:	High and medium water (early June)	
Scenery:	Wild, forested	
Maps:	Lead Mountain, Tunk Lake 15, Tunk Mountain; DL 24 and 25	

Portages:	5.0 mi L Rock Dam 10 yd
	10.0 mi R Long Falls 0.5 mi
	14.0 mi R Sprague Falls 150 yd

This is a beautiful, little-used river, much like other eastern-Maine streams. The rapids are granite ledges and piles of boulders. Access to the put-in is through Denbow Heath Peat Mine. Ask for and obtain permission at the mine before accessing the river.

Rock Dam is a short ledge drop about 3 feet high that should be looked over closely. Spring River enters right at 7.0 miles. Long Falls, 0.25 to 0.33 mile long and difficult, definitely must be scouted. The first pitch should probably be carried; it is strong, complicated, and narrow. There is a nice Class II–III pitch around the corner below. The main portage trail is on the railroad tracks.

There is a good take-out at Sprague Falls. These falls should be portaged on the railroad tracks for 150 yards.

Sprague Falls ➤ Narraguagus River	4.0 mi

The last section to the Narraguagus River is mostly smooth.

Pleasant River

The Pleasant River flows from Pleasant River Lake, just south of ME 9 in Beddington, to Columbia Falls. It should be distinguished from the Pleasant River that is a tributary of the Piscataquis in the Penobscot watershed and others. The Pleasant has three distinct personalities: the upper portion is a fine wilderness trip with some whitewater; the middle portion meanders through an extensive heathland ending at Saco Falls; and the lower section is mostly smooth and settled to Columbia Falls, where it becomes tidal.

Pleasant River Lake ➤ Columbia Falls	33.5 mi
Description:	Flatwater, quickwater, Class I, II, III
Date checked:	2000
Navigable:	High water (early May)
Scenery:	Wild, towns

Maps:	Tug Mountain 15, Cherryfield 15, Columbia Falls; DL 25
Portages:	27.5 mi L Saco Falls 2.0 mi
	33.5 mi Falls

The Pleasant River starts at an outlet on the southern end of Pleasant River Lake. The river can be reached by taking a dirt road south from ME 9 at about the T30 MD Township line, which is marked. Drive straight on the dirt road for 2.75 miles. Keep to the left as several roads run off to the right to lakeside camps. The trip starts at a small wooden bridge and a dam at the southern end of the lake.

The Pleasant River drops over a series of narrow ledges to a pool 70 yards below. These ledges may be impassable in all but very high water. The best route is to the left. The river then passes through a number of marshes with numerous signs of beaver activity; lodges are scattered through the marshes, and dams block the river at several points.

After 5.5 miles, the river narrows and enters a stretch of Class III rapids west of Beech Hill at a point about 0.5 mile from the "Allison Worcester camp" on Tug Mountain quadrangle. The "hill" is almost indistinguishable in the rolling blueberry barrens. The most prominent landmark is a large boulder, which sits in the middle of the river.

Here, the river narrows to about 20 feet. It cascades some 75 yards through Class II and III rapids. This section should be scouted because it is rocky and there is little room to maneuver. **Caution!** Fallen trees may cross the river at this point, forming strainers. After these rapids, the river continues narrow and fast-moving for 0.25 mile. After another 6.5 miles, there is a road access (12.0 mi) before you enter an extended marsh. Paddlers wishing to take out here should spot a car on the dirt road, which can be reached by turning east off ME 192 almost directly opposite the Deblois airfield.

Pleasant River meanders for 14.0 miles through the heath, following such a convoluted route that it requires almost a full day of paddling. (This great heath is one of the longest peat wetlands of its type in the northeastern United States.)

After the heath, the river passes through a forested area with low, alder-lined banks. The approach of Saco Falls is indicated by several old farm buildings on the left (27.5 mi). The river flows past islands and ledges composed of large rocks and then narrows very sharply before dropping to the falls. Only the first 50 yards of the rapids can be run on the left; scout on the right. There is a take-out on the left in the pool below the rapid. Boats can be carried 150 feet up a gravel path leading to a paved road. **Caution!** An unfinished dam stands below the pool, the footing of which causes a drop of several feet. The falls are 100 yards below; the banks of the river are steep and the current fast.

The river thunders under a bridge several hundred feet over a series of giant rock steps at Saco Falls. Since this would be a 0.25-mile-long and difficult portage; it is better to end the trip here.

Advanced paddlers may choose to continue for the 2.0 miles from Saco Falls to Arty's Bridge. There are Class III boulders and ledge drops that you scout from river left. There is at least one more portage, river left, in this very beautiful section of the Pleasant.

Putting in at Arty's Bridge, 2.0 miles downstream (29.5 mi), the river is mostly smooth. Several hundred yards below the bridge is a short set of Class II rips, and another set of rips (31.5 mi), where some dragging may be necessary in low water, about 2 miles above Columbia Falls. The river passes under a railroad bridge to the take-out on the left just above the US 1 bridge. This is also the site of a Maine Atlantic Salmon Commission counting fence and a public boat landing. Below here the river passes over some falls to tidewater.

Machias River

The Machias River rates with the Allagash, the Penobscot, and the Saint John as one of Maine's most scenic waterways. It offers semiwilderness travel with lakes, swamps, intermittent rapids up to Class III, ledges, a waterfall, and portages—all in a region that is used much less than the Allagash and that is more accessible than the Saint John. When the last of the dams was removed in 1974, the Machias once again became a free-flowing river.

The route from Fifth Machias Lake to the sea offers one of the longest (76.0 miles) and most attractive semiwilderness canoe trips in Maine. The three big lakes have only a few cabins on their shores, and above First Machias Lake there are none along the river.

Extensive clear cutting of timber has occurred throughout the Machias watershed. This has changed the characteristics of the river, causing a much more rapid run-off in the spring and a definite response to rain.

Many years ago, there were two routes to the Machias River from Nicatous Lake. One went up Gassabias Stream, across Gassabias Lake, and over a long portage to Fourth Machias Lake. The other began with a portage into Upper Sabao Lake (sometimes called "Machias Lake") and continued downstream to Lower Sabao Lake at the head of the West Branch. Although the first segments of each route (to Gassabias Lake and Upper Sabao Lake, respectively) are usable now, the remaining portions are impassable.

Fifth Machias Lake ➤ ME 9	40.0 mi
Description:	Lakes, flatwater, Class I, II, III
Date checked:	2000
Navigable:	High water (May)
Scenery:	Wild
Maps:	Nicatous Lake 15, Wabassus Lake 15, Tug Mountain 15; DL 35 and 25
Campsites:	3.0 mi 5th Lake Outlet permit
	3.75 mi R old dam site permit
	8.25 mi R Knight Dam permit
	13.75 mi L 4th Lake (N of Unknown Stream) MFS
	15.25 mi L 4th Lake Outlet permit car
	20.5 mi 3rd Lake Narrows (island) permit 21.0 mi Getchel Lakes Outlet (W side) permit
	21.25 mi Prune Island (S side) permit

23.5 mi 3rd Lake Outlet permit car
27.75 mi R 2nd Lake Outlet (beach)
  permit car
30.25 mi L 1st Lake Outlet permit car

Fifth Machias Lake can be reached from the Stud Mill Road that runs from Princeton to Costigan. A half-mile trail to Greenland Cove leaves that road 4.5 miles west of the crossroads near the northern end of First Machias Lake.

From the end of Greenland Cove it is 2.5 miles across the lake to the beach at the outlet (3.0 mi). This point can be reached by car from the same road by turning north 3.0 miles west of Greenland Cove on Road 42-00-0. This is the usual start for the river trip. From there, Fifth Lake Stream flows through a culvert and then a low, marshy area for 5.25 miles to Knight Dam (8.25 mi). Almost all the way there is quickwater, but a short, easy rapid is less than 200 yards above the old washed-out dam. Then there are 1.5 miles of Class I and II rapids, with five short sections to watch out for. The first three are Class II–III ledge drops that should be scouted. After a little slackwater, you reach the fourth sharp drop: a narrow chute. The fifth tricky spot is just around the next corner. Soon thereafter the rapids end, and after 1.25 miles of flatwater Fifth Lake Stream empties into Fourth Machias Lake (11.0 mi).

In 1974, the dams on Fourth and Third Machias lakes were removed, exposing the land that was flooded many years ago. The shores are now vegetated with white birch (particularly at the upper ends of each lake where the land is flatter) and many grass species. Other shrubs and trees will will appear with time.

Fourth Machias Lake is 4.25 miles long. At the outlet (15.25 mi), the remains of the old dam can be run in high water. Fourth Lake Stream begins with a short Class II rapid, followed by 1.25 miles of quickwater and smoothwater. Shoreline Rapids (16.75 mi), exposed when the dam on Third Machias Lake was removed, is a short Class II pitch that carries you below the old lake level. There is another Class I rapid before Third Machias Lake (17.75 mi) is reached.

It is a 5.75-mile paddle down Third Machias Lake to the outlet (23.5 mi), where the remains of the old dam can be run. A good gravel road runs up the eastern side of the river from First Lake to this point. This is an excellent alternative put-in for those wishing to avoid paddling the three large lakes.

The Machias River begins with 0.5 mile of Class I and II rapids, followed by another 0.5 mile of deadwater. Below the latter is Otter Rips, a 0.25-mile set of Class II rapids that leads to a second deadwater, which is 1.0 mile long.

Long Falls (25.75 mi) begins at the boundary line between T43 MD and T37 MD; it is a 0.25-mile Class III pitch consisting of three ledge drops and a boulder-strewn run-off. There is a portage on the left-hand side that leads to a short stretch of quickwater below the rapids. In the remaining 1.25 miles to Second Machias Lake (27.25 mi), there are almost-continuous Class II rapids. These drops below Long Falls, though unnamed, are significant. A half-mile of paddling on Second Machias Lake and 2.0 miles of flatwater on the river bring you to First Machias Lake (29.75 mi). Just before reaching the latter, the river flows under the Stud Mill Road, which connects Princeton and Costigan.

From the outlet of First Machias Lake (30.75 mi), the river is mostly smooth for 4.0 miles. Then, in the middle of an S-turn, a few easy rapids lead up to Carrot Rips, also called Karrick Pitch (35.0 mi), a short Class II–III drop that should be scouted or portaged on the right bank (watch for poison ivy). A half-mile beyond, the West Branch enters on the right.

Below the confluence with the West Branch (35.5 mi), 4.5 miles of good current mingle with occasional easy rapids. All of the latter, including the Class II rapids at Boot Rips (38.25 mi), are flooded out when the water is really high. As you approach ME 9, stop well before the bridge (40.0 mi), because the river above it has been channeled and few good stopping places are available in the swift current. Airline Rapids, below the bridge, should be scouted (watch for poison ivy again here).

ME 9 ➤ Machias	36.5 mi
Description:	Flatwater, quickwater, Class II, III
Date checked:	2000
Navigable:	High and medium water (May and June)
Scenery:	Wild
Maps:	Tug Mountain 15, Wesley 15, Whitneyville, Machias; DL 25 and 26
Portages:	4.5 mi L Little Falls 0.25 mi
	8.5 mi R First Pitch Wigwam Falls 0.5 mi
	13.5 mi L Upper Holmes Falls 200 yd
	14.0 mi R Lower Holmes Falls 150 yd
	25.0 mi R Great Falls 0.25 mi
Campsites:	0.25 mi L Airline Rapids MFS $ car
	4.75 mi L Little Falls (lower end) permit
	10.0 mi L Wigwam Rapids, Third Pitch (poor) permit
	13.75 mi L Upper Holmes Falls (lower end) permit
	23.0 mi L Smith Landing (poor) permit car
	25.5 mi R Great Falls (lower end) permit

The Machias from ME 9 to the sea is a large river with many sections of flatwater separated by falls and, in high water, heavy rapids. Depending on the water level and the skill of the paddlers, only Upper Holmes Falls, listed above, may need to be portaged. All should be scouted before a decision is made.

The riverbanks approaching Whitneyville are in the process of recovering from the disturbance of a fire and a dam.

Below Smith Landing, the river passes through an area burned in 1956. It is interesting to note the ease with which the fire jumped the river, while at the same time left isolated pockets of the forest unscathed. A good example of this is at Great Falls, where the island at the beginning was burned, but neither bank of the river at that point was touched. Little evidence of the fire remains. The old lake bed has gone to meadow and is very attractive.

The removal of the dam at Whitneyville, which backed up the water to Great Falls, has allowed the river to return to its original channel. When the old lake bottom was first exposed, it was covered with cords of sunken pulpwood, which has now been salvaged.

Airline Rapids, about 0.33 mile long, begins under the ME 9 bridge and should be scouted. It is Class III, can be run in two stages, and may have some heavy waves in high water. There is quickwater for 2.25 miles to two short Class II rapids followed by fast current to Little Falls (4.5 mi). The upper section is Class IV, but the lower portion is Class II. The portage begins on the left and ends at the campsite below the falls. More flatwater continues for 3.75 miles to Wigwam Rapids.

Wigwam Rapids (8.5 mi) extends over a distance of 2.0 miles, with sections of varying difficulty depending on the water level. High water obliterates many riffles; when it does, there remain four more or less distinct pitches. The first, upper Wigwam, begins 0.25 mile below the mouth of Mopang Stream and should be scouted from the good portage, which begins in front of a cabin on the right bank. The upper section contains large boulders that make it Class III when the water is high, Class II when medium. The lower portion of the first pitch is much easier, and there are several places to put in partway down. The first pitch is 0.5 mile long, followed by a half-mile of slackwater and then the last three pitches, which together make up Lower Wigwam. Within the next mile there are many small rapids, which are flooded out in high water; the one that is not is the second pitch, Class II. The approach to the third pitch (10.0 mi) is somewhat blind. This rapid should be scouted from the portage on the left bank, as it is a short, tricky drop over a Class III ledge with an almost riverwide hydraulic (a sneak route on left). The fourth pitch, not far beyond, is a short Class II rapid.

After Wigwam Rapids there are 3.0 miles of slackwater to Upper Holmes Falls (13.5 mi), a 15-foot waterfall with a portage on the left. There is a good road that runs from ME 9 to Holmes Falls and the paddler may desire to take out here.

A third-mile below is Lower Holmes Falls (Class III), which begins at Deadman's Island, on the northern end of which is a memorial to Obadiah Hill, a pioneer who died in 1786. The portage is on the right bank. The dangerous section of the rapids is at the end, and it cannot be seen from the trail. These rapids are separated by a small island that makes scouting difficult. The right side tends to be bony even in moderately high water; the left side is quite pushy and tends to run you up against the ledge on river right.

Flatwater continues for 11.0 miles, passing the mouth of Old Stream (20.25 mi), and is interrupted only slightly by Getchell Riffles which are Class I (21.0 mi) and Bobsled Rips, hardly notable (24.5 mi). At Smith Landing (23.0 mi), a good dirt road leads to ME 192. Great Falls (25.0 mi) is a long, continuous Class III rapid. The easiest route is on the left. Scout first. The portage is on the right bank.

There are 6.25 miles of quickwater to Whitneyville (31.5 mi). The old lake bed forms a wide meadow with views of the surrounding hills, unusual on the lower river. Near Whitneyville are crumbling remains of cribs and piers from logging days. Almost nothing remains of the old dam. A canal was once built on the left above US 1A, creating an island in Whitneyville. The canal is now closed and the approach to US 1A is on the right via a Class II+ rapid.

Beyond the highway bridge in Whitneyville, the river is flat for 1.75 miles except for a Class I rapid at the railroad bridge. Then comes Munson Pitch, a river-wide, Class II ledge run on the left.

The river flattens out for another 1.75 miles, then enters 0.75 mile of easy Class I rapids between rocky bluffs. A short, flat stretch leads to a pretty little gorge with a nice Class II rapid. A final Class I rapid ends in a short slackwater behind the partly broken dam just above the bridge in Machias. There is a fairly large parking lot on the left just above the bridge, which provides a good take-out.

Just below the take-out is Machias Falls, an unrunnable falls. Do not miss the take-out!

Machias River (West Branch)

The West Branch is small, wild, and seldom traveled. It requires higher water than is needed on the Machias River below ME 9, so it must be run early in the spring. There is a convenient campsite halfway down—at Rolford Dam—if the trip is done in two days.

Upper Cranberry Lake ➤ ME 9 (above Airline Rapids)	19.75 mi
Description:	Lakes, flatwater, quickwater, Class I, II
Date checked:	2000
Navigable:	High and medium water (April, May)
Scenery:	Wild, forested
Maps:	Tug Mountain 15; DL 35
Campsites:	0 mi Upper Cranberry Lakes MFS $ car
	9.75 mi R Rolford Dam permit

As you follow the road to the Cranberry Lakes from ME 9 (The Airline), keep right at an intersection about 6 miles from the highway.

From the MFS campsite on Upper Cranberry Lake to the beginning of Cranberry Stream, there are 3.5 miles of lake paddling, with a portage around a culvert connecting the two lakes. Cranberry Stream meanders sluggishly for 2.0 miles to its junction with the West Branch (5.5 mi). The West Branch flows for 1.5 miles from Lower Sabao Lake to Cranberry Stream; it is flat and swampy.

There is an alternative put-in at a bridge about 1.5 miles downstream from the confluence of Cranberry Stream and the West Branch. It can be reached by taking the logging road from ME 9 just west of the Airline Rapids on the Machias River for about 6 miles and then turning left on Road 59-00-0 and then right on Road 39-00-0. This allows the paddler to avoid the flatwater paddling on the Cranberry Lakes and Stream and a much longer shuttle.

Beyond the mouth of Cranberry Stream, the current begins to pick up after 0.5 mile. Then there are 2.75 miles of intermittent, easy Class I and II rapids, with a low logging bridge near the end, before reaching Rolford Deadwater (8.75 mi). Rolford Dam (9.75 mi) is washed out and is runnable.

Between Rolford Dam and the bridge above the confluence with the Main Branch, there are 5.25 miles of mixed flatwater and Class I and II rapids. There are also five ledge drops that should be scouted. All can be run at medium to high water, but in lower water they may have to be lined.

Under the bridge (15.0 mi) is a sixth ledge. If it cannot be run, this is more easily portaged beginning on the left bank. The West Branch soon joins the Main Branch (15.25 mi).

Below the confluence, the Machias River flows with good current and occasional easy rapids for 4.5 miles to ME 9 (19.75 mi). Stop well before the bridge, because the river above it has been channeled, with the result that there are few good stopping places in the swift current. Airline Rapids, below the bridge, should be scouted.

Mopang Stream

The trip from the boat landing on Mopang Lake to the Machias River above Wigwam Rapids is a semiwilderness run of 32.0 miles, with only an occasional cabin or dirt road. Mopang Stream flows through marshes in several locations and past blueberry barrens, so that you get a feeling of space similar to that which travel on lakes provides. The dominant ground cover of sheep laurel and lowbush blueberries, sprinkled with isolated red pine and stands of poplar and gray birch, provides a distinct contrast to most other rivers in Maine.

Below the end of Mopang Stream at Machias Eddy, you come to Wigwam Rapids on the Machias, where a road from Columbia Falls provides access.

The water of Mopang Lake and Mopang Second Lake is clear, but before it flows very far downstream it becomes discolored by organic matter from swamps. The river below Second Lake is small, and its banks are forested as far as the meadow at First Lake. Beyond, it is mostly open.

Mopang Lake ➤ ME 9		8.25 mi
Description:	Lakes, flatwater, Class I, II	
Date checked:	2000	
Navigable:	High water (May)	

Scenery:	Wild
Maps:	Lead Mountain 15, Tug Mountain 15; DL 25
Portage:	3.5 mi L Mopang Lake Dam 15 yd
Campsite:	5.75 mi L First Lake Outlet permit

Mopang Lake is reached by a dirt road that leaves ME 9 (The Airline) at a gravel pit 1.8 miles west of the bridge over Mopang Stream. Keep left at each of two forks. It is 3.5 miles from the landing on Mopang Lake to the dam on Second Lake, which controls the water level on both bodies of water. The rapids below are barely passable at medium water. If the water is high, they should be scouted as far as the culvert 0.75 mile downstream (road close by on left bank); there is a sharp drop over a ledge and sometimes there are trees across the river.

Beyond the culvert (Road No. 5), the stream is Class I, with one or two blowdowns, becoming flat as it approaches Mopang First Lake. The latter is small. Below the old bridge at the outlet (5.75 mi), the river is wider and for the most part flat for 2.5 miles to the ME 9 bridge (8.25 mi), although there are some Class I rips at and below the remains of an old log-driving dam just above the highway.

ME 9 ➤ Machias Eddy   23.75 mi

Description:	Flatwater, Class I, II
Date checked:	2000
Navigable:	High water (May)
Scenery:	Wild
Maps:	Tug Mountain 15; DL 25
Campsites:	10.25 mi R beside Bridge (poor) permit
	15.25 mi R Six Mile Dam permit

Most of the drop in elevation takes place in short pitches and at beaver dams. Only at Penman Rips are the rapids appreciably long and more difficult. The rocks in the riverbed are coarse-grained, so they may scrape a boat with unexpected authority in medium water. Much of the way, the river traverses the blueberry barrens, but in the last 3.0 miles above the Machias River, it passes through conifer forests.

For several miles there are intermittent, easy rapids, after which the stream meanders through the barrens. Beech Hill Brook enters on the right 8.0 miles below ME 9. After winding for another 2.25 miles, the stream passes under two culverts (10.25 mi) near Duck Pond. For the next 5.0 miles to Six Mile Dam (15.25 mi) the current is slow, with an occasional easy rip.

Six Mile Dam can be run, but there are some nasty spikes on the far left side. Below, the rapids are more difficult and more frequent, and there are also some rather high beaver dams. After 3.5 miles you pass beneath a steel bridge, and reach Penman Rips (18.75 mi), Class II, at least. **Caution!** These rapids begin just above a left turn, and at the top there are three ledges. Below the latter, the river is narrow with large boulders for about 50 yards, after which the gradient lessens. The next 4.0 miles to the confluence with the Machias River (23.75 mi) are mostly flat, with occasional rips. There is a take-out here at Wigwam Rapids; the next take-out, at Holmes Falls, is 5.0 miles down the Machias.

Old Stream

This river flows into the Machias River about 5 miles above Great Falls. It flows from a series of lakes in T37 MD. Third and First lakes are wild and Second Lake has only a few cabins along its southern shore. Since Canaan Dam no longer impounds water, a section of the river below First Lake is in the meadowland on the bottom of a once-larger lake.

Much of Old Stream above ME 9 is not far from a logging road. However, below the highway, the river is isolated, and it meanders considerably, occasionally within a narrow valley bordered by steep banks.

As recently as the 1950s, long longs were driven down the river by the Saint Regis Paper Company.

Second Lake ➤ Machias River	25.0 mi
Description:	Lakes, flatwater, quickwater, Class II
Date checked:	2000
Navigable:	High and medium water (May)

Maps:	Wabassus Lake 15, Tug Mountain 15, Wesley 15; DL 35, 25, and 26
Portages:	4.0 mi L Canaan Dam 20 yd
	11.75 mi L Stinking Jam Rapids 50 yd
	15.5 mi L Longfellow Pitch 30 yd
Campsites:	11.75 mi L Stinking Jam Rapids permit
	14.0 mi R head of rapids opposite wooded island permit

There is a roadside rest area on ME 9 (The Airline) beside Old Stream. Since the Airline has been widened, the rest area has a small road to the east of Old Stream. Three-quarters of a mile to the east a logging road leads north past Canaan Dam and Second Lake.

Put in below the culvert at the outlet of Second Lake, where a portage is necessary if you begin farther along the road. The river here is very small and somewhat choked by alder, but it soon opens into a meadow. Just above First Lake there is a washed-out driving dam (now stabilized by boulders and tree saplings), followed by a shallow runout.

Flatwater continues from the outlet of First Lake (1.75 mi) to just above Canaan Dam, where there is another washed-out driving dam. The remains of the dams above and below First Lake are almost unrecognizable in high water.

Canaan Dam (4.0 mi) can be run, but should be scouted. There is flatwater to Glover Pitch, which can be recognized, in addition to the sound of it, by a large ledge on the right bank. These rapids begin with a low rock dam, which is followed by 50 yards of easy Class II. The flatwater and quickwater between Glover Pitch and ME 9 are broken by Hayward Dam, a series of ledges, which should be lined on the right.

Below ME 9 (8.0 mi), there is quickwater for about 0.5 mile, after which the river meanders in a narrow valley between conifer forests. There are a few rips. Stinking Jam Rapids (11.75 mi) is an unrunnable ledge drop followed by Class II rapids. (Take the ledge at the next left turn to the left of center.)

There is a 0.25-mile Class II rapid around an island, and some distance later a runnable ledge before Longfellows Pitch (15.5

mi), a 4-foot ledge, which must be lined or portaged on the left. From that point, there is flatwater nearly all the way past New Stream (24.5 mi), which enters on the left to the Machias River (25.0 mi).

The nearest take-out is 2.75 miles downstream at Smith landing (27.75 mi).

East Machias River

The East Machias River is a pleasing mixture of easy rapids, expansive meadows, and lakes of varying sizes. Because of the rapids close to ME 9, the entire river is runnable only in high water. However, the upper section from Pocomoonshine Lake to Crawford Lake is always navigable when free of ice, and below Round Lake the river can be negotiated at low water with some occasional scraping. There are a few cabins, but most of them are on the lakes below ME 9.

In spring, the 45-mile trip takes three or four days. The island campsite on Crawford Lake and the one on Second Lake are among the nicest in eastern Maine.

Pocomoonshine Lake ➤ Crawford (via Maine River)	10.0 mi
Description:	Lakes, flatwater
Date checked:	2000
Navigable:	Spring, summer, fall
Scenery:	Wild
Maps:	Big Lake 15; DL 36
Campsite:	8.0 mi L 1st island close to East shore (S end) permit

From Pokey Lake, a wide, sluggish river winds through wide meadows and small ponds to Crawford Lake. In the summer, it seems as though you are paddling past seas of grass. Seldom do trees grow within 50 yards of the river, so easy access to dry ground is the exception. There is also little protection from a strong wind.

In the town of Alexander, follow the road from ME 9 that leads north 2.5 miles to Pocomoonshine Lake Lodges, where there is a launching area. In 2.0 miles the Maine River flows from the lake. It heads generally south through Upper Mud

Lake (3.5 mi), and Lower Mud Lake (4.75 mi) to Crawford Lake (7.25 mi). The Crawford Public Landing (10.0 mi) is a short way below the cove, around which the few houses are located.

Crawford ➤ East Machias	35.0 mi
Description:	Lakes, flatwater, quickwater, Class I, II
Date checked:	2000
Navigable:	High water above ME 9 (May)
	High and medium water below ME 9 (May or June)
	Low water (passable with some scraping below Round Lake)
Scenery:	Wild, settled, towns
Maps:	Big Lake 15, Wesley 15, Gardner Lake 15, Machias; DL 36 and 26
Portages:	2.5 mi L Pokey Dam 20 yd
	35.0 mi Dam at East Machias
Campsites:	2.5 mi L Pokey Dam (poor) permit
	21.0 mi L Second Lake (1st point S of outlet) permit

This portion of the East Machias River makes a nice two-day trip in the spring when the water is high and the air is faintly scented with the smell of burned or burning blueberry fields. Since the rapids are not too difficult, this river is more suitable for people with limited whitewater skill and experience than is the Machias or Narraguagus.

Put in at the Crawford Public Landing, which is reached by a side road next to the cemetery. The East Machias River, by name, begins 2.5 miles south of the landing at Pokey Dam, the outlet to Crawford Lake. After portaging the dam on the left, there are easy rapids and quickwater for 1.75 miles before reaching a deadwater (4.35 mi). After 0.75 mile there are more rapids to the Airline bridge (5.5 mi).

From the outlet of Second Lake on the west shore, the river is flat for 0.75 mile. Then, within 1.5 miles, there are five rapids, which get progressively harder, from Class I to Class II. At Wigwam Riffles (22.25 mi) there is a low, runnable weir, and within 0.25 mile there is another rapid.

Crooked Pitch (23.0 mi) is on both sides of an island, with the clearest channel on the right; and Smith Mill Pitch (23.35 mi) and Lower Riffles (23.75 mi) are straight chutes in high water. After 3.5 miles of flatwater, including another large meadow, the river flows into Hadley Lake (27.25 mi). The outlet is 3.75 miles down the eastern shore. In the 1.25 miles between the lake and the ME 191 bridge, there are two easy rapids at low or washed-out dams.

There is a short Class II drop under the ME 9 bridge (32.35 mi) and another easier one past the next road bridge. The remaining 1.75 miles to East Machias are flatwater.

The dam at East Machias (34.5 mi) no longer impounds water. **Caution!** Keep to the left, the inside of the turn, as you approach the town. Stop above the bridge to scout or portage. In medium and high water, much of the debris and protruding steel is obscured. Caution is strongly advised. In low water, you can let down through the gates. Below the dam there are sporty Class II rapids, runnable at all water levels. At low tide, they continue past the last bridge (35.0 mi), but the river fans out and the water gets noticeably shallower.

Northern Inlet and Rocky Lake Stream

Northern Inlet, the tributary of Rocky Lake described here, is the beginning of an excellent summer trip that continues on the East Machias River below the mouth of Rocky Lake Stream. The lower East Machias is passable at all water levels, although sections of a few rapids, particularly Crooked Pitch, are bony in low water. This trip to the sea at the town of East Machias is 25.75 miles long, and it takes two full days when the water level is down.

Off ME 191 ➤ East Machias River	9.25 mi
Description:	Lake, flatwater, quickwater, Class I, II
Date checked:	2000
Navigable:	Passable at all water levels
Scenery:	Wild
Maps:	Gardner Lake 15, Wesley 15

Campsites:	3.5 mi L Mud Landing permit car
	4.5 mi L Rocky Lake (beach at S end)
	permit car

This trip begins at a bridge on a road that leads off ME 191 in T18 ED, 1.9 miles north of the second railroad crossing from US 1 in East Machias. It is a dirt road; 2.8 miles from the highway it crosses Northern Inlet. It continues on to meet ME 9 at a a sharp bend in Crawford, where a side road leads to Love Lake

Being on the right bank below the bridge. For most of the distance to Rocky Lake the stream is deep, wide, and flat. There are, however, about 5 very short, narrow sections with Class I–II rapids in high water; they must be lined or dragged in low water. At the last of these, an old log bridge blocks the stream at high water.

Mud Landing (3.5 mi) is on the left just after the last rapid. It is another access point that can be reached via a dirt road, which leads off ME 191 about 1.5 miles north of the aforementioned railroad crossing. A half-mile farther on, Northern Inlet opens into Rocky lake (4.0 mi).

From the outlet (6.5 mi) near the north end of the lake, Rocky Lake Stream, all flatwater, flows for 2.75 miles past the mouth of Northern Stream (8.25 mi) to the East Machias River (9.25 mi).

The first take-out downstream is at the ME 191 bridge below Hadley Lake, 13.75 miles to the left.

Josh Stream, Gardner Lake, and Chase Mills Stream

Lakes and boggy streams combine for a beautiful 10.0-mile trip through surprisingly wild country. It runs from the isolated and remote Josh Pond to the East Machias River.

Access to Josh Pond via Sunken Lake   1.0 mi

From a wooded peninsula on the western shore of a marsh at the end of a shallow, winding, channel off the southwestern end of Sunken Lake, follow a trail first west along the peninsula, then southwest, avoiding bogs to the left. The route is occasionally flagged by red tape. Cross a wet spot and ascend a low ridge. Turn right onto an old tote road 0.3 mile from Sunken Lake. A half-mile up the tote road turn left at a wooden boundary post. The trail descends south through open woods past a rocky outcropping and a mossy green boulder on the left; then it follows a dry ridge south. In sight of the lake it angles left off the ridge, reaching Josh Pond 300 feet east of the prominent point on the northern shore of the pond. The route is dry and the grades gentle—not a hard carry for its length.

Josh Pond also may be reached by paddling upstream from Gardner Lake Road.

Josh Pond ➤ East Machias   9.5 mi

Description:	Lake, flatwater, Class I
Date checked:	2000
Navigable:	All seasons
Scenery:	Wild
Maps:	Gardner Lake 15, Machias Bay

From the northwestern corner of Josh Pond, beside a grassy bluff with scattered trees, Josh Stream winds slowly through a broad marsh. The channel is wide and deep; wild geese, ducks, and bald eagles may be seen. Gardner Lake Road is 1.5 miles from the pond; lift over the culvert and push over a log jam below. Just before Second Lake, duck under a low bridge.

Paddle 1.5 miles down Second Lake, and turn left past a point and island into Gardner Lake. A campsite is on the left opposite the island. Gardner Lake is beautiful, with forested bluffs and islands. Chase Mills is 3.5 miles down the lake.

If Chase Mills Stream is high, there is 0.5 mile of Class II rapids to run. If it does not look high enough below the dam, carry 0.5 mile southwest down the road and carry 1,000 feet northwest to the stream.

After a few hundred feet of Class I rapids, the stream flattens out; after a mile it flows into the East Machias River. Another mile downstream is the village of East Machias on the right. In the past, this route, together with the Orange River, was an important route from Cobscook Bay to the Machias. This trip is still possible with 1.75 miles of carrying in three portages. It can be extended for miles by exploring Rocky Lake, Roaring Lake, Harmon or Clifford Streams, and the northern arms of Second Lake.

Whiting Bay and Dennys Bay

Whiting Bay leads from the Orange River out to Dennys Bay and on out to Passamaquoddy Bay. Any paddling on tidewater demands experience and consideration of the weather and wind direction as well as the state of the tide.

Whiting ➤ Reversing Falls   7.5 mi

At low tide, the head of Whiting Bay is just deep enough to float a loaded boat. To Leighton Point (2.5 mi) the Bay is narrow, often constricted by rocky points, very scenic. The tide runs at 3 to 5 knots. Where the bay widens beyond Freds Island there are mild currents down either shore. In the main channel down the center, there may be 1- to 2-foot waves.

At Reversing Falls, most of the tidal flow squeezes between Falls Island and Leighton Neck. A large reef exposed at all but high tide forms a big eddy with large wave trains along the eddy lines. The channel between the reef and Falls Island has a long line of 3-foot waves. The west channel has impressive boils and swirls. The mean tide range is 20 feet, and the rapids are probably Class III at midtide. At high tide, all this mayhem stops briefly for about 10 minutes.

Orange River

Orange River is the outlet for series of lakes, of which Rocky Lake is the largest, flowing east to Whiting Bay. It is an attractive, semiwild flatwater trip available anytime. Rocky and Sunken lakes are in remote country.

Rocky and Sunken Lakes

Sunken Lake can be reached from Rocky Lake via a broad, shallow channel dotted with beaver lodges. Since the dam at Halls Mills burned, the lake has shrunk, and the northwestern and southwestern bays shown on the USGS Gardner Lake 15 map have returned to marsh. Wildlife is common. (The dam is proposed to be rebuilt in 2002.)

Rocky Lake extends 3.0 miles north, and Rocky Lake Stream is navigable into the marshes nearly a mile more. Rocky Lake deserves its name: rugged bluffs and bare rock knobs grace every view.

Halls Mills ➤ Whiting	6.25 mi
Description:	Flatwater, Class II
Date checked:	2000
Navigable:	Spring, summer, fall (low water-wading below US 1)
Scenery:	Forested, rural
Maps:	Gardner Lake 15, Whiting; DL 26 and 27
Portages:	2.5 mi L
	5.25 mi L LLP Dam and falls at US 1 0.25 mi
	(6.25 mi L Whiting Dam and rapids to tidewater)

In high water, the small connecting stream is runnable. Coming down Rocky Lake, take the left channel and lift over the remains of an old dam. The brook twists through alder to a culvert that is runnable if not blocked by debris. **Check first!** A few hundred feet beyond is Dumpling Falls, a steep, straight flume dropping 4 feet (Class II) to the flatwater of Orange Lake. In low water this 0.25 mile must be carried.

One-mile-long Orange Lake is pretty, but not as wild or rugged as Rocky Lake. One mile of marshy, gentle river with only one riffle under a bridge leads to the next lake, shaped like an X. One half-mile down the lake a short carry at a house on the left connects to Roaring Lake, which wander 1.5 miles back into wild country.

Continuing down "Lake X," take the right channel, then the left in 0.25 mile. After 0.75 mile, turn right again. At the old Lubec Light and Power dam, land on the left carefully. Beyond the dam is a Class III–IV chute under the old bridge and a Class IV falls under the new bridge.

To continue to Whiting, turn right and cross the old bridge. Cross US 1 and turn left at a closed-up house. Follow a dirt road 100 feet, and turn left into the woods down a trail to the river below the bridges. the carry is 0.25 mile long.

In the summer, the next 0.25 mile will be low and require some wading. In the spring, there is a Class I–II rapid on the left-hand bend and beyond the next right-hand bend a Class II drop. The remaining 0.75 mile to Whiting is flatwater. Land on the left along US 1 to finish an Orange River cruise or to portage to Whiting Bay. Below the dam at Whiting is a long series of Class II rapids that are normally too shallow to run even in the spring. Carry along US 1, and then cut through a grassy area to the head of tide. The length of the carry is about 600 yards at low tide, significantly less at high tide. Beyond is the rapid tidal river known as Whiting Bay.

Dennys River

The Dennys River flows out of Meddybemps Lake in the town of Meddybemps first southward, then southeast to Dennysville, where it flows into an arm of Passamaquoddy Bay. It is mixed smooth and rapid, with a good current and a number of rips, which provide a varied interest to the run.

Meddybumps ➤ ME 86	18.0 mi
Description:	Flatwater, quickwater, Class I, II
Date checked:	2000
Navigable:	High and medium water
Scenery:	Wild
Maps:	Calais 15, Gardner Lake 15, Pembroke; DL 36 and 26

There is an excellent put-in just east of the river on a private driveway courteously opened to the public, and to the left off

ME 191. It is a short, dead-end road that runs to the river. Ask for and obtain permission before crossing property lines.

Below the dam at Meddybemps Lake, the quickwater soon slows down for the 7.0 miles of mostly smoothwater through a swampy country to the site of Gilman Dam. This can be reached from the west by high-clearance vehicles via a rough logging road from East Ridge Road 2.5 miles south of ME 191.

It is 1.5 miles to Gardner Rips and another 1.5 miles to Ayers Rips. Here, the river becomes much more winding, and after passing around the northern end of the Whaleback reaches Stoddard Rips in 2.0 miles. Little Falls, 2.0 miles below, is somewhat more of a rapid. Just below here, the river turns south for a short bit and in 1.5 miles reaches Camp Rips. There is a good take-out on the right below Camp Rips. It can be reached by taking the dirt road off ME 86 at the Robinson's Cottages sign about 0.5 mile west of the bridge in Dennysville.

Below this take-out, the paddler travels under a railroad bridge and enters a Class III–IV gorge. It can be scouted on the right and is generally run on the right. There are also several possible take-outs in the town of Dennysville.

ME 86 ➤ Dennysville	2.75 mi
Description:	Class I, II, III
Date checked:	2000
Navigable:	Medium water
Scenery:	Forested
Maps:	Pembroke; DL 26 and 27

Scout the Class III, IV gorge that is 200 feet beyond the bridge. It can be run by keeping as close as possible to the ledge along the right bank. Intermittent Class I–II rapids continue for the next half-mile. Soon Cathance Stream enters on the right (0.75 mi). Tidewater begins just below the Dennys River Sportsmans Club (1.5 mi). At midtide, a Class II run can be made through Dennysville to take out on the left bank at the US 1 bridge where the river widens into Dennys Bay. A Maine Atlantic Salmon Commission counting fence (weir) crosses the river in Dennysville.

Cathance Stream

Cathance Stream rises in Lake Cathance, which is located in Cooper and Township 14, and flows south and east to the Dennys River shortly above Dennysville.

Lake Cathance ➤ ME 86		9.0 mi
Description:	Quickwater, Class I, II	
Date checked:	2000	
Navigable:	High water	
Scenery:	Wild	
Maps:	Gardner Lake, Pembroke; DL 36, 26, and 27	

There two places to put in on the western side of Cathance Lake, from ME 191. The outlet leaves from a long bay on the southeastern side of the lake. To put-in at the outlet take the 90-00-0 road from ME 191. After 1.0 mile, go left on the 90-05-0 road to the river.

Because the grade is unusually consistent, there are no rapids of special note—rather pleasant, mild, talking water. The rapids are steepest at the start, gradually moderating, with the last 2.0 miles quickwater.

A series of unrunnable drops begins just above the ME 86 bridge. Portage, and put in below the bridge. In 4.0 miles you come to the Great Works Flowage, an excellent wildlife area. Portage the Great Works dam. One mile below, where Dodge Road crosses, there as a small flume you can run. The granite walled feature is 6 feet wide and about 60 feet long. From the flume down to the take-out on the Dennys River in Dennysville, the Cathance is a riffle run.

Saint Croix River

The Saint Croix River flows from North Lake on the Maine–New Brunswick border and runs generally south, forming the southern portion of the international boundary. The upper part is largely a succession of lakes; the middle section has a number of Class I and II rapids, which are runnable much of the year; and the lower portion also has some rapids, although it is more developed.

Report to customs in advance when planning to cross the border on your trip.

Orient ➤ Vanceboro	36.0 mi
Description:	Lakes, flatwater, quickwater
Date checked:	2001
Navigable:	Spring, summer, fall
Scenery:	Forested, cottages
Maps:	Amity 15, Danforth 15, Forest 15, Vanceboro 15; DL 53, 45, and 46
Portages:	16.0 mi L (Canadian side)
	36.0 mi R Vanceboro

The highest point on the river that is easily accessible is at the northern end of Grand Lake, where you can put in just below the U.S. Customs office on Boundary Road east of Orient. From here, you can go eastward through the thoroughfare to North Lake if desired. But the more usual route is to proceed directly down Grand Lake, the first of the Chiputneticook Lakes.

At the northern end, Grand Lake is narrow (less than 1 mile wide), but after about 5 miles it opens out into a very large body of water. Although there are a few settled spots here and there, most of the lake is wild. After about 7 miles in the larger part of the lake, you approach the southern end, where you should be careful to keep on the eastern side, where in 1.0 mile more you will arrive at the outlet. On the southwestern side, there is a long arm, some 4 miles, which runs down to a dead end. This makes a pleasant paddle between high hills, if you wish to make a side trip.

At the outlet, there is 1.0 mile of fast current past Forest City to the long deadwater below. This deadwater is followed 2.0 miles north to a steep drop, necessitating a long carry on the Canadian side (left). After 1.0 mile more of river, Spednik Lake is reached. This is a long, narrow, and winding lake, which is followed 19.0 miles to Vanceboro. There the dam should be carried on the right, that is, on the American side.

There are alternate portages from Mud Lake to Spednik Lake (see USGS Forest 15). The first runs from west to east and reaches Spednik Lake 0.5 mile north of Forest City Landing. The second begins just before entering the narrows at the northern end of Mud Lake and runs northeast to Booming Ground Cove on Spednik Lake.

Vanceboro ➤ Kellyland		33.0 mi
Description:	Lakes, flatwater, Class I, II	
Date checked:	2001	
Navigable:	Spring, summer, fall; controlled release	
Scenery:	Wild	
Maps:	Vanceboro 15, Kellyland 15, Waite 15; DL 46 and 36	
Portage:	33.0 mi R Kellyland Dam 100 yd	
Campsites:	6.5 mi R Tunnel Rips	
	9.5 mi R Little Falls MFS	
	13.0 mi L Grassy Island	
	19.5 mi R Loon Bay MFS car	
	25.0 mi L High Banks	
	29.5 mi R Spednic Falls permit	

The Saint Croix has runnable rapids when most other streams in New England are too low. This is because the dam on Spednik Lake is used to regulate part of the flow of water to the generator at Grand Falls Dam. The other regulated drainage area that supplies water to the power plant is that of the Grand Lake chain, but it enters the Saint Croix at Grand Falls flowage. Therefore, it does not affect the river between Vanceboro and Kellyland.

The rapids below Vanceboro are all relatively easy, Class I and II, with Little Falls being the most difficult. Topographical maps name a dozen rapids in the first 20.0 miles to Loon Bay, but most of them are easy and some are apt to be flooded out in high water. If one gate at Vanceboro is open 5 feet, the river below it will be "high."

The best part of the river is the 30.0 miles between Vanceboro and Grand Falls flowage, and it can easily be run in two days. The middle portion of the river is accessible by car at Loon Bay, and there is another road that reaches Grand Falls flowage near Spednic Falls. Information on these roads is most easily obtained from the District Ranger in Topsfield (just east on ME 6).

As you begin the trip, you pass under a railroad bridge, which was the scene of an early act of sabotage prior to the United States' involvement in World War II. The bridge was blown up to prevent the Canadian Pacific from hauling supplies destined for England.

"Kill-me-quick" rapids, which is directly below the dam at Vanceboro and the highway bridge, ends under the railroad bridge.

It is followed by 1.5 miles of flatwater, then an easy Class I–II rapid, and then Wing Dam Island. There is an optional, slightly technical route available to the right of Wing Dam Island—caution at end of pool; it is a sharp II–III chute.

At the end of Wing Dam Island (1.0 mi), you will reach Elbow Rips (easy Class I). It is 1.5 miles to Mile Rips (easy Class II) and another 2.5 miles to Tunnel Rips (easy Class II). The trip to George's Rips (easy Class II) is 0.5 mile. It is 1.0 mile to Hall's Rips (easy Class II) and another 1.5 miles to Little Falls (Class III). Little Falls may be run on either side; it is easier on the right, more technical on the left. There is a good portage trail on the right for those who wish to partake.

Then it is 1.0 mile to Fork Rips. (Old-timers maintain that the original name was Pork Rips, not Fork Rips, as listed now.) It was here that a barrel of salted pork was lost when a freight canoe was upset in the logging days one hundred years ago. Another mile brings the paddler to Cedar Island Rips (easy Class II). After Cedar Island, watch for a clearing on the right with a large, white birch tree. Here is the grave of a baby found in the river by loggers, and it has been maintained by them since the late 1800s.

It is then 1.0 mile to Tyler Rips (easy Class II), and 2.0 miles to Albee Rips (easy Class II). There is a large picnic and camping ground on the left (Canadian) side. It is 1.0 mile to Rocky Rips (easy Class II), with another Canadian campground on the left. Then it is 1.5 miles to Split Rock Rips (Class II), 1.0

mile to Meetinghouse Rips (Class II), and 2.5 miles to Haycock Rips (Class II), which empties into Loon Bay (2.0 miles long). Paddle 1.5 miles below Loon Bay to reach Canoose Rips. **Caution!** Scout here; water level is the key to passage. If it is low, line on left; if medium, paddle chute on left. On the right is a rocky Class III; in the center, a Class IV. Watch for obstructions at Canoose—logs and debris.

Below what is now called Canoose Rips there follows about 1 mile of easy Class I rapids called Canoose Rapids.

Canoose Rapids can be run in three spots: 1) The ledge can be run at virtually any level on far left—steep, but short, easy chute. 2) On the far right there is a rocky winding Class II+ run. 3) The most interesting run is approximately one-third out from the left shore, directly over the ledge—it should be scouted first however; it could be considered Class III at certain water levels. The rapid below Canoose is actually Class II, approximately 0.5 mile long.

At Dog Falls, there is a runnable ledge on either side of the island, easier on the left. Below Dog Falls there is 1.5 miles of moving water/riffles, then 6.0 miles of flatwater to Kendricks Rips. From here on is open flatwater to Kellyland Dam. You pass the flowage, an open body of water with many peninsulas. Paddlers should have a topographical map with them; otherwise, they could spend the day looking for Kellyland Dam.

The first dam (actually the Kellyland Dam; used for many years) is no longer available as a take-out; you must proceed beyond the next point, then head left into the canal to the power generation plant.

Kellyland ➤ Calais		21.0 mi
Description:	Quickwater, flatwater, Class II	
Date checked:	2001	
Navigable:	Spring, summer, fall	
Scenery:	Forested, towns, settled	
Maps:	Kellyland 15, Calais 15; DL 36	
Portages:	9.5 mi L Woodland Dam and rapids 1,000 ft to 0.33 mi	

	19.5 mi L Saint Croix Rapids and Milltown Dam 0.66 mi
	21.0 mi R Calais Falls 0 to 500 ft per tide level
Campsites:	3.5 mi R informal sites on islands

The lower portion of the Saint Croix River is a mixture of complete isolation and heavy industry, flatwater and very difficult rapids, rural countryside and large towns. The former of each pair predominates. It is a very large river because it has picked up substantial drainage from the west. The flow is good all summer, but occasionally it is low if Georgia Pacific's generators are not running.

From the power plant in Kellyland, the river races downstream. After an exuberant but easy Class I mile, it settles down to a slow, deep coast through the forest. It is an attractive, almost wild northern woods setting. If you look underwater in the shallows, you will see sunken logs from the old river drives. Keep to the right of the island at Ash Brook for the deep channel. The deadwater of Woodland Lake begins here. The narrow channel to the left of Mosquito Island is blocked by stranded logs. On the right shore is a boat landing, 6.5 miles from Kellyland.

Beyond here, the wild character of the river is traded for a more-settled, but still attractive, setting, at least once Woodland is passed. Where the lake narrows at Woodland Junction, slip over a log boom, near the left shore. Approaching the dam and pulp mill at Woodland, stay left to pass another boom; land at the left end of the dam to portage.

If the river channel is dry below the dam, carry 1,000 feet down across the first dry channel, up to the power-line pylons, and down and along the major dry channel to where the flow is restored from the mill. The footing is loose and rocky on this carry.

If the river is not dry below the dam, carry 0.33 mile down the railroad tracks and then to the right down to the river at the head of a small rapid.

In the first 0.5 mile are two Class I rapids, then the river is flat but shallow to Bailey Rips, a slightly harder Class I–II rapids. Below the deadwater of Loon Bay is another riffle at Butler Island and another Class I where the river turns left. When the river narrows just below Haywood Island, there is a little Class I–II rapid.

At Upper Mills the river runs through a curving Class II rapid 0.66 mile long, ending in a broad, shallow bay. The next 3.5 miles to Milltown are flatwater curving through marshes and hardwood forest. Take out on the left (Canadian) shore to carry Saint Croix Rapids and the Milltown dam. Carry 0.66 mile either along the railroad or the road paralleling it on the left to a landing below the dam on the left shore.

Saint Croix Rapids are really a falls, Class IV–V. The pool behind the dam is short and complicated by a boom, so the carry is not worth breaking into two carries (around the falls and dam separately).

Below Milltown is 0.5 mile of Class II rapids ending at Union Mills. At high tide, this is the end of flowing river. At low tide, a pool extends 0.5 mile to Calais (pronounced "Cowlus") Falls, which drops to tide. The low-tide carry is on the right, 500 feet long. At midtide, the rapids are a heavy Class II–III. At high tide, the falls are drowned, not even a ripple left. Take out on the right just beyond the bridge in Calais.

Grand Lake Stream

Grand Lake Stream flows from West Grand Lake to Big Lake, the first in a series of lakes that connects with Grand Falls flowage on the Saint Croix River. The flow is dam-controlled, with the drainage area being the entire Grand Lake chain. One-and-a-half gates open at the dam provides a good Class II, III run through everything except Big Falls, which has several large holes and would be very difficult to run. The dam is reached over a public road from US 1 north of Princeton.

There is a USGS gauging station on left bank at Big Falls, 0.5 mi southeast of village of Grand Lake Stream, and 0.8 mile downstream from outlet dam of Grand Lake.

West Grand Lake ➤ Big Lake   3.0 mi

Description:	Class II, III
Date checked:	2000
Navigable:	High and medium water; controlled release
Scenery:	Rural, towns
Maps:	Wabassus Lake 15, Big Lake 15; DL 35
Portage:	0.75 mi L Big Falls 75 yd

If the water is high enough to run the rapids below the bridge in town and low enough to run Little Falls (reached by a road down the left bank 2.0 miles to a picnic area), the rapids will be Class II except for Big Falls, which should be carried.

Put in below the dam from either bank. Class II rapids extend 0.75 mile to Big Falls, around a sharp S-curve starting to the right with a house on the left bank; line or carry on the left. Rapids continue another 1.0 mile to the picnic area at Little Falls. (Camping not permitted.) This is a Class III–IV drop. There is a riverwide hole at the bottom, and it is best punched on the far right.

After another 1.0 mile, the rapids end at a group of cottages. You must obtain permission from one of the landowners in advance to take out here. If you continue to Big Lake, you will enjoy a beautiful paddle through the marsh. There is a public boat launch along the northern shore of Big Lake.

Appendix A

Safety Code of American Whitewater
(formerly the American Whitewater Affiliation

The following code, adopted in 1959 and revised in 1998, is reprinted with permission of American Whitewater, P.O. Box 636, Margaretville, NY 12455.

I. Personal Preparedness and Responsibility

1. Be a competent swimmer, with the ability to handle yourself underwater.

2. Wear a life jacket. A snugly-fitting vest-type life preserver offers back and shoulder protection as well as the flotation needed.

3. Wear a solid, correctly fitted helmet. This is essential in kayaks or covered canoes, and recommended for open canoeists using thigh straps and rafters running steep drops.

4. Do not boat out of control. Your skills should be sufficient to stop or reach shore before reaching danger. Do not enter a rapid unless you are reasonably sure that you can run it safely or swim it without injury.

5. Whitewater rivers contain many hazards which are not always easily recognized. The following are the most frequent killers.

   A. *HIGH WATER* The river's speed and power increase tremendously as the flow increases, raising the difficulty of most rapids. Rescue becomes harder as water rises, adding to the danger. Floating debris and strainers make even easy rapids quite hazardous. It is often misleading to judge river level at the put-in, since a small rise in a wide, shallow place will be multiplied many times where the river narrows. Use reliable gauge information whenever possible, and be aware that sun on snowpack, hard rain, and upstream dam releases may greatly increase the flow.

B. **COLD** Cold drains your strength and robs you of the ability to make sound decisions on matters affecting your survival. Cold water immersion, because of the initial shock and the rapid heat loss which follows, is especially dangerous. Dress appropriately for bad weather or sudden immersion in the water. When the water temperature is less than 50 degrees F., a wetsuit or drysuit is essential for protection if you swim. Next best is wool or pile clothing under a waterproof shell. In this case, you should also carry waterproof matches and a change of clothing in a waterproof bag. If, after prolonged exposure, a person experiences uncontrollable shaking, loss of coordination, or difficulty speaking, he or she is hypothermic, and needs your assistance.

C. **STRAINERS** Brush, fallen trees, bridge pilings, undercut rocks, or anything else which allows river current to sweep through can pin boats and boaters against the obstacle. Water pressure on anything trapped this way can be overwhelming. Rescue is often extremely difficult. Pinning may occur in fast current, with little or no whitewater to warn of the danger.

D. **DAMS, WEIRS, LEDGES, REVERSALS, HOLES, AND HYDRAULICS** When water drops over a obstacle, it curls back on itself, forming a strong upstream current which may be capable of holding a boat or swimmer. Some holes make for excellent sport. Others are proven killers. Paddlers who cannot recognize the difference should avoid all but the smallest holes. Hydraulics around man-made dams must be treated with utmost respect regardless of their height or the level of the river. Despite their seemingly benign appearance, they can create an almost escape-proof trap. The swimmers only exit from the "drowning machine" is to dive below the surface when the downstream current is flowing beneath the reversal.

E. **BROACHING** When a boat is pushed sideways against a rock by strong current, it may collapse and wrap. This is especially dangerous to kayak and decked-canoe paddlers; these boats will collapse and the combination of indestructible hulls and tight outfitting may create a deadly trap. Even without entrapment, releasing pinned boats can be extremely time-consuming and dangerous. To avoid pinning, throw your weight downstream towards the rock. This allows the current to slide harmlessly underneath the hull.

6. Boating alone is discouraged. The minimum party is three people or two craft.

7. Have a frank knowledge of your boating ability, and don't attempt rivers or rapids which lie beyond that ability.

   A. Develop the paddling skills and teamwork required to match the river you plan to boat. Most good paddlers develop skills gradually, and attempts to advance too quickly will compromise your safety and enjoyment.

   B. Be in good physical and mental condition, consistent with the difficulties which may be expected. Make adjustments for loss of skills due to age, health, fitness. Any health limitations must be explained to your fellow paddlers prior to starting the trip.

8. Be practiced in self-rescue, including escape from an overturned craft. The Eskimo roll is strongly recommended for decked boaters who run rapids Class IV or greater, or who paddle in cold environmental conditions.

9. Be trained in rescue skills, CPR, and first aid with special emphasis on the recognizing and treating hypothermia. It may save your friend's life.

10. Carry equipment needed for unexpected emergencies, including footwear which will protect your feet when walking out, a throw rope, knife, whistle, and waterproof matches. If you wear eyeglasses, tie them on and carry a spare pair on long trips. Bring cloth repair tape on short runs, and a full repair kit on isolated rivers. Do not wear bulky jackets, ponchos, heavy boots, or anything else which could reduce your ability to survive a swim.

11. Despite the mutually supportive group structure described in

this code, individual paddlers are ultimately responsible for their own safety, and must assume sole responsibility for the following decisions:

A. The decision to participate on any trip. This includes an evaluation of the expected difficulty of the rapids under the conditions existing at the time of the put-in.

B. The selection of appropriate equipment, including a boat design suited to their skills and the appropriate rescue and survival gear.

C. The decision to scout any rapid, and to run or portage according to their best judgment. Other members of the group may offer advice, but paddlers should resist pressure from anyone to paddle beyond their skills. It is also their responsibility to decide whether to pass up any walkout or take-out opportunity.

D. All trip participants should consistently evaluate their own and their group's safety, voicing their concerns when appropriate and following what they believe to be the best course of action. Paddlers are encouraged to speak with anyone whose actions on the water are dangerous, whether they are a part of your group or not.

II. Boat and Equipment Preparedness

1. Test new and different equipment under familiar conditions before relying on it for difficult runs. This is especially true when adopting a new boat design or outfitting system. Low volume craft may present additional hazards to inexperienced or poorly conditioned paddlers.

2. Be sure your boat and gear are in good repair before starting a trip. The more isolated and difficult the run, the more rigorous this inspection should be.

3. Install flotation bags in non-inflatable craft, securely fixed in each end, designed to displace as much water as possible. Inflatable boats should have multiple air chambers and be test-inflated before launching.

4. Have strong, properly sized paddles or oars for controlling craft. Carry sufficient spares for length and difficulty of trip.

5. Outfit your boat safely. The ability to exit your boat quickly is an essential component of safety in rapids. It is your responsibility to see that there is absolutely nothing to cause entrapment when coming free of an upset craft. This includes:

   A. Spray covers which won't release reliably or which release prematurely.

   B. Boat outfitting too tight to allow a fast exit, especially in low-volume kayaks or decked canoes. This includes low-hung thwarts in canoes lacking adequate clearance for your feet and kayak footbraces which fail or allow your feet to become wedged under them.

   C. Inadequately supported decks which collapse on a paddler's legs when a decked boat is pinned by water pressure. Inadequate clearance with the deck because of your size or build.

   D. Loose ropes which cause entanglement. Beware of any length of loose line attached to a whitewater boat. All items must be tied tightly and excess line eliminated; painters, throw lines, and safety rope systems must be completely and effectively stored. Do not knot the end of a rope, as it can get caught in cracks between rocks.

6. Provide ropes which permit you to hold on to your craft so that it may be rescued. The following methods are recommended:

   A. Kayaks and covered canoes should have grab loops of 0.25" rope or equivalent webbing sized to admit a normal-sized hand. Stern painters are permissible if properly secured.

   B. Open canoes should have securely anchored bow and stern painters consisting of 8–10 feet of 0.25" line. These must be secured in such a way that they are readily accessible, but cannot come loose accidentally. Grab loops are acceptable, but are more difficult to reach after an upset.

C. Rafts and dories may have taut perimeter lines threaded through the loops provided. Footholds should be designed so that a paddler's feet cannot be forced through them, causing entrapment. Flip lines should be carefully and reliably stowed.

7. Know your craft's carrying capacity, and how added loads affect boat handling in whitewater. Most rafts have a minimum crew size which can be added to on day trips or in easy rapids. Carrying more than two paddlers in an open canoe when running rapids is not recommended.

8. Car-top racks must be strong and attach positively to the vehicle. Lash your boat to each crossbar, then tie the ends of boat to the bumpers for added security. This arrangement should survive all but the most violent vehicle accident.

III. Group Preparedness and Responsibility

1. Organization. A river trip should be regarded as a common adventure by all participants, except on instructional or commercially guided trips as defined below. Participants share the responsibility for the conduct of the trip, and each participant is individually responsible for judging his or her own capabilities and for his or her own safety as the trip progresses. Participants are encouraged (but are not obligated) to offer advice and guidance for the independent consideration and judgment of others.

2. River Conditions. The group should have a reasonable knowledge of the difficulty of the run. Participants should evaluate this information and adjust their plans accordingly. If the run is exploratory or no one is familiar with the river, maps and guidebooks, if available, should be examined. The group should secure accurate flow information; the more difficult the run, the more important this will be. Be aware of possible changes in river level and how this will affect the difficulty of the run. If the trip involves tidal stretches, secure appropriate information on tides.

3. Group equipment should be suited to the difficulty of the river. The group should always have a throw line available, and one line per boat is recommended on difficult runs. The list may include: carabiners, prussick loops, first-aid kit, flashlight, folding saw, fire starter, guidebooks, maps, food, extra clothing, and any other rescue or survival items suggested by conditions. Each item is not required on every run, and this list is not meant to be a substitute for good judgment.

4. Keep the group compact, but maintain sufficient spacing to avoid collisions. If the group is large, consider dividing into smaller groups or using the "buddy system" as an additional safeguard. Space yourselves closely enough to permit good communication, but not so close as to interfere with one another in rapids.

   A. A point paddler sets the pace. When in front, do not get in over your head. Never run drops when you cannot see a clear route to the bottom or, for advanced paddlers, a sure route to the next eddy. When in doubt, stop and scout.

   B. Keep track of all group members. Each boat keeps the one behind it in sight, stopping if necessary. Know how many people are in your group and take head counts regularly. No one should paddle ahead or walk out without first informing the group. Paddlers requiring additional support should stay at the center of a group, and not allow themselves to lag behind in the more difficult rapids. If the group is large and contains a wide range of abilities, a Sweep Boat may be designated to bring up the rear.

   C. Courtesy. On heavily used rivers, do not cut in front of a boater running a drop. Always look upstream before leaving eddies to run or play. Never enter a crowded drop or eddy when no room for you exists. Passing other groups in a rapid may be hazardous: it's often safer to wait upstream until the group ahead has passed.

5. Float plan. If the trip is into a wilderness area or for an extended period, plans should be filed with a responsible person who will contact the authorities if you are overdue. It may

be wise to establish checkpoints along the way where civilization could be contacted if necessary. Knowing the location of possible help and preplanning escape routes can speed rescue.

6. Drugs. The use of alcohol or mind-altering drugs before or during river trips is not recommended. It dulls reflexes, reduces decision-making ability, and may interfere with important survival reflexes.

7. Instructional or Commercially Guided Trips. In contrast to the common adventure-trip format, in these trip formats, a boating instructor or commercial guide assumes some of the responsibilities normally exercised by the group as a whole, as appropriate under the circumstances. These formats recognize that instructional or commercially guided trips may involve participants who lack significant experience in whitewater. However, as a participant acquires experience in whitewater, he or she takes on increasing responsibility for his or her own safety, in accordance with what he or she knows or should know as a result of that increased experience. Also, as in all trip formats, every participant must realize and assume the risks associated with the serious hazards of whitewater rivers. It is advisable for instructors and commercial guides or their employers to acquire trip or personal liability insurance:

   A. An "instructional trip" is characterized by a clear teacher/pupil relationship, where the primary purpose of the trip is to teach boating skills, and which is conducted for a fee.

   B. A "commercially guided trip" is characterized by a licensed, professional guide conducting trips for a fee.

IV. Guidelines for River Rescue

1. Recover from an upset with an Eskimo roll whenever possible. Evacuate your boat immediately if there is danger of being trapped against rocks, brush, or any other kind of strainer.

2. If you swim, hold on to your boat. It has much flotation and is easy for rescuers to spot. Get to the upstream end so that you cannot

be crushed between a rock and your boat by the current's force. Persons with good balance may be able to climb on top of a swamped kayak or flipped raft and paddle to shore.

3. Release your craft if this will improve your chances, especially if the water is cold or dangerous rapids lie ahead. Actively attempt self-rescue whenever possible by swimming for safety. Be prepared to assist others who may come to your aid.

   A. When swimming in shallow or obstructed rapids, lie on your back with feet held high and pointed downstream. Do not attempt to stand in fast-moving water; if your foot wedges on the bottom, fast water will push you under and keep you there. Get to slow or very shallow water before attempting to stand or walk. Look ahead! Avoid possible pinning situations including undercut rocks, strainers, downed trees, holes, and other dangers by swimming away from them.

   B. If the rapids are deep and powerful, roll over onto your stomach and swim aggressively for shore. Watch for eddies and slackwater and use them to get out of the current. Strong swimmers can effect a powerful upstream ferry and get to shore fast. If the shores are obstructed with strainers or undercut rocks, however, it is safer to "ride the rapid out" until a safer escape can be found.

4. If others spill and swim, go after the boaters first. Rescue boats and equipment only if this can be done safely. While participants are encouraged (but not obligated) to assist one another to the best of their ability, they should do so only if they can, in their judgment, do so safely. The first duty of a rescuer is not to compound the problem by becoming another victim.

5. The use of rescue lines requires training; uninformed use may cause injury. Never tie yourself into either end of a line without a reliable quick-release system. Have a knife handy to deal with unexpected entanglement. Learn to place set lines effectively, to throw accurately, to belay effectively, and to properly handle a rope thrown to you.

6. When reviving a drowning victim, be aware that cold water may greatly extend survival time underwater. Victims of hypothermia may have depressed vital signs so they look and feel dead. Don't give up; continue CPR for as long as possible without compromising safety.

V. Universal River Signals

These signals may be substituted with an alternate set of signals agreed upon by the group.

STOP: Potential hazard ahead. Wait for "all clear" signal before proceeding, or scout ahead. Form a horizontal bar with your outstretched arms. Those seeing the signal should pass it back to others in the party.

HELP/EMERGENCY: Assist the signaler as quickly as possible. Give three long blasts on a police whistle while waving a paddle, helmet, or life vest over your head. If a whistle is not available, use the visual signal alone. A whistle is best carried on a lanyard attached to your life vest.

ALL CLEAR: Come ahead (in the absence of other directions proceed down the center). Form a vertical bar with your paddle or one arm held high above your head. Paddle blade should be turned flat for maximum visibility. To signal direction or a preferred course through a rapid around obstruction, lower the previously vertical "all clear" by 45 degrees toward the side of the river with the preferred route. Never point toward the obstacle you wish to avoid.

I'M OK: I'm OK and not hurt. While holding the elbow outward toward the side, repeatedly pat the top of your head.

VI. International Scale of River Difficulty

This is the American version of a rating system used to compare river difficulty throughout the world. This system is not exact; rivers do not always fit into one category; regional or individual interpretations may cause misunderstandings. It is no substitute for a guidebook or accurate first-hand descriptions of a run.

Paddlers attempting difficult runs in an unfamiliar area should act cautiously until they get a feel for the way the scale is interpreted locally. River difficulty may change each year due to fluctuations in water level, downed trees, recent floods, geological disturbances, or bad weather. Stay alert for unexpected problems!

As river difficulty increases, the danger to swimming paddlers becomes more severe. As rapids become longer and more continuous, the challenge increases. There is a difference between running an occasional Class IV rapid and dealing with an entire river of this category. Allow an extra margin of safety between skills and river ratings when the water is cold or if the river itself is remote and inaccessible.

The Six Difficulty Classes

Class I: Easy. Fast-moving water with riffles and small waves. Few obstructions, all obvious and easily missed with little training. Risk to swimmers is slight; self-rescue is easy.

Class II: Novice. Straightforward rapids with wide, clear channels which are evident without scouting. Occasional maneuvering may be required, but rocks and medium-sized waves are easily missed by trained paddlers. Swimmers are seldom injured and group assistance, while helpful, is seldom needed. Rapids that are at the upper end of this difficulty range are designated "Class II+".

Class III: Intermediate. Rapids with moderate, irregular waves which may be difficult to avoid and which can swamp an open canoe. Complex maneuvers in fast current and good boat control in tight passages or around ledges are often required; large waves or strainers may be present but are easily avoided. Strong eddies and powerful current effects can be found, particularly on large-volume rivers. Scouting is advisable for inexperienced parties. Injuries while swimming are rare; self-rescue is usually easy but group assistance may be required to avoid long swims. Rapids that are at the lower or upper end of this difficulty range are designated "Class III-" or "Class III+" respectively.

Class IV: Advanced. Intense, powerful but predictable rapids requiring precise boat handling in turbulent water. Depending on the character of the river, it may feature large, unavoidable waves and holes or constricted passages demanding fast maneuvers under pressure. A fast, reliable eddy turn may be needed to initiate maneuvers, scout rapids, or rest. Rapids may require "must" moves above dangerous hazards. Scouting may be necessary the first time down. Risk of injury to swimmers is moderate to high, and water conditions may make self-rescue difficult. Group assistance for rescue is often essential but requires practiced skills. A strong Eskimo roll is highly recommended. Rapids that are at the lower or upper end of this difficulty range are designated "Class IV-" or "Class IV+" respectively.

Class V: Expert. Extremely long, obstructed, or very violent rapids which expose a paddler to added risk. Drops may contain large, unavoidable waves and holes or steep, congested chutes with complex, demanding routes. Rapids may continue for long distances between pools, demanding a high level of fitness. What eddies exist may be small, turbulent, or difficult to reach. At the high end of the scale, several of these factors may be combined. Scouting is recommended but may be difficult. Swims are dangerous, and rescue is often difficult even for experts. A very reliable Eskimo roll, proper equipment, extensive experience, and practiced rescue skills are essential. Because of the large range of difficulty that exists beyond Class IV, Class 5 is an open ended, multiple level scale designated by Class 5.0, 5.1, 5.2, etc. Each of these levels is an order of magnitude more difficult than the last. Example: increasing difficulty from Class 5.0 to Class 5.1 is a similar order of magnitude as increasing from Class IV to Class 5.0.

Class VI: Extreme and Exploratory. These runs have almost never been attempted and often exemplify the extremes of difficulty, unpredictability, and danger. The consequences of errors are very severe and rescue may be impossible. For teams of experts only, at favorable water levels, after close personal inspection and taking all precautions. After a Class VI rapids has been run many times, It's rating may be changed to an appropriate Class 5.x rating.

Appendix B

Northern Forest Canoe Trail

The Northern Forest Canoe Trail is a 740-mile waterway from Old Forge, New York, to Fort Kent, Maine. The trail follows Native American travel routes, and now serves to encourage canoe/kayak travel in the Northern Forest regions of New York, Vermont, New Hampshire, and Maine.

Below is an outline of the route, from west to east. This is not sufficient information to make the trek (just enough to get you interested), but you can get detailed information from:

Northern Forest Canoe Trail
P.O. Box 572
Waitsfield, VT 05673
(802) 496-2285
www.northernforestcanoetrail.org

New York: Begin at Old Forge, ascend the Moose River via the Fulton Lake Chain, and portage to the Raquette River. Descend the Raquette and portage to the Saranec River. Descend the Saranec to Lake Champlain.

Vermont: Cross Lake Champlain and ascend the Missisquoi River to the North Branch of the Missisquoi River. Ascend the North Branch of the Missisquoi River to above Mansonville, Quebec. Portage to Lake Memphremagog. Paddle down Lake Memphremagog to Newport, Vermont. Portage to the Clyde River. Ascend the Clyde River and portage to the Nulhegan river. Descend the Nulhegan River to the Connecticut River.

New Hampshire: Descend the Connecticut River to the Upper Ammonoosuc River. Ascend the Upper Ammonoosuc River and portage to the Androscoggin River. Ascend the Androscoggin River to Lake Umbagog.

Maine: Portage the Rapid River to the Richardson, Mooselookmeguntic, and Rangeley Lakes. Portage to the South Branch of the Dead River. Descend the Dead River to

Spencer Stream. Ascend Spencer Stream to Little Spencer Stream. Ascend Little Spencer Stream to Whipple Pond and portage to the Moose River. Descend the Moose River to the Penobscot River. Descend the Penobscot River to Chesuncook Lake. Cross Chesuncook Lake to Umbazooksus Lake and portage to the Allagash River. Descend the Allagash (Wilderness Waterway) to the Saint John River. Descend the Saint John River to the mouth of the Fish River at Fort Kent.

Eastern Maine Canoe Trail

Maine was once crossed by an extensive network of canoe trails. Established by the ancestors of the indigenous Abenaki peoples, these trails gave access to all parts of the state, and beyond, linking watersheds with short overland portages. The canoe-trail network was pivotal to later European exploitation of Maine's inland resources. Loggers, trappers, missionaries, even armies traveled along, and carried their boats from watershed to watershed via this network.

Today, of course, roads have replaced canoe trails for commercial uses, but many segments of the canoe network still get heavy recreational use. With a few exceptions, there is little current use of the cross-drainage portages that once tied the network together.

In order to increase public awareness of both the historic and recreational value of this network, Native Trails is attempting to revitalize parts of it. Drawing from a variety of research sources, we have combined sections of several old routes to create the Eastern Maine Canoe Trail (EMCT), a modern recreational canoe trail running from Vanceboro, on the Canadian border, to the Penobscot River.

The EMCT traverses some of the most scenic paddling country in Maine. It passes along the watersheds of the Saint Croix, Machias, Passadumkeag, and Penobscot Rivers on its 130-mile journey. Approximately seven of these miles are portages linking the watersheds and avoiding major obstacles like dams or falls. Additional portages may be required depending on the skill level of the paddler undertaking this route.

While not technically difficult, the EMCT will test the wilderness skills of all. A complete run of the route requires knowledge not only of downriver paddling, but also lining, polling, map reading, and lake travel, as well as good camping skills.

The Route

The EMCT is passable through most of the paddling season. Four to seven days are recommended for the passage, but an adventurous traveler will find many additional days of exploration along the way. The run from east to west is easiest; more time will be required for a west-east run.

Most of the EMCT runs through privately owned land; care and respect of this land is important to keeping the trail open. Fire permits are required all along the trail, and official camping sites are rare. Basic backcountry low-impact camping technique is a must!

East ➤ West

Begin on the Saint Croix River in Vanceboro, descend the Saint Croix to Grand Lake Flowage. Paddle west through the town of Princeton to Big Lake. A 2.0-mile portage to West Grand Lake begins near the mouth of Grand Lake Stream. Skillful polers may shorten this portage substantially. The trail winds through the West Grand Lakes to Sysladobsis Lake where a 1.0-mile portage leads to 4th Machias Lake. At the south end of this lake, a 2.0-mile portage leads across state-owned land to Gassabias Lake. Here the paddler descends Gassabias Stream, wading when necessary to Nicatous Lake. Nicatous Lake is the hub for paddling trails in this area. Following old portages, the paddler can reach the Union, Narraguagus, and West Machias Rivers. The EMCT heads north, down Nicatous Stream to join the Passadumkeag River. Shortly after this is a portage around the Grand Falls. The last mandatory portage is around a dam on the Passadumkeag. The EMCT ends in Passadumkeag village at the junction with the Penobscot River.

Allagash Convenience

The Allagash, as beautiful and remote as it is, continues to be at the center of a pitched debate. In broad terms, the debate is over convenience and preservation. On one side are those who would like greater and easier (less arduous) access to and use of the Allagash. On the other are those who believe that the river should remain the wilderness paddling experience it was designated to be when the State of Maine created the Wilderness Waterway in 1966.

In the Wilderness Waterway Act, and in the subsequent federal Wild and Scenic designation (1970), language stating that the Allagash was to be a "wilderness canoeing experience," and maintained in "maximum" or "optimum wilderness character" was invoked repeatedly. This language is the main ammunition the preservation-minded folks use to counter the movement toward easier access and convenience. They also insist that a paddling trip on the Allagash never used to be easy, and it should not be now. "Work a little bit, and do it right!" they exclaim.

But with improved roads, better vehicles, and increasing demand for non-paddling recreation on the Allagash, there has been state legislation to increase and/or improve access points along the river. So-called sportsmen's groups and others contend that the Allagash does not even meet the federal definition of "Wild" because it is regulated by a dam (Churchill Lake). And so these sporting groups wish to "improve" old and existing access points, which would allow more day users onto the river.

Naturally, this raises the ire of traditionalists, including guides and outfitters, and conservation groups, who have filed suit to block permits allowing access improvements. These folks wish to protect the resource and the experience it offers.

Unfortunately there is small middle ground in this dispute. Even if there is a "resolution" or "agreement," one side is going to lose. Though this dispute boils along, you can have a great trip on the Allagash, especially if you make the commitment to take the time to do it in a traditional way. You will be rewarded with the satisfaction of having done it right, even if you could have done it more conveniently.

Androscoggin River Source to the Sea Canoe Trek

Each July paddlers in the Androscoggin River Source to the Sea Canoe Trek revel in the beauty of this river, as it flows from its headwaters in northeastern New Hampshire to the tidewaters in the Gulf of Maine. The event serves as a floating meeting of the Androscoggin River Watershed Council, formed to promote and protect the 170-mile-long waterway and its 3,450-square-mile watershed.

Free and open to the public, the Trek celebrates the renaissance of this formerly polluted New England river. Most Trek participants join the moving river festival as a day trip, but a few hardy souls paddle the entire nineteen days. The Canoe Trek is supported by volunteers, state and local agencies, foundations, and local sponsors.

Learn about trout, water quality, pollution prevention, and Abenaki legends on the river. There is even a special day for wooden canoes!

Celebrate and join the Androscoggin River Watershed Council, a new group that will work to improve environmental quality and promote healthy and prosperous communities in the Androscoggin River Watershed. Information about the Council will be provided during the trek.

Experience the renaissance of a river that has been a key part of New England's heritage.

Who comes on the Trek?

Anyone who wants to go paddling, learn about the river, and have fun!

Is the river difficult?

Read the *River Guide* you are holding!

Do I have to go for the whole 19 days?

Absolutely not! Most people come for the day. Information on camping and lodging near the river is available for those who want to paddle consecutive days. A hardy few paddle the whole river source to the sea!

What about getting back to the beginning?

Trekkers will be shuttled back to the day's starting point at the end of the paddle. On some sections, boat shuttles will be arranged to get around dams and other obstacles.

I'd like to learn about the river, but I don't want to paddle. What else can I do?

Most days of the Trek have special events onshore, usually in the evenings, for interested people. Check the Trek brochure for events—cookouts, slide shows, tours, and other fun.

How much does it cost?

Free! All you have to do is bring a canoe or kayak, lifejackets, a lunch, and suitable clothing. And of course bring a desire to have fun and learn about the wonderful Androscoggin River. Need a paddling partner? The section leader can help find a partner.

Where can I rent a canoe or kayak?

Saco Bound 603-477-2177

Milan General Store 603-449-7327

Bethel Outdoor Adventures 207-824-4424

Wild River Adventures 207-824-2608

Ring's Marine Service 207-865-6143

North Auburn Cash Market 207-783-7378

How do I find out more?

Call Trek Coordinator Sue Lincoln at 207-824-0191 or slincoln@nxi.com.

Atlantic Salmon

Some Maine rivers are the last remaining habitat for Atlantic salmon. Prior to industrialization in the nineteenth century, almost all rivers in New England were salmon habitat. But dams and pollution destroyed the rivers, and the salmon disappeared. In a few rivers in eastern Maine, salmon have survived, and continue to—just barely. The species, despite the concerted effort of governments, fish lovers, anglers, and others, has reached critically low numbers.

Accordingly, the U.S. Government, on November 19, 2000, listed wild Atlantic salmon as endangered on eight Maine rivers. Those rivers are the Dennys, East Machias, Machias, Pleasant, Narraguagus, Ducktrap, Sheepscot, and Cove Brook. The Fish and Wildlife Service and the National Marine Fisheries Service said wild salmon numbers are at an all-time low: they estimate that only about 300 mature wild salmon returned last year to the eight rivers targeted for protection.

Endangered listing means, among other things, that: no one may take (that is, disturb) a protected Atlantic salmon, a recovery plan must be developed, critical habitat must be identified. The endangered listing probably has little effect on the recreational paddler.

The listing does have a serious impact on Maine. From the salmon aquaculture industry to blueberry farming, the effects could ripple through Maine's economy. Captive, farm-raised salmon must not interbreed with wild salmon, in order to preserve the latter's genetic purity. Pesticides from Maine's blueberry farms must not pollute these eight rivers. Nor may they withdraw too much water from these rivers for irrigation.

When you paddle on these rivers, remind yourself that they are beautiful, both for yourself and the salmon. Your paddling will not disturb the fish in the slightest way. And yet, human impact on wild salmon has, paradoxically, through the Endangered Species Act's protections, enhanced the quality of the river for your recreational excursion.

AMC and the Relicensing of Hydroelectric Dams

AMC has been both a regional and national leader in the relicensing of hydroelectric dams. The waters of our rivers are publicly owned. Hydroelectric dams may be granted a license to dam and divert water to generate power for thirty to fifty years. In effect, the dam owner is a tenant, and the public is the landlord.

Thanks, in part, to efforts by the AMC, a federal law passed in 1986 requires that during the licensing process the Federal Energy Regulatory Commission (FERC) must now consider a river's environmental and recreational value on an equal basis with its value as a power source when it issues the terms of a new hydro-dam license.

Dams frequently reduce water quality, block fish movement, flood out boating opportunities, and at times turn flows on and off like a faucet spigot. When hydro dams were licensed over a half-century ago they had to meet few standards. Many of these original licenses are or will soon come due for renewal for new thirty- to fifty-year licenses. The AMC works hard to achieve updated license conditions during these renewals. This includes mitigation for dams' impacts on rivers' recreational opportunities and ecosystems as well as a better balance of priorities.

The AMC has been a successful leader in achieving considerable gains in river protection both through the relicensing process and by negotiating settlement agreements with willing dam owners. The AMC helped pioneer major relicensing settlements on the Kennebec, Androscoggin, Rapid, Connecticut, and Deerfield Rivers to name a few. Today more than 40,000 acres of protected river shorefront, improved flows in several hundred miles of river, and guaranteed water releases for whitewater boating, plus over $20 million in river enhancement funds have resulted from the AMC's work.

Ken Kimball

USGS Gauges in Maine

The U.S. Geological Survey maintains gauges in many locations throughout the region. Many of these transmit data that is posted on the Web at http://me.wateRiverusgs.gov/. The list below is provided for information only.

On many rivers you will find hand-painted gauges, on bridge abutments, for example. These gauges are meaningless except if you know and are familiar with the river in many water levels or you were the one who painted the gauge in the first place. Never substitute a gauge reading, particularly when you may not be familiar with the river, for your own commonsense, river-reading judgment.

It is the belief of the editors, therefore, that gauges are of secondary value to river runners, and this river guide only inconsistently mentions them.

Saint John River Basin
Saint John River at Ninemile Bridge
Big Black River near Depot Mountain
Saint John River at Dickey
Allagash River near Allagash
Saint Francis River near Connors
Fish River near Fort Kent
Saint John River at Fort Kent
Aroostook River near Masardis
Aroostook River at Washburn
Williams Brook at Phair

Saint Croix River Basin
Saint Croix River at Vanceboro
Grand Lake Stream at the city of Grand Lake Stream
Saint Croix River at Baring

Machias River Basin
Pleasant River near Epping
Old Stream near Wesley

Narraguagus River Basin

East Bear Brook near Beddington
West Bear Brook near Beddington
Narraguagus River at Cherryfield
Cadillac Brook near Bar Harbor
Hadlock Brook near Northeast Harbor

Penobscot River Basin

Seboeis River near Shin Pond
East Branch of the Penobscot at Grindstone
Mattawamkeag River near Mattawam
Piscataquis River at Blanchard
Kingsbury Stream at Abbot
Piscataquis River near Dover
Piscataquis River at Medford
Penobscot River at West Enfield
Penobscot River at Eddington

Ducktrap River Basin

Ducktrap River near Lincolnville

Sheepscot River Basin

Sheepscot River at North Whitefield

Kennebec River Basin

Kennebec River at The Forks
Spencer Stream at its mouth
Kennebec River at Bingham
Carrabassett River near North Anson
Sandy River near Mercer
Sebasticook River near Pittsfield
Kennebec River at North Sidney
Kennebec River at Augusta
Cobbosseecontee Stream at Gardiner
Kennebec River at Gardiner

Androscoggin River Basin

Diamond River near Wentworth

Androscoggin River at Errol

Androscoggin River near Gorham

Wild River at Gilead

Androscoggin River at Rumford

Swift River near Roxbury

The Basin outlet at North Auburn

Townsend Brook near Auburn

Bobbin Mill Brook near Auburn

Little Androscoggin River near South Paris

Androscoggin River near Auburn

Royal River Basin

Royal River at Yarmouth

Presumpscot River Basin

Presumpscot River at Westbrook

Saco River Basin

Saco River near Conway

Saco River at Cornish

Index

About the AMC

Since 1876, the Appalachian Mountain Club has helped people experience the majesty and solitude of the Northeast outdoors. We offer outdoor skills workshops, guided trips, and lodging options for all levels of outdoor adventuring. Our pro- grams include trail maintenance, air and water quality research, and conservation advocacy work to preserve the special outdoor places we love and enjoy for future generations.

Join the Club!

Take a hike, ride a bike, paddle a canoe. We believe that people who enjoy climbing mountains, splashing in streams, and walking on trails have more fun and take better care of the outdoors. Join the fun today. Call 617-523-0636 or visit www.outdoors.org for membership information. AMC members receive discounts on workshops, lodging, and books.

Outdoor Adventures

From beginner backpacking to advanced backcountry skiing to guided hiking and paddling trips, we teach outdoor skills workshops to suit your interest and experience. Our outdoor education centers guarantee year-round adventures. View our entire listing of workshops online at www.outdoors.org.

Huts, Lodges, and Visitor Centers

With accommodations throughout the Northeast, you don't have to travel to the ends of the earth to experience unique wilderness lodging. Accessible by car or on foot, our lodges and huts are perfect for families, couples, groups, and individuals. For reservations call 800-262-4455.

Books and Maps

We can lead you to the best hiking, biking, skiing, and paddling destinations from Maine to North Carolina. With more than fifty books and maps published, we're your definitive resource for discovering wonderful outdoor places. To receive a free catalog call 800-262-4455 or visit our online store at www.outdoors.org.

Contact Us

Appalachian Mountain Club
5 Joy Street
Boston, MA 02108-1490
617-523-0636
www.outdoors.org

Leave No Trace

The Appalachian Mountain Club is a national educational partner of Leave No Trace, Inc., a nonprofit organization dedicated to promoting and inspiring responsible outdoor recreation through education, research, and partnerships. The Leave No Trace Program seeks to develop wildland ethics—ways in which people think and act in  the outdoors to minimize their impacts on the areas they visit and to protect our natural resources for future enjoyment. Leave No Trace unites four federal land management agencies—the U.S. Forest Service, National Park Service, Bureau of Land Management, and U.S. Fish and Wildlife Service—with manufacturers, outdoor retailers, user groups, educators, organizations like the AMC and the National Outdoor Leadership School (NOLS), and individuals.

The Leave No Trace ethic is guided by these seven principles:

- Plan ahead and prepare.
- Travel and camp on durable surfaces.
- Dispose of waste properly.
- Leave what you find.
- Minimize campfire impacts.
- Respect wildlife.
- Be considerate of other visitors.

The AMC has joined NOLS—a recognized leader in wilderness education and a founding partner of Leave No Trace—as the sole national providers of the Leave No Trace Master Educator course through 2004. The AMC offers this five-day course, designed especially for outdoor professionals and land managers, as well as the shorter two-day Leave No Trace Trainer course, at locations throughout the northeastern United States.

For Leave No Trace information and materials, contact:

Leave No Trace, Inc.
P.O. Box 997
Boulder, CO 80306
800-332-4100
www.LNT.org

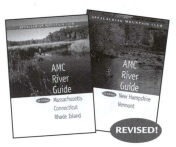
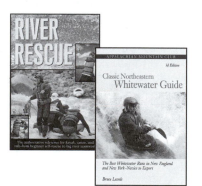